In the Arena

In the Arena

The Board of Directors' Guide to the Successful Operation of a Homeowners Association

Chris D. Gilleland

chrisgilleland@chrisgilleland.com

Professional & Tradesman Publishing & Media Company

Attention: Quantity discounts are available to homeowner associations, companies, educational institutions, professional organizations for reselling, educational purposes, subscription incentives, gifts, or fund raising campaigns. Contact Chris Gilleland at chrisgilleland@chrisgilleland.com or 704-347-8900.

ISBN: 0692918949
ISBN 13: 9780692918944

This book is dedicated to my parents John & Rebecca Gilleland and my son Remington P. Gilleland

Contents

Introduction · xv
Congratulations · xv
Word Use · xv
Why Serve On A Homeowner Association Board of Directors · xvi
Who Is Responsible · xvii
First Homeowners Association · xviii
Home Values · xix
Return on Investment = HOA · xxii
Misconceptions · xxiii
The Media = The Perception = The Reality · · · · · · · · · · · · · · · xxvi
Why Do We Even Need an HOA · xxxii

Association Basics · 1
Association Terminology · 1
Governing Documents · 5
Amending Governing Documents · 7
The Association Structure · 10
Meetings · 14
Annual Meeting Paperwork · 18
Proxies · 21
Quorum · 24

Speaking at Your Annual Meeting · · · · · 27
Heated Association Meetings · · · · · 28
Member in Good Standing · · · · · 30
Association Financials · · · · · 32
The Year-End & the Association's Financials · · · · · 35
Audit or Review or Compilation · · · · · 36
Annual Budget · · · · · 38
Increasing Assessments · · · · · 41
Membership Questions and the Annual Budget · · · · · 46
More On Why Dues Are Different From Association to Association · · · · · 49
Accounting Controls · · · · · 51
Accrual & Cash Accounting · · · · · 54
IRS Reporting · · · · · 54
1099-MISC · · · · · 55
Lien for Assessment · · · · · 56
Collection Process · · · · · 57
Federal Fair Debt Collection Practice Act · · · · · 64
Delinquencies and the Desire to be Neighborly · · · · · 68
Payment Plans · · · · · 70
Reserves · · · · · 71
Investment Vehicles · · · · · 74

Board Basics · · · · · 78
Board of Directors · · · · · 78
Difference between Director & Officer · · · · · 80
President Role · · · · · 81
Vice President Role · · · · · 86
Secretary Role · · · · · 88
Treasurer Role · · · · · 90
Popularity Contests · · · · · 94

Fiduciary Duty · · · 95
Conflicts of Interest · · · 96
Board Meetings · · · 97
Board Meeting Legal Proceeding · · · 99
Board Meeting Proxies · · · 105
Open Board Meetings · · · 105
Online/Teleconferencing Board Meetings · · · 108
Conducting Board Business · · · 109
Board Meeting Packet · · · 110
Robert's Rules · · · 111
Board Meeting Minutes · · · 114
Tips on Taking Minutes · · · 116
Redaction · · · 117
Sunshine Laws - Board Openness · · · 118
Collaborative Decision Making · · · 120
Association Committees · · · 123
Forming Committees · · · 126
Finding Volunteers · · · 127
When Board Members Resign · · · 128
Board Resolutions · · · 129

Membership · · · 131
Membership Communications · · · 131
Productive Membership Communications · · · 133
Challenging Personalities · · · 134
The Slippery Slope of CC&R Enforcement · · · 136
Going Above & Beyond · · · 139
Rules & Regulations · · · 142
Pets - Rules & Regulations · · · 147
All Bite, No Bark · · · 148
Fines and the Concept of Reasonableness · · · 152

Legal · 154
Steering Clear of Court · 154
Legal Discovery & Electronic Communications · · · · · · · · · · 158
Elements of Legal Discovery · 160
Eliminating or Adding Amenities · 162

Vendors · 168
Hiring a Contractor · 168
Finding Vendors · 171
Bid Fatigue · 179
When a Vendor Relationship Has Problems · · · · · · · · · · · · · 181
A Project Checklist · 181
Interview a Potential Vendor · 182
The Association & the 1099 Contractor · · · · · · · · · · · · · · · 185

Selecting an Association Management Company · · · · · · · · · · · 188
Selecting an Association Management Company · · · · · · · · 188
Finding a management company that is a fit
for your community · 192
Contacting References · 219

Other Association Vendors · 221
Selecting an Attorney · 221
Collection Companies · 224
Selecting a Bank · 226
Selecting a Landscaper · 229
Selecting an Insurance Agent · 233
Selecting a Pool Company · 235
How to Hire a Plumbing Company · · · · · · · · · · · · · · · · · · · 237
Hiring a Roofer · 239
Hiring a Public Insurance Adjuster · · · · · · · · · · · · · · · · · · · 241

Hiring Civil Engineers · · · 244
Hiring a Security Company · · · 244
Selecting a Certified Public Account (CPA) Firm · · · 245
Caveat Emptor (Buyer Beware) · · · 246
Hiring Members to Perform Work for the Association · · · 248

Common Association Issues · · · 250
Backflow Prevention · · · 250
Asphalt Preventive Maintenance · · · 252
The Importance of Gutter Cleaning · · · 254
Flashing or Weatherproofing · · · 255
French Drain · · · 257
Trees · · · 257
Tree Trimming · · · 261
The Cost to the Association of Overwatering · · · 262
Searching for Unseen Water Leaks · · · 264
Preventing Water Damage · · · 268
Termites · · · 271
Winter Planning for the Association Landscape · · · 275
Ponds · · · 276
Retention Ponds · · · 280
Water Evaporation or Pool Leak · · · 282
Drainage Issues · · · 284
Foundations - Drainage Issues · · · 286

Insurance · · · 289
The Basics of Insurance and the Homeowners Association · · · 289
Overview of Typical Association Insurance Coverage · · · 291
What is Insurance Coverage & What is Not Insurance Coverage · · · 293
What are Insurable Risks · · · 293

Insurance Cancellation · · · 295
Claims and a Plan of Action · · · 297
Annual Insurance Review · · · 299
More on Directors & Officers Insurance · · · 300
The Association's Insurance Agent · · · 301
Filing an Insurance Claim · · · 302
The Risks in Changing the Association's Insurance Carrier · · · 305
Fidelity Bond · · · 306

Issues That Arise · · · 309
Commercial Activity within the Association · · · 309
Going Gated · · · 315
Short-Term Rentals · · · 317
Withholding Dues Payments · · · 321
Squatters Rights/ Adverse Possession · · · 323
Too Many Board Members · · · 326

"The Man In The Arena"

Appendix · · · 331
Balance Sheet · · · 331
Income Statement · · · 332
Cash Disbursement · · · 333
Affidavit of Mailing · · · 334
Bid Sheet – Asphalt Repair & Seal Coat · · · 335
Bid Sheet – Painting · · · 336
Bid Sheet – Pool Maintenance · · · 338
Bid Sheet – Landscape Maintenance · · · 339

About the Author · · · 349

Disclaimer

This book is presented solely for educational and entertainment purposes. The author and publisher are not offering it as legal, accounting, engineering, insurance, construction or other professional services advice. While best efforts have been used in preparing this book, the author and publisher make no representations or warranties of any kind and assume no liabilities of any kind with respect to the accuracy or completeness of the contents and specifically disclaim any implied warranties of merchantability or fitness of use for a particular purpose. Neither the author nor the publisher shall be held liable or responsible to any person or entity with respect to any loss or incidental or consequential damages caused, or alleged to have been caused, directly or indirectly, by the information or programs contained herein. No warranty may be created or extended by sales representatives or written sales materials. Every homeowner association is different and the advice and strategies contained herein may not be suitable for your situation. You should always seek the services of a competent professional.

Introduction

■ ■ ■

CONGRATULATIONS

If you are reading this, congratulations! You probably have been elected to serve on a homeowner association board of directors. Or you may be considering running for the board of directors. Or possibly you may be a member of a homeowner association wishing to obtain a better understanding of the inner workings of an association. Whatever the case may be, this book serves as an overview and resource guide to aid in the successful operation of an association.

■ ■ ■

WORD USE

USE OF "GENERALLY" AND "USUALLY"

Because of the many different state statutes governing homeowner associations and the fact some states have no statutes, the author is required to generalize on many points and topics. In addition, because of the many different attorneys producing association governing documents that guarantee almost no two sets are written the same, the author is again required to generalize. Consulting individual state statutes or seeking guidance from an experienced association attorney for clarification may be needed.

USE OF "ASSOCIATION"

For simplicity's sake, the term "Association" is used for all common interest communities such as single family home associations, town home associations, condominium associations and co-ops.

USE OF "GOVERNING DOCUMENTS"

Because declarations, bylaws, articles of incorporation, rules and regulations have many different authors, and because particular provisions may be found in multiple documents, for simplicity's sake the term "governing document" is used as a catch-all.

USE OF "ASSESSMENT" AND "DUES"

Assessment and dues refer to the membership's financial contribution to the operation of the association. These terms are used interchangeably throughout this book.

■ ■ ■

WHY SERVE ON A HOMEOWNER ASSOCIATION BOARD OF DIRECTORS

Again, if you are serving on a board of directors, congratulations! It can be an honor and privilege to be elected by your fellow association members to serve on your homeowner association board of directors. But why serve in the first place? Serving on an association board of directors can be a fulfilling and enjoyable endeavor, but can also be a stressful and underappreciated position. In most instances, a position that has no compensation for the work performed, other than the feeling of contributing to the betterment of the community.

The vast majority of successful board members serve with two primary objectives: to give back to their community and to improve the community's overall property values. This is achieved by operating the association in an efficient manner and building harmony within the membership. The efficiency in operations is achieved by collecting and spending association assessments in the most effective ways and by the enforcement of the Covenants, Conditions & Restrictions (CC&Rs) of the association. Community harmony is achieved by efficiently operating the association and by having the best interests of the entire association membership at heart.

■ ■ ■

WHO IS RESPONSIBLE

President Truman had a sign on his Oval Office desk that read "The Buck Stops Here." That expression originated from an old poker term "passing the buck," which means the card player can pass the responsibility of dealing to someone else. Boards have to make a great many decisions, with many being difficult. Within an association the buck stops at the board of directors.

Most board members realize serving is a far cry from a popularity contest and that at the end of the day the board is responsible for whatever happens. Be it good, bad or indifferent, the board must be responsible to the membership. While this may sound dire or ominous, it is not meant to be. It is just part of the job.

The overwhelming majority of the membership will understand if a board makes a mistake. They will understand as long as the board used good judgment and the facts at hand to make its original decision and that the board attempted to correct the mistake (if the mistake is correctable.) What the membership generally does not tolerate is a mistake not being addressed and the board not taking ultimate responsibility.

On December 19, 1952, President Truman addressed the National War College and as part of his talk said, "You know, it's easy for the Monday morning quarterback to say what the coach should have done, after the game is over. But when the decision is up before you and on my desk, I have a motto which says, 'The Buck Stops Here.' The decision has to be made."

■ ■ ■

FIRST HOMEOWNERS ASSOCIATION

The first association, or more precisely the first condominium association, can be traced back to first century Babylon. The first semblance of homeowner associations in the United States was the private streets and neighborhoods of St. Louis, Missouri. Benton Place is deemed by many to be the first homeowners association, opened in 1867. One hundred of these streets and neighborhoods were laid out in St. Louis and in nearby suburbs. The CC&Rs of these private neighborhoods mandated that the homeowners not only owned the streets but the water and sewer lines. Currently many of these neighborhoods are flourishing enclaves surrounded by troubled, crime-ridden areas of St. Louis. Author, architect and urban planner Oscar Newman found that these private neighborhoods were less likely to experience the high crime and poverty rates found in surrounding areas. From Newman's research, it is safe to say that ownership in one's neighborhood or association over the short and long term is beneficial to the standards of living and property values.

■ ■ ■

HOME VALUES

Why do homes within Homeowner Associations sell for more?

There is always debate about the value or perceived value of owning a home within a homeowners association. The debate usually revolves around three factors: the expense of living within an association, the membership assessment and the CC&Rs. The discussion of the many advantages of an association may be challenging because of the many preconceived views. Understanding the underlying benefits aids in this discussion.

The cost of the membership assessment is usually the most common debate discussion topic. That being said, assessment costs are usually the most straightforward to explain and justify. Straightforward in that: cost is the easiest to support with hard facts, i.e. the association's annual budget.

When association members wish to debate their assessment, the annual budget is the best tool to utilize. It may seem obvious, but the annual budget with the income and expenses spelled out in detail is often overlooked and under-considered for this discussion. What surprises many board members is that some in the membership do not have a fundamental understanding of the responsibilities and related expenses of the association.

No matter the level of understanding, it is difficult for a member who is provided a budget to not gain a better understanding once the budget is reviewed. Often members find a newfound respect for what their assessments pay for and the related benefits. It is not uncommon to find members believing their assessment money is being mostly wasted until they review in detail the annual budget.

The primary second debate topic is the CC&Rs. While a few association members may consider the CC&Rs an onerous burden, fortunately the vast majority of members see the CC&Rs very positively. The few association members who have issue with the restrictive CC&Rs many times only look at a narrow instance or, more precisely, something that has impacted them personally.

A kind of compare and contrast is one method to utilize when discussing the benefits of CC&Rs with a member who has an unenthusiastic perception. As with CC&R violations, what is often found is that some members deem their violation minor in nature and fail to see any far-reaching ramifications beyond their violation. The member who paints their shutters an unapproved color may not realize that their paint choices are probably not the real issue, but that of another member who paints their shutters purple. Or one member may consider working on their car just changing the oil, while another neighbor may consider working on their car hanging an engine from a tree in their yard. Often heard when these what-if analogies are used: "something like that would never happen in our association." Yet, if CC&Rs are not enforced anything can happen.

A research study about community associations from 2005, "What Are Private Governments Worth?" by Amanda Agan and Alexander Tabarrok from George Mason University, is still pertinent today. This research study found that community associations can add a 5-6 percent increase in property values over similar homes in nearby non-association communities.

Writing in *Regulation* magazine, the authors say that the increase in home value attributed to community associations is "especially remarkable when one considers that (HOA) residents pay twice for many local services—once in taxes, and then again in HOA fees." The authors also pose valid questions, such as: Do community associations increase home values because they offer better-quality services than local government, or because they offer services that local governments cannot offer (like more restrictive zoning) or do not offer (like greater security)?

The premise of the research paper is: "Constraint is the essence of all government. The important question is whether constraining others is worth the price of constraining oneself. If that constraint is valuable in the case of HOAs, then homes within HOAs will sell for more than comparable homes outside of HOAs."

To this end, the researchers gathered home sales data from five zip codes in northern Virginia for a four-year period. The data included sales price, common home characteristics such as age of home, the number of bedrooms and bathrooms and construction style. Most importantly, the data noted if the home was within an association.

The result of the research determined that, factoring in all the data, homes within community associations were 6.1 percent more valuable than similar homes not located within planned communities. The typical home within the study had a medium sale price of $255,000 and thus an increased value of nearly $14,000 because of being within an association.

▪ ▪ ▪

RETURN ON INVESTMENT = HOA

Members of the association many times view the assessment as just another bill to be paid. Members may even believe they are not really receiving anything of value for their assessment payments. This perspective of the association just having a bunch of restrictions that serve no real benefit is unfortunately common. However, in actuality, these restrictions protect the overall property values of the community. The common amenities, such as a pool, are a huge benefit because the expense is shared among the other members and is a positive resale factor.

Obviously, along with protecting the overall community property values, the individual member's home value is protected and enhanced. The standards in the association's governing documents ensure the association's common areas are properly maintained, and they also restrict activities that have a negative impact on property values. If there were no association and there were deed restrictions, homeowners would be forced to file legal action against their neighbors for deed violations.

Most members do see the association's amenities as a positive and do not begrudge that part of the assessment going to the upkeep. If the installation costs and continuing maintenance costs of most major amenities are taken into consideration, this is a huge savings over an individual member solely purchasing most amenities. When it comes to resale of an association home, amenities can many times be the one factor that tips the buying decision.

■ ■ ■

MISCONCEPTIONS

MISCONCEPTIONS OF HOMEOWNER ASSOCIATIONS

Emotions can run high when members have an issue with the actions of the board of directors or the association's governing documents. This is where membership misconceptions and misunderstandings can most often arise, which can lead to problem issues that can be avoided. Because board members and association managers are minutely aware of the inner workings of the association, this familiarity can sometimes lead to Directors not realizing that members may not have a good understanding of how the association functions.

THE SHADOW GOVERNMENT MISCONCEPTION

It may not exactly border on a conspiracy theory, but some members believe the board of directors is a secretive body that tries to do everything without disclosure. State statutes and most associations' governing documents require reasonable disclosure of almost all association business, with the exception of legal or potential legal matters. The board of directors has a fiduciary duty to be as transparent as possible. Fortunately, the majority of boards understands this and makes every effort to be transparent to the membership. Disclosure issues normally arise when a member's request is too broad, such as a request to see all the records of the association. Considering the age of an association, this broad of a disclosure request could fill many boxes and take an enormous amount of time and expense to compile.

"THE BOARD CAN TAKE ANY ACTIONS IT DESIRES" MISCONCEPTION

In actuality, the board can only do whatever the governing documents or state statutes allow or require. It is very common for members to believe the board makes up the rules as they go along. Depending on the association's governing documents, changing or amending a provision is generally not a simple endeavor. Thus, arbitrarily changing something is not a viable option. The "board can do whatever" issue usually arises when a member does not have an understanding of the association's governing documents. Fortunately, this issue can be the simplest to resolve by showing the member the particulars or justification in the governing documents or state statutes.

"THE BOARD LOVES GETTING THE ASSOCIATION'S LAWYERS INVOLVED" MISCONCEPTION

Realizing the expense, few if any boards wish to involve an attorney. However, in today's environment legal guidance is not a luxury but insurance against larger expenses down the road. In certain areas of the country that are more prone to litigation, associations are frequent targets. In California it has been estimated that at any given time 7 out of 10 associations are actively involved in non-collection related litigation. Justifying the utilization of legal guidance can be one of the most difficult misconceptions to respond to because of the counterfactual nature of legal matters. Explaining to members the intricate and many times delicate nature of the issues that arise within an association can aid in this discussion.

"THE BOARD TAKES DUES AND PUTS THEM INTO THE ASSOCIATION'S SAVINGS (RESERVES) ACCOUNT" MISCONCEPTION

Reserve funding misconceptions are probably the most misunderstood aspect of the financial matters of associations. The misconception generally revolves around a common theme: "Why are you taking money out of my bank account to put into an association savings account?" Just explaining that the board of directors has a fiduciary responsibility to fund reserves usually will not satisfy a member's apprehensions about reserves. Reserves are for future capital improvements so that special assessments from the membership are not required. Well-funded reserves increase the overall property values because reserves are a frequent question of potential home buyers. Also, special assessments generally increase membership delinquencies, which definitely do not improve property values within the association.

"THE BOARD MEMBERS ARE PAID TO BE ON THE BOARD OF DIRECTORS" MISCONCEPTION

When this misconception comes up, it generally draws laughter from board members, but can be a common belief of some in the membership. Most governing documents prevent board members from receiving any form of compensation, and certain state statutes prohibit this as well.

"THE BOARD IS BEING PETTY WITH CC&R ENFORCEMENT" MISCONCEPTION

This comes up when the member perceives their CC&R violation as being minor in nature. While it can be difficult to argue the point on certain violations, it is not a long stretch from a member changing their car's oil to a car up on blocks. A member's violation may not seem like a major issue, but relaxed enforcement is a slippery slope when the lesser items are not being addressed.

"THE BOARD PLAYS FAVORITES" MISCONCEPTION

This is the most common misconception that board and association managers hear. When it comes to CC&R enforcement or any other substantial matter, if there are favorites in the membership, it will have no bearing on the matters in almost all instances. This seems to be such a prevalent misconception because when it comes to CC&R enforcement, members see other members with the same or similar violations not being notified of the violation. Countering this misconception can be the most challenging of all because of the sensitive legal nature of CC&R enforcement. Generally, the only counter is to state that all CC&R issues are being dealt with and that the legal nature of some of these violations will unfortunately have to be resolved in court, so specific violations cannot be discussed publicly.

■ ■ ■

THE MEDIA = THE PERCEPTION = THE REALITY

Negative newspaper and broadcast news stories about homeowner associations are always prevalent in the media. The stories usually have an emotional narrative and most of the time appear decidedly one-sided against the association or the association's board. The most common theme of these stories is that association boards are out-of-control and taking advantage of the membership. Rarely is it pointed out that the association is controlled by the membership and that the membership elects the board of directors. These facts do not lend themselves to supporting the overall premise of the story that an association is not bullying someone.

These negative stories are detrimental to associations as a whole because they can result in a negative opinion of associations by the public, while overlooking the countless benefits. These negative stories and public sentiment can lead to ill-conceived legislation that may fail to resolve any issues, making the administration of an association more difficult and costly. If nothing else, negative perceptions can hurt property values.

This should concern every association board of director and every association member because, with enough negative attention from the media, politicians become involved, wanting to correct these "injustices" by passing legislation. This legislation normally constrains associations from operating effectively and efficiently. Unfortunately, when legislation has been enacted the usual result has been to increase operational costs for associations while reducing the board's authority. These politicians many times have never lived within an association and may not have a good understanding of the many benefits and responsibilities. Without this association experience, they fail to realize the unintended consequences of their legislation.

Several years ago, the author was asked to speak with individual legislators when a state legislature was proposing a bill that would severely limit association collection authority on a delinquent member. During discussions with one particular legislator, they revealed that they had never lived within an association and basically did not know why an association needed to collect assessments in the first place. After a brief discussion with this legislator about common expenses and operational budget requirements, they still felt that collections were just too extreme and that other remedies needed to be utilized. Unfortunately, this legislator did not have any suggestions on what those other remedies could be. When it was pointed out to them that the paying members would have to pay more to offset those who could not be collected from, the legislator did indicate that this was a viable approach that they did not have a problem with. Fortunately, by the dedicated efforts of a vast number of board members and other interested parties lobbying other legislators, this legislation did not gain any traction.

The reality is that no matter what the media reports, it is imperative to keep everything in perspective. Perspective is that in the United States approximately 63 million Americans live within an association, which means that almost 1 in 5 Americans lives under the governance of an association. A great gauge of these so-called problems is a Zogby survey taken in 2012 that discovered that 92 Percent of association members said they are satisfied (70 percent) or neutral (22 percent) when asked about their association experiences. Just 8 percent expressed dissatisfaction with living within an association.

Again, the real problem that associations have is not the reality, but the perception. The media or politicians will many times focus on one extreme situation with one individual member and not factor in that the vast majority of people who live within an association are perfectly satisfied with how the association functions. A great example is the author's meeting with a legislator who produced a three-ring binder and stated the binder "was full of complaints" against a homeowner association board and that something needed to be done immediately to rectify this vast problem. Upon examination, the binder contained eleven complaints or issues going back over five years. Considering that there are an estimated 15,000 associations in that state, just eleven complaints puts the matter in perspective. Interestingly, all but two of the eleven complainants dealt with architectural issues. While architectural matters can be a pressing issue within an association, it is doubtful that lawmakers understand the complexity of the issue. Hopefully, they do not feel a need to weigh in on what type of bush can be planted in front of someone's home.

Changing the perception begins with communicating effectively and getting the facts out to the media and politicians. There are two primary misconceptions that, if countered, will address the majority of what is used to attack associations. The first misconception is that associations are undemocratic, and the second misconception is that associations are petty in dealing with the membership violations.

The charge that an association is undemocratic is unfounded. Quite to the contrary, associations are the most democratic institution in many states. When under membership control, boards of directors are elected to their positions by the members at duly-held annual meetings. If problems arise, most association governing documents specify how to remove association board members and entire boards. In North Carolina, for example, state statutes allow for as little as 10% of the membership to call a special meeting and recall the entire board with 10 days' notice. Ironically, elected state and local politicians in North Carolina are not subject to recalls like most association boards.

The second misconception is that associations are petty in dealing with the membership regarding CC&R enforcement. Many times in a news story, a CC&R violation will be made to look minor in nature without giving the entire background or reasoning behind the board's enforcement. A great example is a member changing their car's oil in the driveway. This may not seem like a gigantic problem, but it is important to point out that the real concern is: Where does this maintenance end? With rotating tires, brakes, replacing the transmission? Uniform and reasonable enforcement heads off issues before these issues become problems.

The media and politicians need to understand that every reasonable and legal effort is made to seek conformity of members. Neither party wins when issues escalate. The member loses, and the association loses. The goal of an association board should always be to be viewed as extremely reasonable.

DEALING WITH REPORTERS

- Disregarding or slowly responding to these inquiries can have television crews knocking on the front door unannounced.
- Disregarding or slowly responding to inquiries can result in the following being said on television: "We have left repeated messages with the board of directors of the association, and they have not responded."

When contacted by a television reporter or newspaper reporter:

REPORTER INQUIRIES BY TELEPHONE

Obtain the name of the person calling and the media organization.

It goes without saying: always be polite. Remember that the reporter is doing their job.

Find out the anticipated time of release of the information in print or broadcast. This may be referred to as a deadline.

Ask the reporter to email or fax their questions over so that you can contact the appropriate person on the association board to respond. Written questions are best so that an appropriate and formulated response can be given. Talking off-the-cuff in front of a television camera or on the telephone can result in unflattering quotes. Written responses to questions are more difficult to misquote.

REPORTER INQUIRES IN PERSON

If confronted by a television or newspaper reporter unexpectedly, remember again that the reporter is just doing their job.

Make sure to understand each question from the media before answering. If an answer cannot be given, take the reporter's number and advise them that someone with the information will contact them as soon as possible.

Always avoid saying, "No comment." If a response is necessary it sounds much better to say, "It is not appropriate to comment at this time."

Never attempt to make "off the record" statements. Nothing is off the record.

■ ■ ■

WHY DO WE EVEN NEED AN HOA

When serving on a board of directors for any length of time, it is common to hear members complain about the "unreasonable" restrictions of an association or, "Why do we even need a home-owner's association?" Without a doubt, some members may not see the need for any restrictions, but many times they fail to understand the ramifications of loose or non-enforcement of these restrictions. One thing is certain: an association that has CC&Rs and enforces these CC&Rs increases the overall property values for everyone in the association.

When someone purchases a home within an association, they are agreeing to live by the standards of the association as prescribed by the governing documents. This homebuyer should also expect that the standards are upheld for every association member. With this being said, most homeowners wish for their home and community, at a minimum, to remain the same. Many deciding factors go into purchasing a home, but the old axiom is true that the three most important things to look for in purchasing a home are: "location, location, location." More precisely: "neighborhood, neighborhood, neighborhood."

When CC&Rs are not enforced, it is a slippery-slope to see how far or how bizarre members' tastes or styles may vary from the CC&Rs. Through the years, the author has seen an array of extreme infractions of the CC&Rs. One time, a member began construction on a junior Olympic-sized swimming pool in his front yard due to insufficient space in his backyard. This member reasoned: "Why would anyone have an issue with a past-time such as swimming? And so what if the pool needs to be in the front yard?" Another member in this same association purchased a 50-foot sailboat to completely restore. He parked the sailboat in his driveway and over the course of a weekend had the entire boat disassembled and neatly organized all over his front lawn.

What some members consider perfectly acceptable can vary greatly from the CC&Rs and what 99.99% of the rest of the membership would deem as acceptable. But unless it is an extreme situation such as some of the examples noted, some in the membership will say "what is the harm?" Again, it is a slippery-slope that begins with small infractions. Failure to enforce the CC&Rs may seem like a small issue in most instances, until the association is faced with a member who wants to build a 400-square-foot air-conditioned tree house for their grandchildren. Enforcing CC&Rs may be a thankless task, but it is crucial to maintaining the property values of the association.

■ ■ ■

Association Basics

■ ■ ■

ASSOCIATION TERMINOLOGY

Certain terms are used incorrectly or generically when discussing association issues. For example, the CC&Rs are often incorrectly referred to as the bylaws. Or the membership may believe that they are voting for the officers (as opposed to the Directors) of the board of directors during an annual meeting.

ARCHITECTURAL CONTROL

Architectural control is generally established in the CC&Rs; this given authority allows the association to police community standards and practices. Architectural control is generally the preview of an association committee. This committee is commonly referred to as the Architectural Review Committee (ARC) or Architectural Control Committee (ACC).

ARTICLES OF INCORPORATION

This is the basic charter of an association corporation, which spells out the name, basic purpose, incorporators and any special characteristics such as being nonprofit. These records are maintained by the secretary of state in each state.

ASSOCIATION MANAGER

An association manager is a manager of any combination of homeowners associations. Although traditionally referred to as a property manager, in recent years the profession's title has evolved into association manager.

BYLAWS

This is the written governance of an association. The bylaws are often confused with the articles of incorporation, which only state the basic outline of the company origination. Bylaws generally provide for meetings, elections of a board of directors and officers, filling vacancies, notices, types and duties of officers, committees, assessments and other routine conduct.

COMMON ELEMENTS

A common element is normally defined as any part of the association that the association is responsible for maintaining.

COMMUNITY ASSOCIATION, COMMON-INTEREST COMMUNITIES (CIC), OR COMMON-INTEREST DEVELOPMENTS (CIDS)

CICs include condominiums, townhomes, retirement communities, timeshares and other housing communities made up of individually-owned homes, in addition to shared facilities and common areas.

CONDOMINIUM UNIT

This is a residential or commercial structure where ownership generally involves no land and ownership is established within vertical and horizontal planes of the structure itself. The condominium owner also has an ownership interest in the common elements. Condominiums, while many times configured in a multi-stack "apartment" type structures, can come in different configurations, such as patio homes. Condominiums make up approximately 40% of all associations within the United States.

COOPERATIVE UNITS

Commonly referred to as co-ops, these are structures where ownership is though a corporation and an owner is a shareholder. Co-ops can be residential or commercial, and this form of association comprises approximately 5% of the associations within the United States.

COVENANTS, CONDITIONS AND RESTRICTIONS (CC&RS)

CC&Rs are written and filed with the county register of deeds. They set forth the requirements, limitations and restrictions on use as put in place by the developer of an association. CC&Rs may limit size and placement of homes, exterior colors, pets, ages of residents, use of barbecues and other conduct, in order to protect the quiet enjoyment of the various members of the association. CC&Rs are enforced by the homeowners association or by individual owners, who can bring lawsuits against violators. These documents are permanent or "run with the land," so that future owners are bound to the same requirements.

DECLARANT

The declarant is usually the developer and/or home builder of an association. Generally, the declarant purchases the tract of land and either constructs the primary association structure as with a condominium or divides up the tract and sells individual lots. Generally, the declarant will construct the roads and common elements of the association.

DIRECTOR

This is a member of a board of directors within an association. A director is elected by the membership at an annual meeting of the membership. In most cases, a director may also be an officer on the board of directors. However, a director does not necessarily have to be an officer on the board of directors.

EASEMENT

A recorded land easement is a legally-binding instrument that permits land use by the land owner and restricts other parties who do not own the land in question.

LIMITED COMMON ELEMENTS

These are common elements that are exclusive to one member of the association. An example could be balconies, parking spaces or boat slips.

OFFICER

This is an office on a board of directors: president, vice president, secretary or treasurer. In infrequent instances, an officer does not necessarily have to be a director. Directors are elected by the membership at an annual meeting, and officers are chosen by the directors elected at the annual meeting.

PLAT

One of the initial processes of establishing an association is the filing of the site plat with the county register of deeds. The plat indicates locations of the lots or units and any common areas. A plat is also known as a Recorded Map, Plan Map, or Site Map.

RULES & REGULATIONS

This is the basic governance of an association. The authority of the association to establish reasonable rules and regulations is generally set forth in the CC&Rs. Rules and regulations usually expand on what is established in the CC&Rs. For example, the CC&R may set forth that the association swimming pool is for exclusive use of members and their guests, while the rules and regulations may specify that a member is limited to 3 guests at one time.

TOWNHOME

This is a structure usually attached to other similar structures, where the ownership of the structure includes the land beneath. It is usually configured with two or three levels.

■ ■ ■

GOVERNING DOCUMENTS

COVENANTS, CONDITIONS & RESTRICTIONS (CC&RS)

These are also known as CC&Rs, declarations or master deed. By whatever name or abbreviation, these are written rules, limitations and restrictions on use, mutually agreed to (by virtue of purchasing in such a community) by all owners of homes in a planned community or condominium complex.

CC&Rs may prescribe size and placement of homes, exterior home colors, pets, ages of residents, parking and other conduct in order to protect the quiet enjoyment of all the various members of the community. CC&Rs are generally enforced by the homeowners association and, in extreme cases, by individual members who bring legal action against other association members or boards of directors. CC&Rs "run with the land" and thus are permanent for all practical purposes, so that future owners are held to the restrictions. CC&Rs are filed with the register of deeds in the county in which the association is located.

ARTICLES OF INCORPORATION

This is the basic charter of any corporation (in the case of an association, a nonprofit corporation), which spells out the name, basic purpose and incorporators. Articles must be signed by the incorporating person or persons or by the first board of directors. The starting point for filing and approval of articles of incorporation is usually the state's secretary of state.

BYLAWS

These are the written rules of conduct for a corporation. They should not be confused with the articles of incorporation, which usually just state the basic outline of the company. Bylaws generally provide for meetings, elections of boards of directors and officers, filling vacancies, notices, types and duties of officers, committees, assessments and other routine conduct. Bylaws are in effect a contract among members and must be formally adopted and/or amended. Bylaws may or may not be required to be on file with a government entity.

RULES & REGULATIONS

The board of directors generally has the authority to establish reasonable rules and regulations. This authority is typically found in the CC&Rs, but it can in rare instances be found in bylaws or in the articles of incorporation. These rules and regulations may provide for imposition of fines or penalties for the violation of the CC&Rs.

■ ■ ■

AMENDING GOVERNING DOCUMENTS

As many boards that have amended or attempted to amend are aware, amending the association's governing documents, be they the CC&Rs or bylaws, can be a trying experience that should not be undertaken lightly. The association's attorney should be consulted for guidance. The final amendment must be valid and able to stand up to any possible legal challenges.

The first step is to decide what exactly needs to be changed, added or removed. This may seem obvious, but there may be varying thoughts on this issue.

The second step is to make certain there is a unified consensus by a majority of the board of directors on what needs to be done.

The third step is to form a committee to explore the best method of obtaining the desired results.

The information for amending the governing documents is almost always found within those governing documents under the "Amendment" section. (If this language is absent from the association's governing documents, hopefully the state statutes will provide guidance on how to address the matter.) The following language is typical of what is found in the amendment section:

"Except as is otherwise specifically authorized herein, this declaration may be amended only by the vote of not less than sixty-seven percent (67%) of the votes allocated to home owners."

It is not uncommon to require voting percentages to be 80% or even 90% of the entire membership. If the amendment is to change the common elements interest, it is not uncommon to require 100% approval of the membership and 100% approval of all mortgagees.

"This Declaration may be amended only by the vote, cast in person or by proxy, at a meeting duly held in accordance with the provisions of the Bylaws."

Generally speaking, a meeting must be held in order for the amendment to be ratified. However, depending upon certain situations as may be determined by the association's attorney, there are methods for facilitating mail-in ballots with a ratification meeting of some sort.

THE ASSOCIATION'S LEGAL COUNSEL

Although most governing documents spell out the amendment process, it is always advisable to have the association's attorney guide this process. Efforts to save on legal fees can usually be offset by wasted time and effort for legal missteps that may accompany this process. One misstep can void months of work if a legal point is not followed.

The association's attorney should have in-depth experience in this process. An experienced attorney will understand exactly what needs to be done and outline the process for clarification and implementation. The attorney will draft and record the amendment and provide guidance through the entire process up to filing the amendment, if that is the final step of the process.

REASONS NOT TO AMEND GOVERNING DOCUMENTS

Language that is obsolete or not relevant is usually fine left in place and not worth the effort to amend. The author is aware of association boards that have attempted to remove all the declarant language in their declarations because the declarant was no longer involved. When it comes to the removing declarant language, the author has never observed an association successful in this particular amendment process. And there is really no valid reason to expend the energy and legal expense, since the declarant is no longer an issue.

Since generally, state statutes supersede the governing documents, an amendment is usually not necessary to conform to state statute changes. However, there can be exceptions to this, in which an association may need to adopt a state statute.

POINTS TO CONSIDER

Before amendments are attempted, the pulse of the association membership should be taken through meetings and/or surveys. Since the burden to amend is usually at least 67% of the membership, if there is no groundswell or momentum this can be a futile effort. Involvement of the membership in the entire process can lead to greater support and passage.

Proceed with caution when dealing with a complicated issue or more than one amendment issue. Multiple or hard-to-understand amendments are much more difficult to ratify. This basically comes down to whether or not something is reasonably straightforward. When it is not, the tendency of the membership is to vote against it. This tendency can be overcome sometimes by a dedicated educational or informational program by the board or amendment committee, but it can still be a large challenge.

■ ■ ■

THE ASSOCIATION STRUCTURE

HOW AN ASSOCIATION IS FORMED

A homeowner association or condominium association is a non-profit corporation formed usually by a real estate developer, the declarant, for the purposes of marketing, managing and selling homes/lots or units in a development. The governing documents of the association grant the developer special voting rights in the operation of the association, while allowing the developer to exit financial and legal responsibility of the association by transferring ownership of the association to the homeowners after selling off a predetermined number of homes/lots or units or by exiting after a specific date in the future. Membership in the homeowners association or condominium association by a home buyer is generally a condition of the purchase; opting out of the association is generally not an option. Homeowner associations have become increasingly common in the United States, and it is estimated that as of 2010, 24.8 million American homes and approximately 63 million residents come under the governance of a homeowners association.

THE GOVERNANCE OF AN ASSOCIATION

While a large number of states do not have specific legislative statutes that govern the operation of homeowner associations, a number of states do have detailed and lengthy statutes. If an association is located within a state without related statutes, the association's governing documents prevail.

There are generally four specific association governing documents: (1) CC&Rs (2) bylaws, (3) articles of incorporation, (4) rules and regulations.

The state statute that an association falls under, if any, can generally be determined by reviewing the first several pages of the association's CC&Rs. An association's CC&Rs are on file at the county register of deeds. Articles of incorporation are on file with the state secretary of state. Association bylaws and rules and regulations may or may not be required to be on file with a local or state authority. Bylaws many times are filed as an appendix to the CC&Rs and could be on file at the register of deeds.

The CC&Rs generally tell the association member what can and cannot be done within the association and who is responsible. For example, the CC&Rs may address whether association members could have a fence and what type of fence. The bylaws generally outline how the association is to be operated. For example, the bylaws would tell when the annual meeting is to be held or the responsibilities of the directors.

States have specific Nonprofit Corporation Acts or statutes that address nonprofit corporations. These state statutes regulate how nonprofit corporations are to be administered. Associations are nonprofit corporations and generally reference this act. For example, if an individual association's bylaws do not address a specific proxy issue, the Nonprofit Corporation Act would be the first point of reference in resolving that issue.

WHO IS IN CONTROL OF THE ASSOCIATION

The board of directors is in charge of the association, whether under original developer control or direct membership control. The board of directors is elected at the association's annual meeting. Depending upon the governing documents, board member terms can be one-year terms or multi-year terms. Many homeowner associations hire and retain association management companies also known as property management companies. The association management company works for the association at the direction of the board of directors.

ASSOCIATION BENEFITS

An association provides members with shared community benefits and increased property values by sharing common expenses such as landscaping, swimming pools, etc., and by enforcement of the CC&Rs to achieve a community representative of such values as established in the original governing documents. By sharing expenses and enforcing the CC&Rs, the entire membership benefits as a whole. For example, a member who wishes to paint their home purple with pink trim may personally benefit from this particular color scheme, but it could negatively impact the property values of other members.

ASSOCIATION FUNDING

Generally speaking, each member of an association pays assessments that are used to maintain the common elements of an association. (In certain instances, original developers can be exempt from paying dues until certain phases of construction are completed or exempt altogether depending on state statute.) Some of these common elements can be landscaping, upkeep of association amenities, insurance for commonly-owned elements and operational expenses such as the management company.

THE RESPONSIBILITY OF THE ASSOCIATION MEMBER

Association boards can generally levy special assessments upon the membership in addition to the regular assessment. This can be done in certain instances if the governing documents allow for a special assessment without membership approval. However, most governing documents require membership approval.

Associations in many states can foreclose on a member's home in order to collect regular and special assessments or otherwise place an enforceable lien on the property that, upon the property sale, allows the association to collect otherwise unpaid assessments. Also, in many cases, a member is subject to foreclosure and other legal remedies for CC&R violations.

■ ■ ■

HIERARCHY OF GOVERNING DOCUMENTS: THE HIERARCHY OF AUTHORITY FOR ASSOCIATION GOVERNANCE

1 - Statutory Federal Laws
2 - Statutory State Laws
3 - County Ordinances
4 - Municipality Ordinances
5 - Association Declarations
6 - Articles of Incorporation
7 - Association Bylaws
8 - Association Rules and Regulations
9 - Procedural Resolutions & Guidelines
10 - Other Resolutions
11 - Actions and decisions by Board Officers and Directors

* Court Cases, State and Federal, can also have bearing or supersede in certain instances.

■ ■ ■

MEETINGS

■ ■ ■

THE VARIOUS ASSOCIATION MEETINGS

Association meetings may not all have the same legal requirements and procedures, but whatever the requirements they must be followed. Generally speaking, meeting requirements are found in the association's bylaws, although there may be meeting requirements in the association's CC&Rs and, in certain instances, state statutes. So what is the difference between a board meeting and a special meeting, or an annual meeting and a general membership meeting? Here's an overview.

ANNUAL MEETINGS

Annual meetings or annual membership meetings are required by an association's governing documents. The governing documents generally specify when the meeting is to be conducted and how and when members are to be notified of the meeting. The legal cornerstones of an annual meeting are proper membership notification as prescribed in the governing documents and obtaining the quorum meeting requirements, the quorum being the minimum number of members of an association that must be present at a meeting in order to validate the proceedings or hold a legal meeting.

The annual meeting is the primary meeting of the association each year, where members elect a board of directors, hear officer reports, hear committee reports and discuss items of common membership interest. In certain instances, governing documents may have other meeting requirements such as approving a new budget or acceptance of the association financial annual audit. Again, the annual meeting requirements are specifically addressed in every association's governing documents and must be followed in order to have a valid meeting.

SPECIAL MEETINGS

Special meetings are generally limited to a particular topic, such as a special assessment or an amendment to the governing documents. The board can call a special meeting at any time. For example, with an annual meeting, in order to hold a valid special association meeting most governing documents outline the meeting requirements of notification, quorum, etc. An important point to note is that depending upon the course of business to be conducted, the notification may require a longer timeframe and the quorum percentage requirement may be higher. For example, the special meeting requirements to approve a special assessment may be considerably more difficult to achieve.

The special meeting notice should be extremely clear about what will be discussed and what action is to be taken or not taken. For example:

"This special meeting of the membership is being called to discuss repairing the damaged seawall."

"This special meeting of the membership is being called to discuss the plan to repair the damaged seawall and to vote on a special assessment to complete these repairs."

The special meeting language in the second example is clearer and explains what is to be discussed and what action will be taken. This clarity is necessary so that interested members can attend and so that members cannot claim after-the-fact that they were mislead.

Another distinction from an annual meeting is that association members do not necessarily participate in the meeting unless asked directly by the meeting chair, although any member has the opportunity to listen to the discussion and vote on actions when necessary.

GENERAL MEMBERSHIP MEETINGS

General Membership Meetings, sometimes referred to as "Town Hall Meetings," are usually informal gatherings intended to promote association communication, and full membership participation is generally allowed. In certain instances, governing documents may require that these meetings be held a set number of times between annual meetings. General membership meetings are important for improving association communication, but they also allow for discussion on association matters about which the board may need to build a consensus and take later action. Many times these meetings allow the board to gain a better understanding of the pulse of the membership and to garner support or remove a matter from further consideration. Association documents do not generally require strict Roberts Rules of Order or a quorum, especially if no action is being taken.

BOARD OF DIRECTORS MEETINGS

Board of directors meetings are the most difficult meetings to pigeonhole because of the various ways in which governing documents are written. There may be very specific notification requirements or, in some cases, none whatsoever. The governing documents may specifically require a set number of meetings per year, while most have no such meeting requirement. However, whatever the governing documents require with regard to board meetings, these requirements must be followed. For example, if portions of the board meeting are required to be open to the membership, that requirement needs to be followed. Even though it is difficult to pigeonhole all board meetings, one universal constant is that there must be a quorum of the board in attendance before any business can be conducted.

In short, the vast majority of association business is conducted at the board of directors meeting. Board members set policy, oversee the manager's work, select vendors, review operations, resolve disputes, talk to members and plan for the future. The harmony and success of an entire association is often directly linked to constructive board meetings. The membership is usually not allowed to participate in board meetings.

EXECUTIVE SESSION

Executive sessions of the board of directors are held so that boards can address issues involving privileged information and matters of private nature. As a result, members do not have a right to attend executive sessions. Generally, boards of directors may only go into executive session for the following issues:

Legal Issues: Boards may go into executive session in order to discuss litigation and, in certain instances, if the matter at hand might lead to litigation. Meeting in executive session preserves attorney-client privilege. The association's attorney does not need to be present for the board to go into executive session or to discuss legal issues.

Negotiation of Contracts: Boards may consider matters relating to the negotiation of contracts with third parties.

Hearings: Boards should meet in executive session for all CC&R violation hearings.

Personnel Issues: If the association has employees, personnel matters which may include, but are not limited to, hiring, firing, raises, disciplinary matters and performance reviews should be addressed in executive session.

Collection Issues: Without exception, boards should enter executive session for matters relating to membership collections. The decision to initiate foreclosure proceedings can only be made by the board of directors of the association and may not be delegated to an agent of the association.

THE KEY POINT OF ALL MEETINGS
The key point of any association meeting is that the governing documents, bylaws and/or declarations are the road map to be followed.

■ ■ ■

ANNUAL MEETING PAPERWORK

An annual meeting is a meeting of the association membership required by state statutes and the association's governing documents. The annual meeting is held every year to elect the board of directors and inform members of previous and future association activities. It is also an opportunity for the membership to ask questions regarding the decisions and direction of the association.

ANNUAL MEETING NOTICE

Notice of the association annual meeting generally must be in writing and is subject to a maximum and minimum notice period that varies by each association's governing documents. For example, maximum and minimum notice periods can be stated as: "annual meeting notices can be mailed no sooner than 60 days before and no less than 10 days before the annual meeting." The annual meeting notice must state a date, time and location of such meeting.

NOMINATING APPLICATION

A nominating application, as the name might imply, is a form to be submitted prior to the annual meeting for members interested in running for the board of directors. The association's governing documents may or may not require that this be mailed to the membership with the annual meeting notice.

PROXY

A proxy used at an annual meeting is a written instrument that gives a member's authority to another party to act on the member's behalf. The association's governing documents may or may not require that this be mailed to the membership with the annual meeting notice.

AFFIDAVIT OF MAILING

This is a document in which the party who prepared and mailed the annual meeting notice attests that all noticing requirements have been met and all the members were mailed notices. Even if the association's governing documents do not require this form to be completed, it is often completed and placed in the association's files.

AGENDA

An agenda is a list of items to be discussed at the annual meeting. Some association governing documents prescribe a specific agenda and format to be used at the annual meeting. Some governing documents require that the agenda be mailed along with the annual meeting notice.

OWNERSHIP LIST/MEMBERSHIP LIST

Ownership lists are generally required for verification of the membership and in order for members to sign in and receive ballots.

BALLOTS

This is a process for voting in writing.

DELINQUENCY REPORT

This is a list of delinquent members. Some association governing documents prohibit members who are delinquent or in litigation with the association from voting and even, in some instances, from attending the meeting.

WELCOME TO THE ANNUAL MEETING FORM

This is a great form to distribute at annual meetings to make sure everyone has an understanding of the annual meeting process.

WELCOME TO THE ASSOCIATION ANNUAL MEETING

Welcome! The Board wishes to thank you for your interest in the homeowner's association and attending the Annual Meeting of the Association.

The governing documents of your association have established the procedures for how the meeting is to be held. There is a set agenda as prescribed in your association's governing documents. Because of this, please do not interrupt the meeting unless you are addressed by the president/chair of the annual meeting.

Please note that at the bottom of the agenda there is an open floor discussion session, which allows the membership to voice issues of a nature that involve and relate to the entire membership. During this open floor discussion please avoid discussing issues that solely affect individual matters such as individual maintenance, others in the membership, etc. Issues of an individual nature can be discussed after the annual meeting, or you can request to be added to the agenda of the next Board of Directors meeting.

Sincerely,

The Association Board of Directors

■ ■ ■

PROXIES

Proxies are an important aspect of many association membership meetings. This is especially the case when associations have high quorum requirements and low membership meeting turnout. Because association governing documents can vary and individual state statutes can also vary, the following information is a general outline of the use of proxies within associations.

A proxy is the formal authority given to another party by an association member to act on their behalf in their absence, generally at an association membership meeting. This party may or may not necessarily be a member of the association. Proxies cannot be used for board of director meetings since this would constitute a delegation of fiduciary responsibilities that cannot be delegated.

While there is typically no standardized proxy form, in most instances this authority must be given in writing. The exception, unless prohibited by the association's articles of incorporation, bylaws or state statute, is in certain instances of telephonic transmissions. Even if this telephonic communication is not accompanied by written document, it is acceptable if the board secretary can reasonably assume that the proxy was authorized by the member.

The proxy form must be signed by the member, either personally or by the member's attorney-in-fact. Generally speaking, a proxy form in electronic format that bears the member's electronic signature is considered valid.

A proxy is generally effective when accepted and filed by the association's secretary. Proxies can be written to be valid for a particular meeting or a longer time-period. This time-period can vary according to the association's governing documents or state statute.

Generally speaking, a proxy is revocable by the member who appointed the proxy. Some governing documents and state statutes allow for and some prohibit the use of irrevocable proxies. A proxy is revocable by the appointing member attending the meeting and voting in person, or by the appointing member delivering a written statement to the board secretary revoking said appointment. A proxy can also be revoked by the member submitting a subsequent proxy, which automatically revokes the prior proxy when accepted and filed by the secretary.

If the association governing documents and state statute allow, there are two types of proxies: first, the general proxy, which allows the appointed member the authority to vote as they see fit regarding any business brought up at a meeting; second, the limited proxy, by which the appointing member directs the appointed proxy-holder on how to exercise the proxy.

The wording that comprises a proxy form can vary. However, a proxy form should have a phrase similar to the following: "I John Smith appoint Jane Jones as my proxy." Then there should be a place for the member to sign and date the proxy. While state statutes and governing documents may have additional requirements, this wording is generally the minimum. Unless the governing documents or state statutes mandate a specific proxy form, the board secretary generally accepts other forms.

Two primary concerns often arise when it comes to the use of proxies: first, members who submit proxies and do not attend meetings are less informed; second, a member obtaining a vast number of proxies can influence membership votes.

States and some associations have implement limits on the use of proxies in attempts to reduce these two concerns. It is not uncommon for associations to amend their bylaws to prevent members from bringing more than a set number of proxies to a meeting. The state of Arizona implemented legislation that severely restricts the use of proxies in favor of mail-in ballots.

With both of these concerns taken into consideration, when a member signs a general proxy they are giving their authority to another party to make decisions on their behalf. Short of a new statute or document amendment, there is not much an association board of directors can do to relieve either of these two concerns.

When members complete proxies for a membership meeting and designate those proxies, the proxy must be designated to a specific person or possibly a board officer. Designating proxies to "The Board of Directors" would generally not be acceptable because that is a not an identifiable individual. Designating to the board secretary could be considered valid if there is an individual holding that board position.

■ ■ ■

QUORUM

A quorum is the number of members required to be present before a meeting can legally be conducted. Quorums are necessary for annual membership meetings and board of directors meetings. If association business is to be conducted, special membership meetings require a quorum as well.

For board of directors meetings, unless the bylaws or possibly the articles of incorporation state differently, a quorum is a majority of the board members. Membership meeting quorums can be almost any percentage of the membership. Membership meeting quorum requirements can range from as little as 5% up to 75%, with typical associations being in the 10% to 20% range.

Special membership meetings may have a higher quorum requirement than an annual meeting. This is typical when special meetings are held to raise dues or vote on a special assessment. This higher quorum threshold is especially common if the annual meeting quorum requirements are exceptionally low.

The necessity of the mandated quorum percentage being met is to confer authority upon decisions made by the board of members going forward. Thus, if a quorum is not present, no association business can legally be conducted. If business is conducted, such as board elections, these elections can rightly be challenged as improper. Any decisions that these "board members" make would be illegitimate and, as a consequence, delegitimize any decisions made by the rest of the board of directors.

A proxy is authorization from an association member to another party, not necessarily to another association member, to act or vote in their place. Unless the governing documents prohibit a proxy's use, proxies can be used for annual membership or special membership meetings in order to help establish a quorum. However, proxies cannot be used for board of director meetings, since this would constitute a delegation of fiduciary responsibilities that cannot be delegated.

If the meeting quorum is difficult to obtain because of a high turnout percentage requirement, a common acceptable means to help meet quorum is the "member in good standing" provision found in many governing documents. This provision often has wording similar to: "A Member shall be considered to be a 'Member in Good Standing' if such Member is not past due in their assessment or not in litigation with the association." In the section of an association's governing documents regarding membership voting rights and other sections, there is many times wording similar to: "Only members in good standing are permitted to participate in the annual meeting." This can reduce a quorum requirement by reducing the number of homes that are factored into the quorum.

For example, in a 100-home association the quorum requirement is 25%, which equates to 25 members in person or by proxy for a quorum. If 10 members of the association are not in good standing, this quorum is factored on 90 homes instead of 100, which reduces the required number from 25 members to 23 members to constitute a quorum. If the governing documents are not clear on which members can and cannot vote, the association's attorney should be consulted for clarification.

Another possible solution to high quorum requirements is the annual meeting provision in an association's governing documents that allows for subsequent annual meetings. This provision allows for follow-up annual meetings at a lower quorum requirement if a quorum is not obtained at the initial annual meeting. If there is such a provision, the quorum is usually halved in subsequent annual meeting attempts.

If there is no specific percentage quorum requirement addressed in an association's governing documents and no state statute provides guidance, the standard quorum defaults to 51%.

■ ■ ■

SPEAKING AT YOUR ANNUAL MEETING

"According to most studies, people's number one fear is public speaking. Number two is death. Death is number two. Does that seem right? That means that, to the average person, if you have to go to a funeral, you're better off in the casket than doing the eulogy." Comedian Jerry Seinfeld

For most people, speaking in front of an association is never an easy task. However, there are steps that can be taken to help overcome the trepidation. If the message is coherent, informative and interesting, that is 99% of the battle. Here are some key points to capture and keep an association audience's attention:

- Speak to the association member's issues. Begin the talk by generally discussing the issues facing the association and, more specifically, the issues facing the membership. Portray the issues or problems on everyone's mind. Beginning the talk with these considerations should grab the membership and direct the conversation in the right direction.
- Use the KIS Principle: Keep the message simple and relative. Drill down on the main message points. Be selective about the facts and deliver the main points.
- Try to anticipate the membership's predominant point of view on the topic beforehand and plan accordingly. And *vice versa*, try to anticipate any minor points of view that may need addressing.
- Slow down. Novice speakers have a tendency to speak fast and in some instances so fast that the audience cannot keep up with what is being said. Take a breath and pause to let the message sink in and resonate. Practice breathing at

particular important points when rehearsing the talk. Slow and deliberate speech is the marking of seriousness and contemplation.

- Be composed in the message. A large part of being persuasive is how the speakers carry themselves while talking. Appearing relaxed and confident comes across much better than appearing nervous and much better than appearing lofty.

One key point is to not take questions or let the membership interrupt. Allowing the membership to interrupt can throw the talk off track. Remind members to hold their questions until the open discussion part of the meeting.

Without any doubt, the most important aspect of the message preparation is practice, practice, practice. Remember the old joke: "A man is lost in New York City and asks a street performer; 'Sir, how do you get to Carnegie Hall?' The street performer answers without hesitation: 'Practice, practice and more practice.'"

■ ■ ■

HEATED ASSOCIATION MEETINGS

For most board members, meetings are a fact of life, and over time board members obtain valuable experience in dealing with issues that arise. Part of this valuable experience is becoming adept at participating effectively and managing meetings. This experience is a useful skill, not only in an association meeting, but also in unrelated matters that everyone becomes involved in during their life.

With this valuable experience of participating effectively and managing meetings, sometimes one or two meeting participants will dominate the discussion, steer it off topic and interrupt others, causing long and uncomfortable or unproductive meetings. Whether used by the meeting chair or a participant, there are techniques that can be used to help engage others, limit intrusions and minimize distractions.

- Table the discussion. If a conversation is getting particularly heated, the chair or a participant can move to table the discussion for a later date. This helps clear the air and allows a calmer and more meaningful conversation at the next meeting. It also sends the signal that debates will be conducted rationally and with respect.
- Discuss Independently. When a meeting attendee takes a topic off course, everyone's time is wasted. A good tool for the chair to use, or for another attendee to suggest, is to ask the member to discuss the matter independently with the board after the meeting. Saying, "Let's talk about that topic after the meeting so we can talk more," is an easy way to get back on the subject without alienating the sidetracked speaker.
- Use a timed agenda. The timed agenda is a useful tool for keeping a meeting moving efficiently.

  When a chair begins a meeting by saying, "We have a full agenda today," he or she sets the stage for productivity. Periodically referring to the agenda time schedule during the course of the meeting keeps all attendees focused on the discussion.
- Call on members. To engage more reserved members of the group and balance the impact of more vocal participants,

it's helpful to call on members by name to ask for their opinions. "What do you think, Mary?" or "Do you have some input here, Steve?" ensures that all members are valued.

■ ■ ■

MEMBER IN GOOD STANDING

When an association member fails to pay their assessment or violates the CC&Rs, how does the board respond? For past due assessments the association has the standard collection processes, and for CC&R violations the board has standard enforcement processes. What if these standard processes are not enough to force the member to bring their account current or to force CC&R compliance?

Another alternative to use in conjunction with the standard compliance processes is to revoke or suspend a member's association privileges. To determine whether the association has the ability to suspend a member's privileges, the association's bylaws are the first governing document to review. The heading or wording may vary from the bylaws of one association to another; however, "Member in Good Standing," is probably the most utilized term. For example:

Section 4.1. MEMBER IN GOOD STANDING. A Member shall be considered to be a "Member in Good Standing" if such Member:

a. Has, at least ten days prior to the taking of any vote by the Association, fully paid all Assessments or other charges levied by the Association, as such Assessments or charges are provided for hereunder;
b. Is not in litigation with the association;

c. Has discharged all other obligations to the Association as may be required of Members hereunder or under the Association Documents.

The Board shall have sole authority for determining the good standing status of any Member at any time and shall make such determination with respect to all Members prior to a vote being taken by the Association on any matter. The Board shall have the right and authority, in its sole discretion, to waive the ten-day prior payment requirement if extenuating circumstances exist. Any Member not conforming with the provisions of this Section 4.1 shall be declared by the Board not to be a Member in Good Standing and shall not be entitled to vote on matters before the Association, hold a position on the board of directors or utilize any of the Association's amenities until such time Member in Good Standing status is attained and so declared by the Board.

While the above example is very detailed, some associations' bylaws may offer sparser language or possibly not have any bylaw provisions regarding suspending member privileges. When the language of members in good standing is vague or does not offer enough detail, the association's attorney should be consulted. If the association's governing documents fail to address this issue, amending the bylaws to include such language may be a viable option. Amending bylaws is generally much easier and more straightforward than amending declarations. The association's attorney should be consulted on amending governing documents.

No matter what the association documents require about notifying members about revoking privileges, written notification is always advisable before these privileges are revoked. In certain situations, even if it is not required by the governing documents, a hearing before the board of directors to discuss the suspension may be advisable. Giving the member notice of the pending suspension and an opportunity to speak with the board of directors always comes across well in court, if the action eventually ends up in litigation.

■ ■ ■

ASSOCIATION FINANCIALS

Financial soundness is the foundation of all homeowner associations. Poorly financially-operated associations typically have lower property values and more volatile memberships. An association board of directors should always consider the financial stability of the association as the top priority. This financial stability involves everything from the collection of delinquent member assessments to the best utilization of the vendors who serve the association.

The starting point of the financial soundness of any association is reading and understanding the financial statements. The association's financial statements are the summary of the financial activity of the association during any given period of time. Financial statements are the final product of the accounting function. Homeowner associations should at a minimum produce three financial statements: Balance Sheet, Income Statement and the Cash Disbursement Report. To complement these three reports, a membership Aging Report should be produced to track delinquent members.

THE BALANCE SHEET

The Balance Sheet is the most basic of the financial statements, which includes the association's assets and liabilities/equities as of a specific date. The Balance Sheet is a fast and easy way to determine the financial health of an association.

Assets are the resources that the association has for future benefit. Assets include items such as funds in the operating checking account, funds in money market accounts, certificates of deposit and possible capital equipment.

Liabilities and Equities are obligations to others. A Balance Sheet for an association's Liabilities and Equities will generally contain Capital Reserves and Retained Earnings. Reserves are funds set aside for future capital maintenance obligations and are thus liabilities. Retained Earnings is the balance of net income less losses over the years that the association has been in existence: profits (excess income) retained by the association. Retained Earnings are an equity account. The retained earnings (+/- net income/loss) amount is not indicative of how much cash the association has but, rather, represents how much unobligated cash (assets) the association has.

There is a category of Net Income or Net Loss calculation on the Balance Sheet. Net Income is the total of excess income over expenses, while Net Loss is the excess expenses over income. There is an example of a Balance Sheet in the appendix.

THE INCOME STATEMENT

Whereas the Balance Sheet shows balances as of a specific date, the Income Statement shows the flow of financial activity and transactions over a specific period of time, typically a month. There are incomes from dues, etc., and expenses from association operations.

The Income Statement has two primary parts: Operating Income and Operating Expenses. The Operating Expense has subparts to explain expenses. Every income and expense item has a number corresponding to the chart of accounts. A chart of accounts is a financial organizational tool that provides a numerical listing for every financial category account in an accounting system. An account is a unique record for each type of asset, liability, equity, revenue and expense.

Income statements can vary in layout. The example in the appendix has seven columns with numbers reflecting either income or expenses. Income statements can have as few as one numbers column containing the "Actual" income and expense for the accounting period in question.

A good tip to make reading and understanding the income statement with multiple columns easier is to take a sheet of paper and cover all but the first column and look at only one column at a time. This first "Actual" column is actually what was brought in and what was spent in the operations of the association in the time-period of the statement. The next column is the "Budget," and this is what was budgeted to be received or spent. The third column, "Variance," is the difference between the first two columns.

The next three columns are Year-to-Date calculations, as opposed to the first three columns, which deal with a one-month time-period. The last column, "Annual Budget," is the annual budgeted amount. When it comes to reading an income statement, breaking the statement down by covering up columns and reading one at time makes the task manageable.

CASH DISBURSEMENT REPORT

A Cash Disbursement shows the detailed activity of checks written or electronically transferred from the association's operating checking account to pay the association's expenses. The disbursements on the Cash Disbursements Report can be reconciled against the "Actual" column on the Income Statement and *vice versa*. There is an example of Cash Disbursement in the appendix.

MEMBERSHIP AGING REPORT

A Membership Aging Report is a report that lists members who are delinquent or have outstanding or unpaid assessments. The aging report is the primary tool for monitoring collections.

■ ■ ■

THE YEAR-END & THE ASSOCIATION'S FINANCIALS

Association tax preparation should be completed by a qualified outside third party CPA firm. Potential cost savings of utilizing others to perform this task are not offset by the problems that inexperience or lack of competence can cause. For example, the author was asked a number of years ago to review the financials of an office park condominium association. The board treasurer used the same bookkeeper to do the association's tax returns that he used to do his small businesses returns. While the bookkeeper was a very nice person and the board treasurer defended her to the very end, it did not change the fact that she had made several major mistakes on their tax filings for over a decade, which had cost the office association over $10,000. In this association's case, their new CPA could only file amended returns that recovered several thousand dollars.

One aspect that makes associations' financials different is that, while individual tax returns are due by April 15, corporation tax returns in a December 31 fiscal year are typically due by March 15.

The Internal Revenue Service requires associations who have hired third-party contractors to complete Form 1099, if certain requirements are met. Currently a 1099 does not have to be completed by the association if the contractor is incorporated or less than $600 worth of services were provided in the fiscal year. Once a 1099 is completed, it must be mailed out to the independent contractor by January 31. The IRS Copy 1099 duplicate copy must be filed to the IRS by the last day of February.

If the association has employees, year-end filings include the quarterly and year-end payroll reports for both federal and state. In addition, a W-2 must be completed for each association employee. Employee earnings also have to be reported to the Social Security Administration and Employment Security Commission.

■ ■ ■

AUDIT OR REVIEW OR COMPILATION

Independent third-party financial examinations are a good business practice for all homeowner associations. Even if the association's governing documents do not require some type of financial examination every year, yearly examinations are money well spent. There are three levels of accounting evaluations that associations utilize: Audits, Reviews and Compilations. Audits are the most thorough and thus the most expensive of the three. Compilations are the least thorough and are used for specific financial areas that need review.

When negotiating with the outside CPA firm for a financial examination, it is always advisable to have annual federal and state tax filings included.

- An audit is the most thorough examination of the association financials. The audit provides the auditor's opinion on whether or not the financial statements are presented fairly, in all material respects, in conformity with the applicable financial reporting standards. In an audit, the auditor is required by auditing standards, Generally Accepted Accounting Standards (GAAS), to obtain an understanding of the association's internal financial controls and assess any potential fraud risk.

  In an audit, the auditor is required to verify the transactions within the association's financial statements by verifying through inspection, third-party confirmations and other procedures. The auditor may also issue a disclaimer of opinion or an adverse opinion (if appropriate). Audits are a good business practice and demonstrate to the membership that their dues are being handled properly.
- Reviews, while not as thorough as audits, are financial reports that provide the board of directors with a level of assurance that, based upon the accountant's review, the association's financials are in conformity with accounting principles.

  A review involves the CPA performing procedures (primarily analytical procedures and with limited inquiries) that provide a reasonable basis for obtaining some level of assurance that there are no material modifications that should be made to the financial statements in order to be in conformity with applicable accounting principles.

In a review, the CPA designs and performs analytical procedures, inquiries and other procedures as appropriate. A review does not certify the association's internal accounting control or an in-depth assessment of fraud risk. A review is not an in-depth testing of accounting records or other procedures ordinarily performed during an audit.

- A compilation in the realm of homeowner associations is generally utilized to examine one specific accounting issue that concerns the board of directors. For example, compilations are sometimes used to verify beginning membership balances from the prior homeowner association's management company, when the prior management company's accounting records are in question.

  A compilation does not do a complete examination, as would be determined by an audit. A compilation is a very narrow examination of a specific accounting record.

■ ■ ■

ANNUAL BUDGET

A budget is often referred to as a shot-in-the-dark, but accurate and realistic annual budgets are possible with proper forethought. Budgets are essential in the planning of the upcoming fiscal year. Budget shortfalls and failures to properly fund reserves can have a negative effect on the financial stability of the association and can hurt overall property values. When an association starts under-funding annual budgets, it can be difficult, if not impossible, to correct in future years without extreme measures. Fund-raising measures such as special assessments and bank loans are best avoided and, with proper planning, can be avoided in most situations. A realistic annual budget now can prevent future special assessments and drastic dues increases in future budget years.

Calculating a nonprofit association's budget is different from that of for-profit corporations. For-profit corporations estimate income and profits first and then expenses. A nonprofit association estimates expenses first and then the income or dues needed to cover those expenses; in this way, dues amounts are the end result.

1st: Review the previous year's budget as compared to the actual expenses incurred.

2nd: Identify inflation effects from increases in utilities and other services.

3rd: Identify any special projects or areas of focus in the upcoming year.

4th: Reserve funding: is a reserve study needed to help plan for future capital improvements? A board may possibly want to budget for a reserve study in the upcoming year.

5th: Calculate the annual income needed: Annual Expenses + Annual Reserves = Annual Dues Amount. This amount is divided equally amongst the membership or by the ownership percentage, as prescribed in the association's governing documents.

A key point to keep in mind regarding dues increases is that gradual increases to keep up with inflation are always much more palatable to memberships than drastic increases in one budget year. No one likes dues increases, and it can be unpleasant to serve on a board when there is a dues increase. However, delaying this increase will eventually make matters worse in the coming years.

If the governing documents limit increases and there is an unavoidable shortfall in the annual budget, a budget plan for deferring or eliminating certain expenses is often the only acceptable option. Expenses such as landscaping can be reduced by limiting additional items such as mulching the flowerbeds or seasonal flowers. Care must be exercised in delaying painting and other preventative maintenance items. Failure to paint or clean gutters can cause wood rot and other water damage that creates future expenses that greatly exceed any benefit from delaying these expenses.

While nothing can generally be done for an association's past budgeting shortfalls, proper planning for the future can greatly improve the financial stability of the association

QUICK POINTS REGARDING BUDGETS

While calculating future expenses, always consider whether or not a prior year expense was a one-time expense and will not occur again in the coming year.

When calculating seasonal expenses such as pool and landscaping, the year-to-date expenses may not be representative of a total annual expense. For example, the pool expense is much higher in summer months than in winter months.

Almost all association governing documents require an annual budget to be prepared and approved, generally at least 30 days prior to the beginning of a fiscal year.

If an association's board approves a budget with a dues increase and the association's governing documents do not specify a notification date for an increase, a 30-day notification by mail is standard.

When dues are increased, coupons with the new dues amount noted are usually sufficient notification of an increase to the membership, unless the association governing documents require another form of notification.

■ ■ ■

INCREASING ASSESSMENTS

To quote from Christopher Bullock's 1716 *The Cobbler of Preston*, 'Tis impossible to be sure of any thing but Death and Taxes." Another truism that could be added is: expenses go up. Assessments, as any other expense, go up. Some may read this and remark that this is obvious, but it is not uncommon for some in the membership not to grasp this situation. As with many association issues, planning and communication are an effective strategy.

With all associations, expenses go up each year as reflected in the annual budget. First and foremost, these expense increases should always be offset by matching assessment increases. The reasoning is that these gradual yearly assessment increases are viewed much more favorably by the membership than an extreme increase down the road. When these large annual increases do occur, there can be a great deal of animosity as a result.

Another important point about not increasing the assessment when expenses increase is the restraints of the governing documents. Most association governing documents cap or limit annual assessment increases. So, if the assessment does not keep pace with increases in the association's expenses, the governing documents may prevent increases in the future in order to cover operational shortfalls.

If the increase is gradual, or if the increase is large, the annual budget is the first line of defense. As always, the annual budget should reflect the best efforts of the board to predict the upcoming expenses of the association. A lackadaisical approach to budgeting or even a simple error in a budget can quickly erode membership confidence in the association's expenses. For example, an item on the budget that was a onetime emergency expense unlikely to reoccur can make the budget appear inflated.

Adequately communicating an assessment increase to the membership begins with a clear and precise description of the facts of the matter. Because of the busy nature of our society, communications must be clear and precise, and this is best accomplished in communicating the situation on one page or less. Elaborate explanations and multiple pages of text are better presented in bullet points and pie charts on one page as an "overview." This assessment increase overview is designed to accomplish the overall goal of the membership reading and comprehending the matter.

At the end of this section is an example of an assessment increase overview. There are four parts to this overview: The increase, Why there is an increase, Where the money is going (pie chart), What members received for their money and what they will be getting for their money going forward.

- The increase: "We are writing to inform you of your 2018 dues rate for your home...making the new 2018 monthly dues rate $181.10."

  This increase aspect is the most crucial to communicate to the membership. This section sets forth the legal requirement of notice. Many times, in order to enforce an assessment increase in court, there has to be written notice to the membership.
- Why there is an increase: "The primary reasons for this increase...Sewer line breaks...Age of the community..."

  Providing detail to the membership on why the dues "must" increase goes a long way in relaying concerns. The more specifics on this aspect the better. If the association water bill went up 8.5% along with the electricity bill going up 4%, this is most pertinent to the increase dialog.
- Where the money is going (pie chart): "Per the 2018 budget the $181.10 monthly dues are allocated as follows..."

  A pie chart or similar visual vehicle reinforces the funding needs of the association. This is especially true with members who only skim the overview for the high points. This type of graphic also helps dispel the incorrect perception some members may have that their dues are not being spent wisely.
- What members received for their money and what they will be getting for their money going forward: "Many large

projects have been completed in the past two years, and the overall financials are healthy...the primary challenge in 2018 will be removal and potential replacement of dead and overgrown trees/bushes...throughout the community... Maintaining the landscaping and appearance is an important factor in supporting property values."

While this part of the overview may speak for itself, it is always best to end on a positive point.

HAPPY GLEN HOMEOWNERS ASSOCIATION

November 30, 2017

To: All Members of the Happy Glen Homeowners Association

From: Board of Directors for Happy Glen Homeowners Association

Re: New Monthly Dues Rate for 2018 Year

Dear Member,

We are writing to inform you of your 2018 dues rate for your home located in the Happy Glen Homeowners Association. Enclosed is a copy of the 2018 Budget for your records. There will be an increase in the monthly homeowners dues of 5% which is equal to $8.62 extra per month, making the new 2018 monthly dues rate $181.10. This is an annual increase of $103.44 per unit resulting in $18,619.20 of additional revenue for the year.

The primary reasons for this increase in association dues are as follows:

- Sewer line breaks and anticipated proactive repairs to lines to prevent sewage from backing up into our homes.
- Age of the community being twenty plus years now means increased replacements & repairs needed.
- Anticipated costs of landscaping removal of trees and other replacements due to tree roots damaging sidewalks, driveways, etc. throughout the community.
- Repairs to three detention ponds located in the community to prevent failure and flooding of community.
- This allows for reserves to be funded at current level.

Per the 2018 budget the $181.10 monthly dues are allocated as follows:

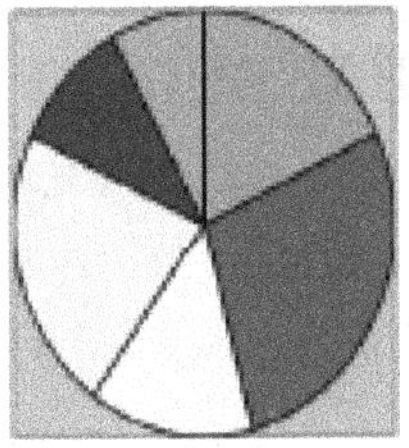

- Repairs & Maintenance (Bldg, pool, plumbing) $32.49
- Utilities (water/sewer/electric) Termite & Pest Control $50.48
- Building & Liability Insurance $25.34
- Landscaping Maintenance $39.86
- Reserves $18.11
- Administrative & Misc $14.82

Many large projects have been completed in the past two years and the overall financials are healthy and delinquencies remain low. We anticipate the primary challenge in 2018 will be removal and potential replacement of dead and overgrown trees/bushes throughout the community as well as addressing erosion/drainage. Maintaining the landscaping and appearance is an important factor in supporting property values. Coupon booklets will be mailed out shortly, unless you are set up on auto-draft. If you are on auto-draft they will automatically adjust the amount drafted starting January 2018. If you pay online with your bank please make sure that you change the dues rate to $181.10 per month effective January 1, 2018.

With kindest regards,

Board of Directors
Happy Glen Homeowners Association

▪ ▪ ▪

MEMBERSHIP QUESTIONS AND THE ANNUAL BUDGET

Memberships have questions about what they are paying for with their dues. The best practice for a homeowner association board is to always have open communication with the membership when it comes to most matters and especially when it comes to annual budgets and dues. Communication is vital to ease possible concerns and to inform the membership of what they are paying for each dues pay period. Some in the membership may have no real understanding of what they receive for their dues.

Copies of the budget can go a long way toward reassuring the membership that their monies are spent wisely. Many associations go as far as providing expense breakdowns in their monthly newsletters and at their annual meeting, in order to stress that a certain percentage goes to the maintenance of the pool and a certain percentage goes to the landscaping, etc. A better understanding by the membership of expenses is always beneficial.

"Why Are Our Dues Higher?"

It is common to hear from members something like: "I have a friend who lives at Happy Glen HOA, their dues are lower than ours, and they have more amenities." Many times this can be a tough question to answer without firsthand knowledge of Happy Glen. However, there are numerous factors that influence dues amounts:

Size of the Association: Economics of Scale; for example, an association with 100 homes will generally have the same pool maintenance expense as an association with 200 homes.

Age of the Association: Age for obvious reasons can affect maintenance expenses of an association.

Amenities of the Association: Operations of certain amenities such as pool lifeguards and the cleaning of clubhouses can drastically affect budgets.

Features of the Association: Security fences and gates, security guards, parking decks, ponds/lakes and other features that are not routine for some associations can have major impacts on annual budgets.

Reserves of the Association: While most associations are funding their reserves, not *all* associations are funding their reserves.

If these key points do not shed light on the matter, request that this member obtain a budget of the association referred to. This will provide a wealth of information that can generally answer the question in short order.

An association board president with whom the author works was confronted with this very question several years ago at their annual meeting regarding a neighboring association of similar size, age and amenities. This association's dues were reported to be on average $50/month less than his association's. However, upon further investigation, this neighboring association turned out to have had at least one special assessment per year and in some years two special assessments over the previous five years, in order to meet general operating expenses. Taking these special assessments into account, the neighboring association's dues were on average $35 a month higher.

The key to the membership understanding and accepting the association's budget is communication. The membership has a right to know how the dues amounts are determined and how these dues are going to be spent. If this communication is done effectively, the membership often obtains a new perspective of what goes into the operation of their association. After all, there are no trips to Paris for the board of directors in the budget, and arguing about utility bills can be similar to complaining about the weather.

■ ■ ■

MORE ON WHY DUES ARE DIFFERENT FROM ASSOCIATION TO ASSOCIATION

"Why are our dues higher than the association next door?" Or perhaps: "My sister's association dues are less than our dues." No matter the one-dimensional analysis of another association's dues, a great deal of further research is needed. As with many situations, the answer to this may appear to be straightforward, but the answer is rarely clear-cut.

ASSOCIATION AGE

For obvious reasons, the age of the association generally has the largest impact upon the expenses. As with any aging property, maintenance and preventive maintenance expenses only increase with time. The composition of maintenance items has an enormous impact on expenses. For example, a swimming pool constructed of concrete has a different lifespan and maintenance needs than a pool constructed of fiberglass.

RESERVES

Another factor with the age of an association is the reserve funds. More precisely, the factor is how well-funded or underfunded are the reserves. Ideally, capital expenditure funds are drawn from the reserves and not the general operating funds. If reserves are not sufficient, dues have to be increased to make up the deficiency. Conversely, if there are sufficient reserves, these capital expenditures should not negatively influence normal dues amounts.

COMMON ELEMENTS

The maintenance responsibilities for any particular association is as varied as the colors of a rainbow.

Common elements could be nominal, as is found in many single-family home associations. For example, maybe just a front entrance sign is required. Conversely, association responsibilities could be as comprehensive as those found in condominiums communities. The point here is that no two associations are the same when it comes to common elements.

STYLE OR CONFIGURATION OF HOME

Notwithstanding common elements, the style or configuration of the homes within an association plays a factor in association responsibilities and related expenses. For example, there is a number of associations that have "townhome" configurations (multiple floor dwelling with no unit above or below), but the declarations are written to reflect the dwellings as condominiums. Situations such as this can even be found in single-family home structures that have declarations reflecting patio-home maintenance responsibilities.

UTILITIES & MUNICIPAL SERVICES

Depending upon the municipality or service provider, water/sewer or trash collection may be an individual association member expense or an association expense. Municipalities on multifamily developments will many times only install one master water meter in order to reduce monitoring and billing expenses. Trash collection is another service that municipalities may not provide for associations without additional fees. The author is familiar with two associations that neighbor each other and were built by the same developer; the only difference is that one association was built before the municipality ceased providing trash collection services for new developments.

AMENITIES

Amenities can be one of the most difficult expenses to compare and contrast to another association. Amenities can have varying degrees of maintenance requirements and staffing requirements. For example, one association may employ lifeguards, while another association may not.

ASSOCIATION SIZE/NUMBER OF HOMES

An aspect that is often overlooked with regard to expenses is the size of the association. With certain expenses such as pool maintenance, a kind of economy of scale occurs. Consider the fact that an Olympic-sized pool costs the same to maintain no matter whether the association has 100 homes or 250 homes. So the costs can be spread out over 250 homes instead of only 100 homes.

■ ■ ■

ACCOUNTING CONTROLS

If an association is self-managed or under professional management, the board of directors should have at least a basic understanding of the accounting controls. Association management companies and self-managed associations should adhere to Generally Accepted Accounting Principles (GAAP). GAAP are authoritative practices and standards intended to provide guidelines and detailed procedures for the accounting functions within a company and the preparation of financial statements that result from the accounting functions.

A major aspect of these guidelines and procedures for GAAP are the accounting controls. With regard to association management companies, accounting controls are the methods or procedures that form the complete internal control system of the management company. Accounting controls ensure compliance with accounting policies and procedures and also help safeguard the association's funds and other assets. These controls ensure that the association's financial reports are accurate and completed in a timely manner.

Ideally, an association management company has a substantial accounting department, with a personnel size that allows for segregation of duties. Segregation of accounting duties or functions is one of the key aspects of accounting controls.

For example, a segregation of duties would be the person reconciling the association's bank account being someone other than the person signing the checks. A third person would be responsible for making entries on the association's ledger and producing financial reports. Segregating accounting duties has two benefits: first, multiple parties are double-checking everyone's work for accuracy, and second and most important, dishonest activities are more difficult to conceal.

Since self-managed association boards are usually small, and since the majority of management companies have small accounting departments, the "true" segregation of duties is usually more difficult, but not impossible. If a management company only has one or two people in their accounting department, the association board of directors will have to be more diligent than normal about reviewing the financial statements. As a part of this additional reviewing process, the board of directors should also be receiving bank statements directly from the bank to help safeguard association funds.

Another control for the board would be that only board members sign checks. Because some association governing documents require board members to sign checks, management companies should have a board check-signing process. The management company should be able to implement this process so that it is relatively seamless to the board of directors.

If an association is self-managed, a good control is the treasurer reconciling the checkbook while another board member signs the checks. The rest of the board receives bank statements directly from the bank and reviews them accordingly. While the treasurer and another board member are accounting for the payment process, ideally another board member is involved with scheduling the work that results in eventual payment.

Remote Internet access to the association's records is another great control. Several of the association management software platforms allow for remote view-only access. This 24/7 real-time ability allows the board to view everything from the association's accounting to operational matters, such as violation letters mailed.

> The board should receive copies of the vendor invoices each month along with the financial statements. Reviewing invoices along with the Cash Disbursement Report can be an effective accounting control. Speaking directly with a vendor to confirm the accuracy of a particular invoice, spot checking, is an excellent accounting control.

For self-managed associations, smaller management companies and even large management companies, consulting the association's CPA for guidance regarding controls is advisable. The CPA should be able to review the current accounting controls or lack-thereof and make recommendations for going forward. Control recommendations that are implemented can go a long way in preventing issues down the road.

■ ■ ■

ACCRUAL & CASH ACCOUNTING

Accrual accounting is recording revenues and expenses when they are incurred, regardless of when cash is exchanged. In accounting, the term "accrual" refers to any accounting entry that records revenue or expense in the absence of a cash transaction.

Cash basis is the easiest to understand, in that the accounts reflect the actual flow of income coming in and expenses going out. Income is recognized when it is collected, and expenses are recognized when the expense is paid. The cash method is probably the best accounting method to use, for the primary reason that it is the clearest to explain to members of the association who may not have a background in accounting.

■ ■ ■

IRS REPORTING

Homeowner Associations have to comply with payment reporting requirements for payments made to third-party subcontractors. Section 6109 of the Internal Revenue Code requires a signed IRS Form W-9 (A Request for Taxpayer Identification Number) to be on file for all subcontractors who perform work for the association.

If a signed W-9 is not provided, the association could be required to withhold 28% of any payments to a subcontractor.

The signed W-9 is used to prepare IRS Form 1099-MISC. Form 1099-MISC is prepared by the association and reflects what was paid to the subcontractor in the prior tax year. However, if the subcontractor is incorporated or is paid less than $600 in one tax year, currently a Form 1099-MISC does not have to be completed.

Noncompliance with this tax code could subject an association to fines and other penalties. Failing to follow these prescribed procedures could, in extreme situations, result in an association's bank accounts being levied by the Internal Revenue Service.

■ ■ ■

1099-MISC

Form 1099-MISC is a variation of Form 1099 and is used to report miscellaneous income paid from our association clients to their vendors and other parties who have been paid from association funds. Associations, like all business entities that have paid third parties, are required by the Internal Revenue Service regulations to complete 1099s. The ubiquity of the 1099 form has led to use of the phrase "1099 worker" to refer to the independent contractors.

The form is completed in the name of the association and must be completed and issued to the recipient by January 31 each year. The duplicate IRS filing of the 1099 must be completed by the last day of February each year. This form is not required to be completed for association employees, only for non-employees who have received compensation.

■ ■ ■

LIEN FOR ASSESSMENT

Questions arise from members, usually delinquent members, regarding "what authority does the association have" in collecting dues. Basically, associations are established in two forms: volunteer associations and mandatory associations. As both preceding adjectives indicate, mandatory associations need declaration and in some cases state statute authority in order to collect assessments.

While volunteer associations may have declaration language that allows for the collection of assessments and the establishment of an annual budget, they generally do not have a mechanism to collect or, more precisely, a method to collect, if a member elects not to pay. Mandatory associations must either have CC&R language and/or state statutes to enforce the collection of assessments. For example:

9.3 - In the administration of the operation and management of the Property, the Association shall have and is hereby granted the authority and power to enforce the provisions of this Declaration, to levy and collect assessments in the manner provided in Article X below and in the Bylaws. Any sum assessed by the Association remaining unpaid for a period of thirty (30) days or longer shall constitute a lien on the Unit...

The most significant language from the example above is: "Any sum assessed by the Association remaining unpaid for a period of thirty (30) days or longer shall constitute a lien on the Unit." The unpaid assessments constitute a lien giving the association the legal authority to file a lien and under this particular state statute proceed with foreclosing on this lien.

While there are misconceptions within the membership and general population about the harshness of an association's abilities to collect past-due assessments, the reality is quite the opposite. A very common retort is "my credit card company can't foreclose for me not paying my credit card bill." While this may be true, a credit card company also does not have to issue this person a credit card in the first place. However, an association is required to provide association services, such as amenities and other common expenses, when a person purchases into an association. To make delinquency matters even worse, members who are paying their assessments are forced to subsidize those non-paying members by making up the difference in higher dues amounts.

■ ■ ■

COLLECTION PROCESS

Even though homeowner associations and association management companies do not fall under the federal debt-collector statues, there are numerous other federal and state statues for which boards of directors may need to seek legal counsel in order to avoid any pitfalls of running afoul of any statute.

If financial soundness is the foundation of all homeowner associations, then collections or, more precisely, delinquencies can be the termites in this foundation. Slowly eroding the foundation over time is really no better than a tornado coming through and destroying the entire association in five minutes. At least with a tornado there are generally advisories and warnings in time to take shelter. Unfortunately, with delinquencies an innocuous aging report may be the only warning sign, and this report may not be closely monitored. As a result, delinquencies creep up and up until alarm bells start going off in the form of the association not being able to pay the water or insurance bills. When this dire point is reached, only the most drastic measures work to resolve matters. Everyone in the membership is going to feel the pain, and ironically the board of directors gets most of the blame, not the delinquent members.

Dealing with delinquencies can be one of the most trying aspects of serving on a board of directors, especially as compared to dealing with CC&R violations, because the majority of the time the association member violating the CC&Rs knows that what they are doing is in violation and could choose another course of action. Collection issues arise many times because of circumstances beyond the control of the delinquent members, such as job loss or family health emergency. So again, collections can be one of the most trying aspects of serving on a board of directors. However, the board of directors has a fiduciary responsibility to take reasonable action to collect unpaid assessments in order to ensure the financial stability of the association.

There are many reasons that delinquencies get out of control. The most prevalent is that there is no fair and consistent collection process in practice. Either the board of directors or the third-party management company has not made collections a matter of concern. The author has witnessed a number of avenues by which boards and management companies have obscured the delinquency problem. Camouflaging the problem can be done simply by reducing reserve funding, thus kicking a very big can down the road. The author is aware of a third-party management company's association manager who got so weary of questions about the association's delinquencies report that he stopped providing the board a copy of their Delinquency Report. This tactic worked for the association manager for over a year, until one day the board president confronted a water department worker attempting to lockdown the entire association's water meter for non-payment.

First and foremost, the initial collection process for delinquent accounts must be established and approved by the association's board of directors, not the third-party management company or the association's attorney. As with most everything that happens within an association, the board is ultimately responsible, and if collections violate state or federal law the board has the liability. Of course, this does not mean disregarding counsel from the management agent or attorney, just being aware that the board of directors is ultimately the party responsible for collections.

Fortunately, not a great deal of imagination is needed to establish a fair and consistent collection process. State statutes also need to be consulted to ensure compliance with the individual state laws. State and especially federal collection statutes must be adhered to, because violations have severe consequences. The following is an example of a fair and consistent collection process:

An association assessment is billed, and no subsequent payment is received by the predetermined late date. A late notice should be sent by US mail on the following business day. If the member's account is not brought current after the second late date, a second late notice should be sent First Class US mail. It is important that these late notices be sent First Class US mail, not certified. First Class US mail is the generally-accepted method and required in many cases for the delivery of delinquent notification. Other means of delivery may not be recognized by the court as proper notice of a delinquent account. Avoid sending certified mail unless required by the association governing documents or other statutes. First Class postage is considered "effective delivery," which is defended as "the carrying and turning over of letters, goods, etc., to a designated recipient or recipients." Sending delinquent notices by certified mail or other means such as FedEx in an attempt to obtain a signature is not necessary, and if the notice is not picked up or is refused and returned to sender, the association now has proof that the delinquent member did not receive the notice.

Unless the governing documents or statute provide otherwise, the next step in this collection process—— is the legal "demand letter." The demand letter is the starting point in most lawsuits, not only in collections matters. A demand letter puts the delinquent member on notice of potential legal ramifications if they do not bring their account current.

The demand letter gives the delinquent member a set amount of time in which to bring their account current or contest the matter as not accurate. The amount of time that the letter specifies can vary from one state to another. The demand letter is important for establishing proper notice, time for the member to contest if not accurate and, if statutes allow, the collection of attorney fees related to any collection action.

If there is no response from the member regarding the demand letter by the time allotted, the board of directors should begin "formal" collection efforts with whatever state statutes allow. Collection statutes vary from one state to another. Because of severe legal ramifications for improper collection practices, self-managed homeowner associations should seek legal counsel from an experienced attorney with experience in homeowner association collections.

Many states allow for lien to foreclosure actions. While this is an expensive option, in most cases it may be the only effective collection avenue. Some will make the counter-argument: "Why spend association funds on lien to foreclosure when there is a mortgage or other liens that will take priority in most states?" Priority in this case means that if the association liens and gains legal possession of the home, there is still an outstanding mortgage on the property that has to be paid. The point is that collections are unpleasant and the only party to the matter who actually wins is the collections attorney. However, failing to take action encourages other members to become delinquent, and the association begins to take a downward spiral. The ultimate objective is to get a member in the home paying their fair share of the association's expenses.

In many states, money judgments are generally a waste of time and attorney fees. A money judgment is a court order that awards the plaintiff, in this case the association, a sum of money for the delinquent dues and possibly the attorney's fees. In most cases, money judgments are not attached to the member's home and have no real effective collection mechanism to recoup the funds. This might be where the term "it is not worth the paper it is written on" comes from. For example, in Georgia wages and other income can be garnished from delinquent members, so this can be an effective collection avenue. However, in states with no effective statutes for collecting on money judgments, generally the only recourse is turning the matter over to a collection agency.

The author was once called in to assist an association that had close to $250,000 in delinquent dues. This was the culmination of five years of obtaining money judgments from the association's attorney. For budgetary reasons, this association was forced to close the swimming pool and cut down landscaping to twice a month. At this point, the association was having difficulty paying monthly utility bills.

During his initial meeting with the board of directors, the author was given the year-to-date income statement. Upon review, it was noted that the association had spent just over $40,000 in legal fees that year, and it was only September. The author asked if the association had been involved in a lawsuit, to have such high legal expenses. One board member explained that it was for the association's attorney obtaining money judgments. Another board member asked if it was unusual to see such high attorney fees for money judgments. The author said, yes, but since they were spending that much, the association must be collecting on these judgments.

This was a large nine-member board of directors, and eight of the members had perplexed expressions. They could not recall ever collecting on a money judgment. Further investigation found that, after five years of the association's collection attorney obtaining money judgments, not one had ever been collected. The one board member with an angry look rather than a perplexed expression was the board president. Who, unbeknownst to the author, just happened to also be the association's collection attorney.

Self-help when it comes to homeowner associations is the board of directors taking it upon itself to resolve a delinquent member's account. Depending upon state statutes and how the association's governing documents are written, self-help may or may not be an option. Before undertaking any self-help actions, the association's attorney should be consulted for any potential legal ramifications. Courts traditionally take a dim view of boards of directors who exercise self-help that contradicts the governing documents and, especially, violates state statutes.

Most association boards are familiar with the self-help action that limits delinquent members from utilizing any of the association's amenities. Probably the most common action is turning off a delinquent member's pool access card in order to prevent that member's access. More drastic, and perfectly legal if the governing documents and state statutes do not forbid it, is shutting off the water to a condominium unit served by a common water supply line and a water utility bill paid for the association. For example, in North Carolina, if the governing documents allow for this and the delinquent member is called to a hearing about the suspension of services, this is perfectly legal. Associations in some instances have gone to the expense of installing individual water shut-offs. Again, the association's attorney should be consulted on anything of this nature, because the legal ramifications can be severe if not allowed by state statutes.

For example, in gated communities in Georgia it is a common practice to turn off the automobile gate access to the property, provided the governing documents allow it, although associations cannot restrict entry by foot or impede someone from entering their home. It may not be surprising that communities able to restrict gate access have lower delinquency rates. The association's attorney needs to be consulted on these types of access-restrictive actions to make sure they do not violate state statutes or even possibly federal law.

■ ■ ■

FEDERAL FAIR DEBT COLLECTION PRACTICE ACT

The Federal Fair Debt Collection Act (FDCPA) was enacted in an attempt to help eliminate abusive debt collection practices by disreputable debt collectors, and *vice versa* to ensure that debt collectors who do not use abusive debt collection practices are not prevented from legitimately collecting bad debts. The Act also promotes consistent individual state action to protect consumers against abusive debt collection practices.

Under the FDCPA, a debt collector is broadly defined as "any person who uses any instrumentality of interstate commerce or the mails in any business, the principal purpose of which is the collection of any debts, or who regularly collects or attempts to collect, directly or indirectly, debts owed or due or asserted to be owed or due another." Under this statute definition, the FDCPA would only apply to third-party debt collectors whose principal business is the collection of debt, not original creditors such as a homeowner association or their professional management company.

There have been unsuccessful legal attempts to try to join homeowner associations and their professional management companies to the FDCPA. Fortunately, since neither the association nor the management company is considered an actual "debt collection" company as defined in the FDCPA, there is no applicable legal option for this approach. However, not considering any particular individual state statute that could be similar to the FDCPA or more limiting, it is beneficial for a board of directors to have an understanding of the FDCPA and the serious legal nature of collections overall.

No one wants to utilize unethical or potentially illegal collection methods. Unfortunately, certain collection statutes may not be precise, and in certain situations lines may be unintentionally crossed. In the not-so-recent past, associations would post delinquent members on the mail kiosk or print delinquent member names in the association newsletter. Doing this now would definitely be a violation of the FDCPA and many state collection statutes. A board member sharing a delinquency list with a non-board member could be considered in violation of the Act.

The FDCPA prohibits a vast number of specific abusive and deceptive activities that violate the Act. These abusive and deceptive activities have severe ramifications if utilized in the collection of a debt. What follows are just a few examples of what the act prohibits as abusive and deceptive activities that would violate the Act:

- Failure to cease communication upon written request to do so from the debtor, including notification that the debt collector intends to collect the debt via judicial process.
- Communicating/demanding payment with/from the debtor after the debtor's written request for debt validation with a 30-day validation period.
- Misrepresentation in order to collect a debt by posing as an authority or law enforcement officer or attorney or by threatening arrest or legal action that is not allowable by statute.

> The author is aware of an association board president who happened to be a police officer. This board president proceeded to tell a small gathering how he had helped reduce his association's delinquency issues. Three to four times a month after the association's late date, on the way home from work he would stop by delinquent members' homes. In his municipality he was allowed to take his patrol car home, so he would park the patrol car in the delinquent members driveway, and while dressed in his police uniform he would knock on their doors. He proudly told everyone at the gathering that, out of 350 homes, his association had only two delinquent members.

- Publishing the debtor's name or address.
- Seeking unjustified debts or collection fees not permitted under an agreement or provided for under federal or state statute.

- Communication with third parties and disclosing the nature of debts with third parties.
- Contact by "embarrassing media," such as communicating the debt with a postcard or an envelope that reveals the envelope's contents by information deducted from the outside of the envelope. For example, the name on the return address could be Delinquent Collections of America.

While there may be positive aspects of the FDCPA, there are a great many companies besides debt collectors that have been taken to court and had to defend themselves against frivolous lawsuits. The severe legal ramifications of the FDCPA make fighting these lawsuits expensive to defend and potentially very profitable to unscrupulous attorneys. The collection industry and insurance companies that provide coverage have lobbied Congress for legal relief from these frivolous lawsuits brought on by the FDCPA, but to no avail.

"Seeking unjustified debts or collection fees not permitted under an agreement or provided for under federal or state statute." This is a potential area of concern for a homeowner association board. If the association is managed by a third-party management company, the board needs to verify what is being charged to delinquent members and verify that those charges are in compliance with state and federal statutes.

There are association management companies that charge collection fees, administrative fees or other improper fees to delinquent members. If these additional fees have no basis in law, the board of directors could be ultimately responsible for the third-party management company's wrongdoing. There are even management companies filing liens and charging the delinquent members the cost to do so, thus charging legal fees. In most states, by statute only attorneys can charge for legal services. Setting aside the obvious conflicts-of-interest, even if the management company has an attorney on staff these charges may be deemed excessive and thus not valid to be collected.

Again, even if the associations and their agent, the third-party management company, do not fall under the FDCPA, there are ethical issues with charging excessive fees to delinquent members. And there are certain states with statutes that do regulate original creditors, such as a homeowners association, that may be even more limiting than the FDCPA.

■ ■ ■

DELINQUENCIES AND THE DESIRE TO BE NEIGHBORLY

As discussed one of the many challenges of being on an association board of directors is membership delinquencies. While everyone wants to be fair and consistent with all delinquent members, questions often arise from boards about what more can be done to collect delinquent assessments, or, on the other extreme, boards ask "can we be neighborly in our collection efforts?"

Because of prior collection practices, boards sometimes feel that, since this was done in the past and worked, this method is still a viable collection method. One common collection practice from the past that some associations ascribed to was posting delinquencies in membership newsletters and even on the entrance signs to the community. While extremely effective in the collection of delinquent assessments, it could possibly be a violation of both federal and state statutes.

The flip side of more aggressive collections efforts is the call to be more neighborly by telephoning the delinquent member or visiting with the delinquent member at their home. The primary reason that these methods are not feasible is that speaking directly with a delinquent member provides no proof that the member was informed of their rights under any collections statutes, if this becomes an issue. The burden of proof on proper notification can fall back on the party collecting the debt. That is why the best method is written communication directing the delinquent member to contact the appropriate party in order to address the delinquent account.

Another issue that arises from members and board members is the legalistic language on late notices and demand letters. This language may seem blunt or outright harsh, but when it comes to legal matters and the collection statutes certain language has to be used to be in compliance with the statutes. With regard to federal and state statutes regarding written communications, the association's attorney should draft or review all collection communications to ensure compliance with all applicable statutes.

To make matters worse, there are law firms who specialize in representing debtors against creditors. Because of the complexities and potential federal fines levied for violating the collection statutes, these law firms actively solicit delinquent association members seeking clients.

These law firms review the collection efforts of the association and look for any violations of the statutes. Because of the possible penalties and fines within the federal statutes, if these law firms find anything they threaten to file suit. To sum up the words of a thirty-years serving board president: "these collection laws aren't meant to protect the people owed money. They are written to protect people who owe the HOA money."

The most distressing realization about collections is that all parties lose: the delinquent member has to pay late fees and, in some instances, legal fees, and they may possibly lose their home. The board of directors and association management company lose time and effort collecting those delinquent assessments, when that energy could be applied to other constructive activities that are more beneficial to the entire association.

■ ■ ■

PAYMENT PLANS

The board of directors is usually under no obligation, unless state statutes dictate otherwise, to accept a member's payment plan or propose an alternative plan. However, if a member is in financial distress, many boards will consider a reasonable payment plan. The vast majority of association boards consider working with delinquent members the best course of action. However, defining what a reasonable payment plan can be a sticking point.

The ideal payment plan can vary with each delinquent member's situation. However, it is ideal to wrap up any payment plan within a reasonable amount of time. Ideally, payment plans with time frames of no more than 60 to 90 days are best. While some boards will extend this repayment period further six months to a year. The important point about payment plans are that they have to be realistic on the member's ability to pay. The second point is automatically waving late fees on the outstanding payment plan balance, as long as the member remains current on their recurring dues and the payment plan. Waiving the late fee will hopefully keep the delinquent from digging a deeper financial hole.

■ ■ ■

RESERVES

Capital reserves are funds set aside separately to fund future capital repairs of an association's common elements. Capital items can be roofs, streets, sidewalks, pools, tennis courts, elevators and other common elements.

In some communities, reserves can be a tough sale to the membership. Common objections will be similar to: "Why do we need reserves? We need to pay as we go along" "I plan on moving in a few years, so why do I care about the reserves? Why should I take money out of my personal bank account and put it in the association's bank account for future expenses that I might not even be here to benefit from?" "Why can't we just do special assessments when we need the funds?" "Why should I have to put money aside for a swimming pool that I never use?"

Reserve funds are generally required by an association's governing documents or possibly by state statutes. If not implicitly required, reserves would be a fiduciary responsibility of the board of directors. Even though most governing documents do not specify an amount to be funded, language such as the following is common: "The Association shall establish and maintain an adequate reserve fund."

Mortgage providers may require reserve funding to make loans in an association. When mortgages are initiated by borrowers, lenders require that financial data be provided to support the loan. Lenders are concerned with how their security will be maintained if there are no funds to replace common elements. Lenders are also apprehensive about how their borrower would be able to pay the loan back along with any special assessments that may arise.

Funded reserves reduce the likelihood of special assessments. While special assessments are necessary in certain instances, especially when unexpected expenses arise, funded reserves should curtail the necessity. When special assessments are required to be used, membership delinquencies typically increase. Special assessments can play havoc with the moral of the membership.

Reserves should increase the home resale value for everyone in the membership. However, poorly-funded reserves and frequent special assessments, without a doubt, have a negative influence on property values.

Maintaining reserves makes fair and equal distribution of expenses between the former, current and future membership. Funded reserves prevent the current, possibly new member from paying for repair or replacement of a capital element that they may not have had full enjoyment of for the element's useful life.

THE METHODS & PROCESS OF RESERVES

There are generally three reserve funding classifications or funding goals: baseline, threshold and full.

Baseline funding is the riskiest form, with the objective of just funding "some" dollar amount with the hope that the association does not run out of money and does not need to make up the difference with a special assessment or a bank loan.

Threshold funding is the objective of funding to a specific amount and maintaining that amount. This chosen amount may or may not cover future reserve needs. There can be less risk with threshold than with baseline.

Full funding objectives are funding reserves to meet all known future capital expenditures. This type of funding is the least likely to result in special assessments or bank loans. If feasible, full funding of all capital reserves is the safest funding form.

RESERVE FUNDING – THE PROCESS

The reserve process begins with the association's annual budget. Boards of directors must be pragmatic with regard to expenses and raising dues accordingly. Moderately raising dues gradually to adequately fund operating expenses and reserves is generally more palatable to everyone than a large special assessment years down the road.

RESERVE STUDIES

A reserve study allows an association to better predict what future funds are needed and to budget accordingly today. A reserve study should analyze the present condition of the association's common elements and provide an estimate on the remaining life of this common element. The reserve study should also estimate the cost of repair or replacement at the needed point in the future. Reserve studies can start around $1,500 and go up proportionally from there, depending upon depth and scope.

POINTS REGARDING RESERVES

- Reserves should not be established for general maintenance expenses. For example, painting may not qualify as a reserve item.
- Reserves have to be allocated for a specific purpose. The IRS could take issue with contingency reserves, general reserves and rainy day reserves.
- Adequately-funded reserves increase the overall property values within the association.
- Reserve studies, once completed, should be updated every 5 years. These updates cost substantially less than the initial study.

■ ■ ■

INVESTMENT VEHICLES

It is understood that boards of directors want to maximize the return on the funds in the association's reserve account. Being that inflation and expenses normally go up, maximizing investments is a prudent policy. If the governing documents or state statutes do not provide specific guidance on investment vehicles, determining what is suitable relies on the good judgment of the board of directors.

An investment vehicle is a financial product used with the intention of obtaining a return. For an association these financial products must be "no risk," such as CDs or money market accounts. Other investment vehicles, such as stocks or futures, offer the possibility of larger financial returns, but there is also more loss-exposure risk.

The board of directors has a fiduciary responsibility to preserve the funds of the association. A fiduciary responsibility is the highest standard of consideration, and the board of directors is expected to exercise reasonableness and good judgment in their decision-making. The board of directors exercising reasonableness and good judgment begins with the selection of the right investment vehicle for their association.

Most consider a reasonableness and prudent investment policy to be one where the principal funds of the association are not at risk. The most common investment vehicles for association funds are CDs and money market accounts. These two vehicles allow for growth, liquidity and, most importantly, safety of principal investment. These vehicles are virtually at no risk of principal as long as they are placed in a financial institution with Federal Deposit Insurance Corporation (FDIC) coverage. FDIC currently covers losses from financial institutions up to $250,000.

The higher risk investment vehicles have a loss-exposure risk not only with any potential gain, but of the principal dollar amount initially invested. In almost all association investment situations, the loss of principal would be unacceptable and would expose the board of directors to additional liability. This liability could be in the form of litigation from the membership for failure to exercise fiduciary care.

"Safe and steady" is the mantra for association investment vehicles. Even though interest rates on CDs and money markets may not produce astonishing returns, they do produce returns and not losses.

LADDERED CERTIFICATES OF DEPOSITS

Certificates of Deposit (CDs) are one of the acceptable and standard investment vehicles for associations. CDs are available through banks and carry FDIC insurance. A common method for associations to ensure cash flow and maximize interest income is the "laddered" CD process. This laddered method provides for a safe way to produce cash flow over a fiscal year. This process is especially beneficial for associations that collect assessments at the first of the year.

Laddering involves spreading out individual CDs so that they mature at varying times. The objective is to create a mechanism that generates distribution of funds as they are operationally needed.

For example, an association collects $12,000 on January 1 of their fiscal year. The association uses $1,000 for January operating and then opens a $1,000 one-month CD coming due February 1 for February operating expenses. The association then opens another $1,000 CD maturing March 1 (2-month CD) for March operating expenses, and the rest of the funds are invested so on. Ideally, the interest rate on the longer-term CDs will provide a higher rate of return.

If the association needs a CD before maturity, typically some of the potential interest is forfeited as a penalty, but the principal amount is returned by the bank. If an association's CD investments exceed $250,000, multiple banks need to be utilized to remain within FDIC insurance coverage amounts.

CDARS

Certificate of Deposit Account Registry Service (CDARS) is a program that allows associations the ability to spread their CD funds across multiple banks. The reason for CDARS is to give associations the ability to invest in CDs and remain below the FDIC insurance limits. CDARS work by an association depositing funds into a participating CDARS bank, which spreads these funds around to other CDARS-participating banks.

The benefit to an association is that they only have to deal with one bank, which generates the sole bank statement that contains the information on each certificate of deposit. This one bank acts as the primary custodian for the CDARS deposits, while the banks that the association's funds are spread to are considered subcustodians. CDARS, just like insured cash sweeps, have been thoroughly vetted, and reciprocal deposit placement services, subcustodians, are accepted by the FDIC regulations.

■ ■ ■

Board Basics

■ ■ ■

BOARD OF DIRECTORS

A homeowner association board of directors is a body of elected or appointed members who equally oversee the activities of the association. The board of directors, commonly referred to as "the board," derive their powers, duties and responsibilities from the association's governing documents and, if applicable, state statutes. These governing documents are generally the association's bylaws and, in certain circumstances, the articles of incorporation and CC&Rs. The bylaws usually specify the number of board members, how these board members are to be chosen, issues such as meeting requirements and other issues that deal with the operation of the association.

The association board of directors represents the entire association membership and is bound to act in every member's best interests. The legal responsibilities of the board and board members vary with the nature of the organization and with the jurisdiction within which it operates.

The effective operation of a board of directors begins with the election or selection of individual board members. The association bylaws are generally the governing document that details the process for becoming a board member. The majority of board members are elected at annual meetings by the association members; however, in certain situations board members may be elected at a special membership meeting duly called for that purpose. Special meetings for board elections are usually called when the governing documents do not allow for appointing individual board members to fill director vacancies. Appointing of board members can also occur when associations are under developer control or when vacancies occur.

The governing documents and, more precisely, the association bylaws need to be reviewed regarding elections of board members. Terms in office can vary from one association's bylaws to another. Even the number of board members can vary drastically. This author has worked with association bylaws that called for a 25-member board.

The next step of an efficient operation of a board is the establishment of clear, obtainable goals. Goal-setting for a new board of directors should be one of the first courses of action. These should be reasonably obtainable goals with a limited number of objectives that can be accomplished by the next annual membership meeting.

The actual mechanics or steps of a board meeting begin with the meeting agenda. An agenda is the road map to how the meeting is to function. There should always be a written agenda, and it should be followed without deviation to ensure the proper function of a meeting. The agenda should be timed or, more precisely, the agenda should have the meeting start time and expected completion times beside each agenda item.

Robert's Rules of Order are traditionally used to conduct the business of a board meeting or any other official membership meeting. The use of Robert's Rules may be required by the association's governing documents or state statutes. The degree of formality or how strictly Robert's Rules of Order are followed can vary. However, the basics of Robert's Rules need to be followed, such as motions and voting.

■ ■ ■

DIFFERENCE BETWEEN DIRECTOR & OFFICER

Individuals may serve on a board of directors for many years and not realize there is a difference between a director and an officer. In short, an individual is elected as a director to serve on the association board of directors, and then the directors convene amongst themselves to select the officers.

The definition of an association director is an individual acting on behalf of the membership of an association. A director is responsible, along with other members of the board of directors, for overseeing the operation of the homeowners association and thus protecting the property values of the membership.

Directors owe a fiduciary responsibility to the association membership in the exercise of their duties. Directors have the authority, as granted in the association's governing documents and state statutes, if applicable, to hire and discharge vendors, call meetings of the membership and determine other matters affecting the association.

Depending upon the association's governing documents, directors may or may not be members of the associations. Depending upon the association's governing documents, directors may or may not have to be in "good standing" to serve on the board of directors. Being in "good standing" generally means that the member is not in litigation with the association and is not past-due with their association's assessments.

The directors, or more precisely, the board of directors, elect the officers. The association's officers usually consist of a president, vice president, secretary and treasurer. On an association board of directors, officers have specific roles and duties in regard to the operations of the association. Governing documents, generally the bylaws, specify the officer positions that are to be filled. Officers' duties vary by position and may be specified in the governing documents, but the primary responsibility of the officers is the operation of the associations.

Generally speaking, the association president is responsible for the overall day-to-day activities of the association. However, the president acts under the consent of the rest of the board of directors.

■ ■ ■

PRESIDENT ROLE

The role of the association president is wide in scope and can be difficult to pigeonhole. The ultimate goal of any board of directors is to increase the overall standard of living of the membership and to increase the value of the property within the association. The president is charged with leading this effort.

- The president is tasked with working closely with the other board members, association manager and membership to determine the overall goals of the association.
- The president must have a good understanding of the association's governing documents.
- In the broad view, the president is responsible for the association's fiscal well-being. This includes collecting assessments, guiding the budget process and making sure that reserves are adequately funded.
- The president is charged with making sure there is adequate insurance coverage to protect the association from liability and other hazards.
- The president finds and develops potential volunteers and future association leaders.
- The president maintains close working relationships with the association manager and other association vendors to make certain of the efficient operation of the association.
- The president presides at board meetings and other association meetings. The president prepares meeting agendas and makes certain that proper voting procedures are used.
- The president must not necessarily be a great public speaker, but the president is the representative of the association and must be an effective communicator.

ESTABLISHING GOALS AND PRIORITIES

The president helps establish association goals, and these goals help direct board efforts. The president should also prioritize these goals and, thus, provide a framework for these being accomplished. Clearly-defined goals contribute to the success of the association. Goals can range from "we will lengthen the pool season and pay for it by..." to "we will retain an engineering firm to perform a reserve study."

ASSOCIATION GOVERNANCE

Association presidents are required to interpret and carry out many association governing tasks, such as preparing meeting agendas and conducting meetings. Presidents are also charged with working with the various association committees.

THE ASSOCIATION REPRESENTATIVE

Being the highest office of the board, the president speaks officially for the board of directors and the association. The president usually serves as the liaison between the board and the association manager. An important point a president must remember is that, when speaking on behalf of the association, he or she must report back to the board on what has been said. The president's communications and decisions must be in line with the views of the board.

WORKING WITH THE BOARD

The president must have a spirit of cooperation when working with the board, which many times will have varying opinions and ideas. The president should encourage the other board members to participate because the contributions of board members are vital.

FORMING COMMITTEES

Because of the many actions and topics at any given board meeting, the board cannot always handle all the work in an effective manner. When this occurs, committees can provide an important service to the board of directors and the president.

Committees can focus efforts on topics that need in-depth research, input and thoughtful consideration before a recommendation is made. As an added benefit, committees provide an opportunity for the membership to participate. With board guidance, the president is tasked with appointing committee chairs and explaining the committees' tasks. The president should also establish time frames for committee reports. Once the committee is established, the president should be available to provide additional guidance.

FIDUCIARY RESPONSIBILITIES

The president must put forth more effort than other board members with regard to fiduciary responsibilities because the president's role can be more extensive with regard to negotiating contracts with vendors, dealing with the association manager, etc. Board members and the general membership trust that the president will act in the best interests of the association when performing their duties. However, the president does not have authority to act without board guidance or consent.

BOARD MEETINGS

The president is responsible for conducting efficient board meetings that attend to the matters of the association. Board meetings are for conducting association business and decision-making. The president should always review the association's governing documents for specific meeting guidelines. In general, to conduct an efficient meeting the president should:

- Prepare a timed agenda and distribute it well in advance of the meeting.
- Come to the meeting prepared and insist that the other participants be prepared as well.

- Take charge. Tell the board members the topics for discussion and how the meeting will proceed.
- Have a good understanding of Robert's Rules of Order and use them to conduct an orderly, efficient meeting.
- Stick to the timed agenda. Meeting participants know what to expect when the president follows the written agenda.
- Keep the agenda moving and be considerate of the time constraints of the meeting.
- Focus discussion on the issues at hand and the information that the board members received prior to the meeting.
- Remain businesslike and calm. To effectively manage the meeting, the president must conduct the meeting in a way that promotes a pleasant and efficient meeting.
- Always approach issues in an impartial manner.
- Always remember that everyone on the board is a volunteer and that their time is valuable. An efficient meeting can be completed in an hour rather than in hours.

THE AGENDA

At least several days before the board meeting, the president should prepare an agenda and distribute it to the board. Supporting documentation as it relates to the items on the agenda - i.e. treasurer's report, a president's or manager's report, minutes from the previous meeting and other documents—should be included with the agenda into a board packet. The board packet should lay out the details and create the groundwork for the issues at hand to be discussed. An organized and specific-timed agenda allows the board to work much more efficiently. A tight-timed agenda keeps discussion of issues and actions moving efficiently.

THE AGENDA SHOULD:

- Set a time limit for the length of the meeting and discussion of each agenda item. This keeps board members focused and moving towards a decision.
- Include a descriptive sentence on topics to clarify issues. An action statement of the needed motion, etc., helps identify what is needed to move the issue along. An action statement might read, "We have been asked to allow grills on the clubhouse patio, but the association manager recommends that we not approve because of fire hazard concerns." This type of action statement is more to the point and is results-oriented if used.
- Prepare motions before the meeting. The president should state the motions on the agenda that are expected to be made. Action statements help direct the discussion and make decision-making easier. As an added benefit it also makes it easier to document motions in the meeting minutes.
- List new business on the agenda. Always eliminate any surprises at the board meeting--no decision should be made on issues presented that are not on the agenda beforehand.
- There is an old saying that "no business is old business," but it can be unfinished business. Any action delayed by the board from a prior board meeting can be listed as an agenda item to be reported or acted on.

■ ■ ■

VICE PRESIDENT ROLE

The role of the association vice president can be wide in scope as is the president's, but can also be narrow in scope, depending upon the particular vice president or the board of directors. The vice president may assume additional duties as defined by the board of directors and the association's governing documents.

The vice president is charged with all of the powers required in order to perform the duties of the association president in the absence of the president. The vice president does not possess innate powers or authority to act in the capacity of the association president. Generally, the vice president may only act for the president when the president is physically absent or otherwise unable to act.

ESTABLISHING GOALS AND PRIORITIES:
The vice president works very closely with the president in establishing association goals for the future. As the second position in the association leadership chain-of-command, the vice president many times helps the president prioritize the association's goals.

COUNCIL TO THE PRESIDENT:
In most cases, the vice president works very closely with the president of the association and provides needed input. In this role, the vice president provides a "sounding board" for the president and thus helps define issues.

COMMITTEE LEADERSHIP:
The vice president many times will take additional leadership roles and will chair committees. Because of the large time commitments on the architectural control committee and the landscaping committee, the vice president will chair one of these committees. Chairing these committees is a great way to prepare for broader leadership roles.

LEADERSHIP DEVELOPMENT:

The vice president along with the president finds and develops potential volunteers and future association leaders.

■ ■ ■

SECRETARY ROLE

The roll of the association secretary may be easier to define than that of the association president or vice president, but it is no less varied. Whereas the association president is charged with leading the association, the association secretary is charged with maintaining the records and protecting the association from liability.

The secretary records meeting minutes and board resolutions. The secretary affixes the association's corporate seal to legal documents and verifies the signatures on those documents. The secretary verifies the proxies for the association's annual meeting or any special meetings of the association. The secretary is charged with maintaining all of the association's records and distributing accordingly.

DUTIES OF THE SECRETARY:

The association secretary's duties are classified into three job functions: recording secretary, corresponding secretary and filing secretary. Recording secretary, as it implies, is the taking of minutes and the recording of corporate resolutions. Corresponding secretary is the function of sending notices as required by the governing documents of the association. The filing secretary is the function of maintaining all the records of the association and disposing of old records.

RECORDING SECRETARY:
The recording function is taking meeting minutes, drawing up resolutions, making sure the minutes are approved and distributing approved minutes.

TAKING MINUTES:
Meeting minutes are vital for the documentation of association business. However, there are many misconceptions about what minutes should contain and not contain. Minutes are definitely not a detailed transcription of what was discussed. Minutes should reflect what was accomplished only.

RESOLUTIONS:
A resolution is a determination of policy of the association by the vote of its board of directors. Resolutions are often statements of policy, belief or appreciation, and do not supersede or amend the association's governing documents. For example, a bank may require a resolution for a loan stating that the association has the authority to take out a loan.

The resolution has three parts: authority, reason and extent. For example: Whereas the association's governing documents give authority to the board of directors to take out loans from financial institutions from time to time in order to meet the needs of the association, now therefore be it resolved that a loan be taken out for an irrigation system for the beautification of the association. It is also resolved that the loan will be for no more than $100,000 and with a repayment term of no more than 60 months.

APPROVED MINUTES:

When meeting minutes are approved, the meeting's presiding officer (board president/chair, vice president, etc.) and secretary should sign and date. Once this step is accomplished, the minutes are approved and finalized. These original meeting minutes should be placed in the association minute book. In some instances, copies are forwarded to the association's attorney for legal review or compliance.

CORRESPONDING SECRETARY:

The corresponding secretary is ultimately responsible for all communications to the membership: this includes annual and board meeting notifications and any other correspondence from the association. The actual tasks of generating and mailing are generally delegated to the property management company or agent.

FILING SECRETARY:

The secretary keeps the official association minute book where the association's meeting minutes, corporate resolutions, proceedings and board of director and membership votes are maintained. The secretary maintains an owner's list with corresponding mailing addresses. The association being a legal entity, it must always maintain the records in compliance with state statutes. The records should also be maintained in a manner so as to defend the association in the event of a legal action. The following are typical items that are maintained in the association's permanent files: meeting minutes, articles of incorporation, bylaws, CC&Rs, financial statements and vendor contracts.

■ ■ ■

TREASURER ROLE

The treasurer is the financial voice of the board of directors and the association. The roll of the association treasurer can be narrow in focus and is crucial to the smooth operation of any association. Whereas the association president is charged with leading the association, the treasurer is charged with ensuring the financial well-being of the association.

The treasurer's responsibilities are usually specifically spelled out in the association's bylaws. Generally, the treasurer has the overall responsibility for the association's funds and securities and is responsible for keeping full and accurate financial records. This does not necessarily mean the treasurer physically has to perform accounting tasks, but just ensure they are being done.

DUTIES OF THE TREASURER:

The primary duties of the treasurer are reviewing the financials and taking the lead on the annual budget. Other duties can include signing promissory notes of the association, signing letters of engagement for reviews or audits of the financials by a third-party public accountant. The treasurer is usually responsible for giving the financial report at the association's annual meeting. The treasurer makes sure that the federal and state tax returns are filed in a timely manner. The treasurer should recommend that a reserve study by an engineering firm be made on a regular basis.

ANNUAL BUDGET:

The treasurer should take the lead on the association's annual budget. The treasurer does not necessarily compile the actual budget, but should work closely with the association manager and supporting accounting staff to ensure the budget is reasonable and ready to present to the entire board of directors for further review and approval. If there is a budget committee formed, the treasurer is usually the chairperson of the committee. At any membership budget ratification meeting, the treasurer will take the lead along with the association president in presenting the budget to the membership.

ANNUAL MEETING ROLE:

The treasurer's role at the annual meeting is generally limited to a brief financial report. This financial report should be an overview of the financial condition of the association. Typical reports would be the level of funds in operating and reserve accounts as of the year-end. Delinquencies, if they are at a level that affects the operation of the association, can be mentioned in overall amounts, but individual membership delinquencies should not be discussed. If delinquencies are discussed, the treasurer should be prepared to discuss how the delinquencies are being brought to resolution. If the association is taking on additional indebtedness or issues that could affect the overall financial wellbeing of the association, this should be mentioned during this report.

OUTSIDE CPA FIRM:

The treasurer should take an active role in the search for and selection of an independent CPA firm to prepare state and federal income tax returns and review or audit the financials. The treasurer is the board's liaison to the association's independent auditor.

DELINQUENCIES:

The treasurer is charged with monitoring the collection of delinquent accounts. The treasurer should ensure that the association's management company and attorney are pursuing delinquent accounts efficiently and within the collection guidelines prescribed by the board of directors.

ASSOCIATION INVESTMENTS:

The treasurer should ensure funds are invested to maximize the yield to the association and invested in approved investment vehicles. The governing documents of the association many times will specify how funds are to be invested. They are almost always limited to operating accounts, money market accounts and CDs in federally-insured financial institutions.

Board members may leave office by resignation, death or possibly removal. The governing documents may have provisions allowing the board to remove other board members. The governing documents may have language that, if a board member misses three consecutive meetings, they are automatically removed from the board. The association governing documents may allow for removal by recall of the membership, and some states' statutes have provisions for recall elections. In many instances, removing a board member can be quite difficult if there are no provisions for such in the governing documents or in the state statutes.

Generally speaking, most homeowner association board members cannot receive compensation for serving on the board of directors. The average board member will work 2 to 4 hours a week on association matters. Board of directors should conduct meetings according to the rules and procedures contained in its governing documents.

■ ■ ■

SIGNING CONTRACTS

When signing all association contracts and other association instruments, Board members should include their board title. If the board member does not hold a board office, then "Board Director" should be noted after their signature. Including their board title helps to protect them from possible personal liability. Non-board members can obtain the same liability protection by signing and including "On Behalf of the Board of Directors" if they have such authority.

■ ■ ■

POPULARITY CONTESTS

In 1914 a Kentucky court of appeals ruled that popularity contests did not violate state statutes. While popularity contests may be legal in the state of Kentucky, trying to win a popularity contest can play havoc on a board of directors. This is especially the case when tough decisions have to be made and some in the membership are strongly opposed.

The board of directors has a fiduciary duty to make decisions in the best interests of the association, that being the entire association. A fiduciary duty is the highest standard of responsibility that can be undertaken. It is a duty of care that in most instances negates any other responsibilities, even if fulfilling the fiduciary responsibilities has a negative impact on the person exercising the responsibilities.

Fiduciary responsibility situations appear in many forms during a board member's service on a board of directors. They commonly appear during budget approvals and assessment increases, but even more commonly with CC&R enforcements situations.

Almost all boards of directors strive to have a spirit of community and a live-and-let-live approach to members. Unfortunately, or fortunately, this approach can clash with the association's governing documents.

Most board members realize that being on a board is anything but a popularity contest. Far from it. And the membership that views the board of directors as some kind of popularity contest are many times the same people in the membership violating the CC&Rs or not paying their dues or both. The fortunate aspect is that the overwhelming majority of the membership agrees on why tough decisions sometimes have to be made. This is especially true when the board communicates these tough decisions (non-legal related matters) to the membership.

In a famous New York Court of Appeals case, *Meinhard v Salmon* from 1928, the court determined that fiduciaries must conduct themselves "at a level higher than that trodden by the crowd." So serving on a board puts the board above the matter, whether they like it or not.

■ ■ ■

FIDUCIARY DUTY

Fiduciary duty simply means that the board has an ethical and legal obligation to make decisions in the best interests of the entire association. That's a small explanation for a very big responsibility.

Fiduciary duty includes a duty of loyalty to the association, which means that board members should never use their position to take advantage of the association. They should never make decisions for the association that benefit themselves at the expense of the association and members.

Fiduciary duty also includes the duty to exercise ordinary care. This means that board members must perform their duties in good faith and in a manner they believe to be in the best interest of the association, with such care as an ordinary prudent person in a similar position under similar circumstances would use.

In short, boards must act in the best interests of the association and act reasonably.

■ ■ ■

CONFLICTS OF INTEREST

Conflicts of interest can arise for board members in the performance of many of their board responsibilities: everything from the vendor hiring process to the scheduling of landscaping projects. Since board members have a fiduciary responsibility, board members must ensure that any potential conflicts of interest are dealt with in an appropriate way.

Effectively addressing potential conflicts of interest begins with:

- Board members must fully disclose a conflict or a potential conflict when objectivity cannot be completely ruled out.
- Board minutes should reflect the board members' entire disclosure.

- Conflicted board members should abstain/recuse themselves or even sit out the board's decision on the conflicting matter, including any related executive sessions that may occur.
- Always go above and beyond to avoid the appearance of a conflict of interest. For example, seek multiple vendors, require sealed bids and perform a thorough due diligence process in the hiring of vendors.

■ ■ ■

BOARD MEETINGS

Board of directors meetings are the most effective method for communicating and resolving association issues. A board meeting is a legal proceeding and must be conducted as such. Thus, this is what makes an efficient and proper board meeting so important to the operation of a homeowners association.

An association's board of directors is confronted with an array of issues that must be resolved in a timely manner. A board is charged with what can be the problematical task of obtaining a majority consensus amongst the other board members. The following points are essential for ensuring a productive and successful board meeting.

Agenda: Have a clear and specific written timed agenda. There are generic or stock agendas that are better than no written agenda, but these types of agendas only help control the order of the meeting. Being clear and specific on an agenda means instead of a discussion issue being "General Maintenance," the discussion should read "Resurfacing Pool."

Pre-Distribution: If possible, have the agenda prepared and distributed well before the meeting. Early distribution will help board members prepare for the meeting in advance and improve discussion. When board members can organize their thoughts beforehand about the agenda items, meetings are more efficient and much more is achieved.

Follow the Agenda: While having a clear and specific agenda is helpful, not deviating from the agenda is even more important. "Chasing rabbits" can be one of the most detrimental aspects of running a board meeting. If an item is not on the agenda or has not been added to the agenda at the beginning of the meeting, the item should be added to the agenda of the next meeting. By attempting to deal with a non-agenda item, in many instances the board is unprepared to properly discuss the item and thus cannot make an informed decision.

Limit the Agenda: Limit the agenda to no more than three major issues. Limiting an agenda to three major issues (major issues being items requiring more than 10 minutes of discussion) allows for proper and thoughtful consideration.

Establish a Time Limit: Set a meeting end time at the beginning of the meeting. Most board meeting should be concluded in an hour and half, at most. Longer meetings have a tendency to be less productive and produce dimensioning returns the longer the meeting continues. If meetings typically run long in future meetings, attempt to reduce this time by 10 minutes. The meeting chair will be forced to become more efficient, and the other members will become much more focused knowing that there is a set end-time. When the meeting end-time has arrived, simply end the meeting. Even if every agenda item has not been addressed, add these items to the next meeting agenda, and eventually everything will be addressed.

Follow Roberts Rules of Order: Motions and voting are vital to conducting an efficient and legal board meeting. Each motion needs a "second" before the vote is called. The other benefit of following Roberts Rules, besides the legal framework and the efficiency that is created, is the civility and politeness that result. When Roberts Rules are used effectively, what generally happens is that there is a reverence for other points of view. This reverence helps to facilitate a better understanding and fosters a spirit of cooperation.

Have a Spirit of Cooperation: The one aspect that makes a board of directors function properly is a common spirit of cooperation. This spirit of cooperation means that each member has the best interests of the association at heart and wishes to work towards a common goal of improving the association. Working towards this common goal should be the ultimate goal of every board member.

■ ■ ■

BOARD MEETING LEGAL PROCEEDING

As mentioned previously, a board of directors meeting is a legal proceeding. Maybe because of the routine nature of board meetings, or possibly because of the meeting location not normally being very formal, even board members can overlook the legal nature of the meeting. It is always important to remember this fact when participating in a board meeting. Discussions that are not in executive session are subject to legal discovery in the event of a lawsuit involving the association. Collection matters and architectural violations are the primary instigators of legal recourse that involves associations and their boards of directors.

Meeting minutes must be taken and, once approved, signed and dated by the board secretary and president. Once signed, these minutes are the legal record of the board meeting. Board meeting minutes should be maintained indefinitely in the association's permanent records.

If the governing documents or state statutes require specific procedural board actions or legal actions, these actions must be followed, or the association may risk their actions being challenged in court. For example, if a state statute requires the board of directors to vote on whether or not to send delinquent members to collections, and this vote is not held, a delinquent member's attorney could make an argument that the initial collection action was not properly followed and thus that the action was taken in violation of state statutes.

THE BOARD MEETING TIMED AGENDA

Board Meeting Agenda
Happy Glen Homeowners Association
Happy Glen Clubhouse - 1000 Happy Glen Drive
5:30 P.M. - November 10, 2015

I.	Call to Order - (Meeting Chair)	5:30 P.M.
II.	Establish Meeting Quorum - (Secretary)	5:31 P.M.
III.	Approval of Minutes - (Secretary)	5:35 P.M.
IV.	Financials - (Treasurer)	

	A. Financial Report Review	5:45 P.M.
	B. 2016 Operational Budget Approval	5:55 P.M.
V.	Unfinished Business (Vice-President)	
	A. Pool Surface Refinishing	6:00 P.M.
	B. Clubhouse Painting	6:05 P.M.
VI.	New Business (Meeting Chair)	
	A. Discuss Special Membership Meeting	6:10 P.M.
	B. Fence Approval 8912 Happy Glen Dr.	6:15 P.M.
	C. Violation Issue 9215 Happy Glen Dr.	6:20 P.M.
VII	Schedule Next Board Meeting (Meeting Chair)	6:25 P.M.
VIII	Meeting Adjournment (Meeting Chair)	6:30 P.M.

An agenda can come in various formats or layouts. The main consideration when constructing an agenda is: "Does it provide an efficient and effective way to run the meeting in question?"

Header: The agenda should include the three "Ws" in the header: who? where? when? These points may seem obvious or may not seem necessary, because everyone in the association knows that the monthly board meeting is held in the clubhouse on the second Wednesday of each month. Remember that this is a legal proceeding, and the location of the meeting or date of the meeting might be a material matter in litigation. For example, the bylaws might state that the board meeting has to be held in the clubhouse.

Call to Order: The board president or the meeting chair should call the meeting to order.

Establish Meeting Quorum: The board secretary establishes that a quorum of the board is present. A quorum is usually 51% of the board members present. If the quorum requirement is not met, the only actions that can legally take place are establishing the time in which to adjourn, recess or take steps to obtain a quorum. (These steps could be to contact board members and see if they can attend.) This quorum requirement to conduct board business cannot be waived even by unanimous consent of the entire board of directors.

Even if it is obvious that no quorum is present, the meeting chair should call the meeting to order and announce that no quorum is present and entertain a motion to adjourn or possibly recess if a quorum can be obtained in a reasonable amount of time.

Approval of Minutes: With the ease of distribution, it is a good idea to email minutes to the board in advance of the meeting in order to expedite the approval process. This advance review allows for any adjustments to the meeting minutes, so that a final version can be distributed during the actual meeting.

Meeting minutes do not necessarily have to be voted on by the board for approval. The most efficient way to approve minutes is for the chair to assume the motion and obtain unanimous consent that the minutes be approved as distributed or as corrected. This is simply done by the chair stating: "The minutes are approved as distributed."

Financials: Reviewing the financials along with any supporting documentation such as vendor invoices can take varying amounts of time, depending upon the amount of financial data that must be reviewed. If the financial reports are distributed in advance of the board meeting and reviewed before, many questions can be addressed beforehand or, at a minimum, handled more efficiently during the actual meeting.

Unfinished Business: Items being addressed as unfinished business should ideally be items that need very little additional discussion and are ready to act on. An example would be: a maintenance project debated in a prior meeting, when an additional piece of information was needed to proceed with a vote. In this case, the majority of debate was dealt with in a prior board meeting and can be wrapped up in short order.

New Business - New business requiring more than 10 minutes of debate ideally should be limited to three major issues or less. The primary side-effect of too many issues is that it can prevent proper and thoughtful consideration of all the issues. Too many issues can lead to poor decisions or no decisions being made at all.

EXECUTIVE SESSIONS

Executive sessions of the board of directors are usually provided for by state statute. Association members generally do not have a right to attend executive sessions. The purpose of an executive session is for boards to address issues involving privileged information and matters of a private nature. This can be for legal issues, such as collection efforts or architectural violations that can lead to litigation. Boards may also use executive session to consider issues relating to contract negotiations with third parties. If the association has employees, executive sessions can be used for personnel matters. Membership hearings for CC&R violations should be conducted in executive session. Membership hearings are generally the one exception where a member is entitled to attend the executive session for that portion of the meeting dealing with the member's hearing.

One important point regarding an executive session is that it generally preserves attorney-client privilege, even if the association's attorney is not present. Executive sessions are vital in discussing litigation strategy for pending and potential legal matters. Again, the association's attorney does not have to be present for the board to meet and discuss legal issues and be protected by attorney-client privilege.

ADOPTION OF THE AGENDA

If a board of directors has a tendency to lose focus during the board meeting, formally adopting the agenda may help prevent this problem. Every meeting should begin with the deliberation of the agenda. The chair should ask if any of the board members have additional matters that should be added to the agenda. The chair should then entertain a motion to adopt the agenda. A member should make a motion: "that the agenda be adopted" or "adopted as amended." A second is required. A simple majority passes the motion, in order to restrict meeting business to just the items listed on the agenda.

If a board meeting does not adopt the agenda at the beginning of the meeting, it can change that agenda only by a formal motion to do so. For example, a board member might make a motion that an item be added or deleted or the order of discussion revised on the agenda. This type of motion must have a second and requires a two-thirds majority vote.

■ ■ ■

BOARD MEETING PROXIES

A common misconception arises with proxies and board meetings. Being a member of a board of directors is considered a "nondelegable duty." Board members cannot appoint someone else in their place to attend board meetings or give another board member a proxy to vote in their stead. It does not matter whether the appointed party has a signed power-of-attorney or not.

The reason for the exclusion is that sending a proxy to attend a board meeting is incompatible with the deliberative nature of board meetings and a director's fiduciary duty of due diligence. (Robert's Rules, 11th ed., pp. 428-429.) In order to vote, directors must attend board meetings. If a director is not present when a vote is called, the director cannot vote.

■ ■ ■

OPEN BOARD MEETINGS

Some governing documents and some state statutes may allow the membership the right to attend portions of an association's board meeting. Some governing documents may even allow for membership to participate through an open discussion session of the board meeting. While membership attendance may not necessarily be a hindrance to the productivity of the board meeting, an open discussion session can be a hindrance if not exercised properly.

Whatever the governing documents or state statutes require needs to be adhered to, but this should be the extent of what is done on behalf of the board of directors. For example, if the governing documents allow for the membership to attend, but do not mandate an open-session portion of the meeting for members to address the board, avoid beginning this tradition. If a member or members wish to address the board, this is generally best done in a closed board session with just the rest of the board in attendance. There are legal reasons for this or, more precisely, potential legal issues with letting members make statements in an open forum.

If an open discussion session is required, follow the governing documents or state statue to the letter. If the requirements are vague or not specified, the board should establish a policy on how the open discussion is to be conducted. Generally, all this policy entails is establishing the place in the meeting agenda where this open discussion is to take place. Most boards place this session at the beginning of the board meeting. The second point of the policy is establishing how long someone is allowed to speak. Three minutes is the commonly-accepted forum standard. The final point of the policy revolves around the topic of the discussion, generally limited to just the matters affecting the association as a whole. Importantly, matters of a legal nature or potential legal nature should not to be discussed in this type of forum. Items of a legal nature could include members complaining about other member's architectural violations or a member complaining about an employee of the association. These types of issues should always be discussed in closed session and, in certain situations, may require the attendance of the association's attorney.

If the board meeting is required to be open just to the membership without open discussion, there is still one issue that seems to arise: interruptions from the membership in attendance. The membership may not realize that they cannot simply participate in the board meeting, and the board members need to remember this aspect as well. A board of directors' meeting is specifically for the board to address association business, not to seek input from the membership in attendance. Input from the membership can always be encouraged at specific sections of the agenda, but entering into board discussions can expose the non-board member to legal liability. Members of the board have specific insurance (directors' and officers' insurance) that covers the board's actions during a board meeting. Non-board members entering into board discussions have no protection under the directors' and officers' insurance coverage.

GUESTS AT BOARD OF DIRECTOR MEETINGS

Welcome. The Board wishes to thank you for your interest in the homeowner's association and attending the Board of Director's meeting.

The Board has a set agenda for each meeting and has a great many issues to cover. Because of this, please do not interrupt the meeting unless you are addressed by the Chair of the Board or the President of the Board.

By a vote of the Board or by the Chair/President's discretion, the Board may ask to hear from any interested parties from the floor. If they do so, please address only issues that relate to the homeowner's association.

If the Board goes into executive session, you will be asked to leave or wait elsewhere until the Board goes back into open session. The reason for executive sessions is to allow the Board to discuss issues of a sensitive nature, such as delinquent accounts, legal matters, etc.

Sincerely,

The Board of Directors

■ ■ ■

ONLINE/TELECONFERENCING BOARD MEETINGS

Schedules are more hectic than ever, and board members' schedules are no different. Because of scheduling difficulties and, in some cases, convenience, some boards of directors hold their board meetings via online services such as Skype, GoToMeeting and GooglePlus Hangouts.

With these online services, board members have the ability to hear one another through microphones and speakers and to view each other through video cameras, regardless of where the other board members are located. These services allow board members to share architectural plans, vendor proposals or other documents that are circulated during the meeting.

While these are virtual meetings, they must be conducted in the same legal manner in which a traditional board meeting would be held. There must be a quorum, call to order, minutes taken and no conflict with the association's governing documents or state statutes.

An association's governing documents, along with the state statues, must be reviewed in order to ensure that virtual meetings are allowed and to determine what rules govern virtual meetings. For example, most state statutes require that all board members participating in a virtual meeting be able to "hear" one another simultaneously at this board meeting. An online meeting with no audio element, such as just Instant Messenger, could conflict with this legal requirement.

However, an alternative may be to vote by written consent. Some state nonprofit acts allow board votes by written consent, so a board of directors could use an online forum for debate and vote via email. The association's governing documents and state statutes may require that votes by written consent be unanimous.

THE FINE POINTS OF ONLINE MEETINGS:

- The meeting chair must be proactive and control the debate in a timely and orderly fashion.
- Have a timed and precise agenda with no deviation.
- Everyone must announce themselves before talking.
- Phone/microphone should be muted unless talking, especially if there is background noise.

■ ■ ■

CONDUCTING BOARD BUSINESS

What constitutes the board of directors conducting board business? This question comes up when boards meet outside normal board meetings and association business is discussed. Some could argue that this constitutes a board meeting, while others will argue that, as long as voting on association matters is not conducted, it is not a board meeting.

The first consideration on determining whether the board members being in the same room constitutes a board meeting is: "Are enough present to establish a quorum?" For example, if three of five board members are together in the same room, the quorum requirement is met. Simply stated, those three board members can meet for non-association related matters, but once association matters are discussed, theoretically, a board meeting has occurred. Although the meeting is not called to order or adjourned and no votes are taken, this still could be deemed a board meeting.

■ ■ ■

BOARD MEETING PACKET

The Board package is basically the meeting agenda with the supporting documentation, such as the association financials, supporting invoices and copies of CC&R violation letters. Ideally, the agenda with attached supporting documentation should be sent out to the board of directors before the meeting so that the material can be reviewed beforehand and everyone can be prepared.

Distributing the agenda along with the board package beforehand, and seeking review and comments, improves efficiency and the flow of the actual meeting. When the board arrives at the meeting, everyone already has the current issues analysis, and thus at least 30 minutes of setup and discussion time can be reduced. Everyone should be prepared to discuss the higher-level issues that the preparation has generated. With Google Docs and Dropbox there are a number of technologies that make distribution easy and fast.

The following is a typical homeowner board of directors board meeting package:

Agenda
Minutes - To be approved from prior meeting
Financials - Balance Sheet, Income Statement, Cash Disbursement Report
Membership Delinquency Report or Aging Report
Invoice Copies - For certain expenditures represented on the attached income statement
Maintenance Proposals - To be discussed in Unfinished or New Business
Warning Letters - Copies of CC&R violation letters mailed during prior period
Membership Correspondences to the Board

When presented to the board, the package should be stapled and each page should be numbered to make referencing back to a supporting document more efficient.

■ ■ ■

ROBERT'S RULES

Robert's Rules of Order is the book on parliamentary procedure that is considered the standard. It is recognized as the standard by many statutes and organizations. Parliamentarians, associations, clubs, groups or any organization with a deliberative body generally recognize this book as the authoritative guide to conducting an orderly and equitable meeting.

Brigadier General Henry M. Robert graduated from the United States Military Academy in 1857 and received a commission in the Army. He was once asked to chair a church meeting and became embarrassed because of his lack of knowledge regarding parliamentary procedures. This embarrassment left him determined to better understand parliamentary procedure. During his military service, he was posted to different parts of the United States, where he found varying forms of parliamentary procedures being followed. In 1876, he decided to publish a standardized manual, and this manual eventually became *Robert's Rules of Order.*

Robert's Rules of Order Newly Revised is a great reference for any board of directors. It is advisable to have a copy of *Robert's Rules of Order* at all membership meetings. While *Robert's Rules of Order* has a great deal of reference material within the covers, gaining an overall working grasp of parliamentary procedures is obtainable without memorizing every section of the book.

KEY MEETING POINTS OF ROBERTS RULES

1. The Meeting Chair decides who has the floor.
2. Only one person may have the floor at a time.
3. The person with the floor may only discuss the issue being considered.
4. The Chair must be considerate of other board members wishing to have the floor and give them a reasonable opportunity.

5. All decisions require a motion, a second to the motion and a vote.
6. Once voted upon, no further discussion is allowed.
7. It is the responsibility of the Chair to move the meeting along in a timely fashion.

MOTIONS

All motions must be seconded and are adopted by a majority vote unless otherwise noted. All motions may be debated unless otherwise noted below. Motions are in order of precedence: motions may be made only if no motion of equal or higher precedence is on the floor.

1. Motion to Adjourn: Not debatable. Goes to immediate majority vote.
2. Motion to Recess: Not debatable. May be for a specific time.
3. Motion to Appeal the Chair's Decision: Not debatable. Goes to immediate vote. Allows the body to overrule a decision made by the chair.
4. Motion to Suspend the Rules: Suspends formal process for dealing with a specific question. Debatable. Requires 2/3 vote.
5. Motion to End Debate and Vote or Move the Main Question: Applies only to the motion on the floor. Not debatable. Requires 2/3 vote.
6. Motion to Extend Debate: Can be general or for a specific time or number of speakers. Not debatable. Requires 2/3 vote.
7. Motion to Refer to Committee: Applies only to the main motion. Refers question to a specific group with a specific time and charge.

■ ■ ■

BOARD MEETING MINUTES

The association's meeting minutes are the written legal record of the board of director's meetings. The board secretary is responsible for compiling and, once approved, maintaining these records in the association's files. Minutes are to be maintained indefinitely in the association's records.

Minutes are used to document decisions made during a meeting and also provide a record of actions taken. A common mistake or misconception is that minutes are to be a word-for-word detailed account or essentially a transcription of everything that is said. On the contrary, minutes should state what was accomplished, rather than denote every detail of the meeting's discussion. Generally speaking, an entire meeting's business should fit on one or possibly two pages.

Minutes must be taken for all board and annual meetings. Minutes must also be taken for committee meetings and any special board or special membership meetings. CC&R violation hearings must be documented with minutes.

THE BASIC CONTENT OF MEETING MINUTES:

- Association name
- Specific Meeting Type (board, annual, etc.)
- Date
- Location of meeting (legal address)
- Time meeting called to order
- Names of board or committee members in attendance
- Statement that quorum was established
- Precise wording of every adopted motion

- Notations of failed or withdrawn motions
- Name of the person who made the motion
- Name of the person who seconded the motion
- If a vote was not unanimous, the names of those dissenting should be noted
- Committee reports given or submitted
- If the membership is allowed to address the board, the member's name and discussion topic should be noted. Placing the member's spoken statements or written statements into the minutes would not be appropriate.
- Items that will be discussed at future meetings can be included
- The date, time and location of the next meeting, if determined, should be included
- Time of adjournment
- When the minutes are approved, the secretary and president/meeting chair should sign and date as approved minutes

Meeting minutes provide a historical and legal record of the operations of the association. Matters dealing with personal issues and opinions that have no bearing on association business should never be noted in the association's minutes. Association meeting minutes are subject to membership review and to legal discovery in membership and non-membership lawsuits. So meeting minutes must be precise and brief, and under no circumstance should minutes be subjective. Minutes should be clear and to the point and only a basic summary of business that was conducted, debated and voted upon.

■ ■ ■

TIPS ON TAKING MINUTES

Distribute minutes to board or committee members before the meeting in which they will be approved so they can be reviewed beforehand. This will hasten the approval process during the meeting.

Keep opinions and observations that are not relevant from the minutes.

Items of a legal nature, such as collections, should be redacted before being distributed to non-board members.

If corrections to minutes are made, these corrections must be made in the text of the minutes being approved. The minutes of the meeting at which the corrections are made should merely indicate that the minutes were approved "as corrected." [RONR (10th ed.), p. 452, l. 12-15; p. 458, l. 10-16; see also p.151 of RONR In Brief.]

If it is necessary to correct minutes after they have been approved, such corrections can be made by means of the motion to "Amend Something Previously Adopted." The exact wording of that motion, whether adopted or rejected, should be entered in the minutes of the meeting at which it was considered. [RONR (10th ed.), p. 452, l. 12-15; p. 458, l. 10-16; see also p.151 of RONR In Brief.]

The best outline for taking minutes is the agenda of the meeting.

It is not uncommon or inappropriate for the minutes of an entire board meeting to fit on one typed page.

▪ ▪ ▪

REDACTION

"Redact" is a verb defined by Merriam Webster as: 1) to put in writing: frame, 2) to select or adapt (as by obscuring or removing sensitive information) for publication or release; broadly: edit, 3) to obscure or remove (text) from a document prior to publication or release.

Redaction in the context of an association occurs when the board of directors produces and distributes the board of directors' meeting minutes to the membership. The term "redact" is used to describe removal of certain text from the approved meeting minutes by replacing the text with black rectangles or using a text-editing function to make the text unreadable. A very prevalent example of this is classified government documents that are released under the Freedom of Information Act with classified or sensitive information redacted in this manner.

The board secretary who drafted the original meeting minutes is typically the board member responsible for redacting the sensitive information. This redaction should only be performed after the meeting minutes are finalized and approved. In certain circumstances, the secretary may add additional text to approved minutes after this redaction. The reason for adding this additional text is usually in order to clarify what was redacted in the first place. For example, if an association member was sent to the attorney for collections, this member's name and address would be redacted and the secretary or redactor may note at the place of redaction what was redacted, such as: "Board voted to send a delinquent member to the association's attorney for collections." These additions are not part of the official meeting minutes and should be concise and not embellished.

Sensitive information that should be redacted before distribution to the membership is generally any matter that is of a legal nature or could potentially be a legal issue. Collection issues and lawsuits should be redacted along with CC&R enforcement matters because of the potential for litigation. Failing to redact these types of matters could possibly result in a violation of federal and state statutes regarding public disclosure of delinquent parties. Disclosing legal matters in the board minutes could also result in the board of directors unintentionally waiving the attorney-client privilege.

■ ■ ■

SUNSHINE LAWS - BOARD OPENNESS

Frequently, the term "sunshine law" wrongly comes up with regard to the operation of an association. Sunshine laws are federal statutes, and some states have similarly-named statutes that require governmental meetings to be open to the public whenever possible. The federal sunshine laws are part of the Freedom of Information Act, which has the objective of making the government more transparent and open to public review.

The fundamental tenet of the Freedom of Information Act is derived from Federalist Paper Number 49: "the people are the only legitimate fountain of power." Similarly, as with any elected body, the association board of directors represents the membership and is accountable to the membership.

While the specific sunshine statutes and Freedom of Information Act only apply to government bodies, associations have their own sunshine-type requirements dictated by either their governing documents or state statutes. Whatever the requirements of the association's governing documents or state statutes, a board of directors should always strive to make reasonable accommodations to disseminate information and meet with members.

Generally speaking, the governing documents will usually address association meeting requirements quite thoroughly. However, it is not uncommon for an association's governing documents to not address record retention and dissemination in great detail. If this is the case, the state's nonprofit corporation statutes are the fallback.

State statutes will generally be very specific with what nonprofit corporations are required to do with communications and record-keeping. The membership's rights to review association records commonly arises and, in most cases, if not addressed in the governing documents is found in the state statutes. This particular type of statute will generally mandate what records the members are entitled to and the process for obtaining those records. Hopefully there will be aspects of these document request statutes that make complying with the requests reasonable. For example, a member cannot demand records of the association without doing so in good faith and paying for the procurement expense.

It goes without saying that it is almost always best to be as open as possible when dealing with the membership, the exception being matters dealing with litigation or potential litigation. For a board of directors with this type of policy, generally the worst thing that an association member can say is: "I do not like what the board did in this matter, but they answered my questions and gave me everything I asked for."

■ ■ ■

COLLABORATIVE DECISION MAKING

Association boards and association managers must strive to meet the needs of the entire membership. Unfortunately, within this process the board and manager rarely please everyone. However, engaging in a proactive and collaborative decision-making process can reduce or even eliminate conflicts within the association. At the very least, the membership will understand and be a part of the process, and hopefully this leads to a positive outcome for everyone involved.

A Three-Step Process: (1) The board must establish the objective or goal (2) The board must explain its obligation to address the issue to the membership (3) The board must obtain input and/or approval from the membership

The board must establish the objective or goal: The board establishing the objective may seem like the easy part of the task, but this step can be the most crucial. Unclear or overly-ambitious objectives can undermine the process. For example, a board may state that the objective of the association is to repair all the mailboxes in the association. What does this mean? Paint? Replacing certain mailboxes? Or the objective may be too ambitious and exceed a board's mandate. For example, the mailboxes may need to be replaced, but instead of obtaining the same or equivalent mailboxes, the board plans to obtain mailboxes that cost three times what the current mailboxes would cost to replace.

The board must explain its role or obligation to address the issue to the membership: Depending upon the issue at hand, it may have to be addressed as mandated by the association's governing documents. For example, building a swimming pool when there was no swimming pool originally in the association would call into question the board's mandate for such a project. However, if the clubhouse roof needs to be replaced, the association's governing documents always give the board the authority to repair or maintain.

The board must obtain input and/or approval from the membership: Developing a support base within the membership can be a slow and methodical process, but it is necessary. The board should not expect everyone in the membership to support every decision, and that is why it is crucial to develop a membership support base. All too often, the board and concerned members assume that everyone in the membership will support an issue, especially when it is obviously a critical one. For instance, a sinkhole swallowed the front entrance of an association, and a small group in the membership felt that the front entrance should not be repaired, but that everyone should just begin using the back entrance. In another example, an association's clubhouse and pool, because of erosion, became in danger of falling into the surrounding lake. A group in that membership began making the argument they did not use the pool or clubhouse, so why should they have to pay to fix the erosion problem?

Communication of the overall issue at hand is the first step to developing a support base. Holding back or trying to put a spin on an issue can cause confusion and mistrust. Be sure to explain the benefits or needs. As for the example given above regarding the sinking clubhouse and pool, this affected each individual member's home value. Most issues are not this extreme. However, home values are at the heart of most association issues, and this point can be stressed to great effect. Explaining what happens if nothing is done will often not have the same effect as pointing out the benefits of having an issue resolved.

Preach to the center: All too often, the angry small minority receive all the focus, such as when this small group feels that a viable solution is letting a clubhouse sink into a lake. This does not mean ignoring or disrespecting that group. However, a great deal of energy spent convincing that group of the needs of the association may be energy better spent towards the majority in the membership.

Communicating the issue to build the support base is generally accomplished by mailings, meetings and door-to-door canvassing.

Mailings can take many forms, from letters with outright appeals to surveys to gauge if there is any support for an issue. If the issue is controversial, a survey to test the waters is always best. People in general — and this goes for any association membership — do not like to feel that an issue is being forced upon them. A survey can help inform and also defuse. In the instances in which an outright appeal letter must be sent, it needs to be constructed in such a way as to inform while also conveying the urgency of the matter.

Membership meetings take several forms. While informal informational meetings are a great way to build support in a relaxed atmosphere, depending upon the nature of the issue, formal meetings are best left to the latter stages of approval, after support has gained momentum.

Door-to-door canvassing can be appropriate at any stage and is a great way to build support on a personal basis. Members generally appreciate this approach, and it is a great way to address concerns in a more relaxed manner. Generally, the only drawback with this approach is the time that it requires to accomplish. Many times this approach is taken after an initial mailing or meeting to solidify support.

■ ■ ■

ASSOCIATION COMMITTEES

Committees can be an essential part of any association. Committees are a way to bring association members together with similar objectives and relevant expertise who may otherwise not have a method for gathering information or coordinating actions. Two of the main advantages of a committee are the broad perspective brought to the group by the committee members and the sharing of responsibilities.

An association committee is a deliberative assembly that is subordinate to the association's board of directors. Committees are formed by the board of directors and generally have at least one board member chairing the particular committee. The chairperson organizes a committee meeting through an agenda, which is usually distributed in advance.

The committee chairperson is responsible for running the meeting. This responsibility entails keeping discussions on topic, recognizing committee members to speak and calling for votes after a debate has taken place. The committee chairperson appoints a committee secretary to record minutes of meetings.

Committees may meet on a regular basis or may meet less frequently, or meetings may be called irregularly as the need arises.

There are generally two types of committees that associations establish: working committees and standing committees. Working committees are established in order to accomplish a particular task or oversee an ongoing area in need of temporary oversight. Board nominating committees are working committees because of the temporary duration, such as the upcoming annual meeting.

It is not uncommon for an association to have up to five or more standing committees. Standing committees are permanent in nature and have regular meetings and/or duties. An association's standing committees are usually architectural, legal, financial, communication and social. Sometimes two of these committees will be combined into one.

Architectural Committee: The board of directors appoints the architectural committee to provide guidance on the architectural standards for the association. These standards include the enhancement, preservation and safety of the association. This is accomplished by the committee submission process of review and approval of all plans. The committee also tracks and monitors the enforcement of architectural standards that are in process.

Legal Committee: The board of directors receives guidance on legal and financial risk from the legal committee. This committee reviews and recommends rules and regulations related to the association. The committee may also track and monitor rules violations. When boards of directors feel their governing documents need to be updated or changed, this committee would be charged with the task of making recommendations. This committee is also charged with the responsibility for reviewing insurance policies and insurance claims. The objective of this committee is to reduce potential legal and financial risk to the board and the association as a whole.

Financial Committee: The board of directors appoints a financial committee to provide guidance on the financial matters facing the association. The board treasurer usually chairs this committee. This committee proposes the annual budget and monitors the financials throughout the fiscal year. This committee oversees the outside accounting firm's annual tax preparation and filing, the annual audit of the association's financials and any reserve studies and resulting reserve funding. When necessary, this committee would address any financing issues with regard to bank loans or special assessment issues. The objective of this committee is to improve the overall financial wellbeing of the association.

Communication Committee: This committee can be the liaison between the board of directors, any committees and the association membership. This committee is charged with keeping the association membership informed about the activities of the association. Communication methods such as newsletters, websites and general notices can be the responsibility of this Committee. The communication committee is responsible for recommending improvements to the methods by which information is distributed to the association and received by the board of directors and committees, as well as to how it is followed up by these responsible bodies.

Social Committee: The social committee suggests, oversees and reviews activities, social events and the welcoming of new members. In working with the board, the committee is responsible for establishing and improving the sense of community.

■ ■ ■

FORMING COMMITTEES

Forming committees can be as basic as the guidelines that follow, or establishing committees can be more elaborate if the association's governing documents have other procedures. One important point to stress is that no matter what the committee says or does, the board of directors is ultimately responsible for the actions or inactions of any committee that is formed. The board of directors is also generally the final word or authority on what a committee decides.

TO FORM A COMMITTEE:

Purpose: Defines expected result of committees' work (not what's to be done to fulfill goal)

Responsibilities: Activities/actions that must be performed to fulfill assigned purpose

Organization: Number of members; method to select chair, members; term of office, role of officers and board liaison; desired characteristics

Operations: Time, place, frequency of meetings; meeting minutes; reports to board and when; approval process for committee's use of association funds

If the committee is a working committee with a set goal to accomplish, set the deadline for the committee to report back to the board of directors with the committee's recommendations, when the committee ceases to exist.

■ ■ ■

FINDING VOLUNTEERS

Volunteers are crucial to the operation of the association. With this said, how are these volunteers attracted, recruited and maintained?

Communication is crucial to addressing the issue of volunteerism in an association. Do not assume that the membership knows there is a need for volunteers. Newsletters are one of the best methods for communicating this need to the membership. Outline the volunteer needs of the association, social committee, landscaping committee, etc.

Another good method of finding interested volunteers is to find members who have taken specific interests in their own yards, such as gardening, or members who are continually doing projects in and around their homes. Members who spend a great deal of time working around their homes are often great candidates for landscaping and architecture review committees.

Recognition is paramount to gaining and retaining volunteers. Listing committee members in the newsletter and recognizing them at the annual meeting with applause goes a long way.

■ ■ ■

WHEN BOARD MEMBERS RESIGN

Board members resign from boards of directors for a myriad of reasons. The predominate reason usually revolves around the member's other pressing commitments. Another common reason is that the board member is selling their home and moving out of the association.

Whatever the reason, the first step is to review the association's bylaws for guidance. Generally speaking, most association bylaws address the topic of board vacancies. The bylaws might go into detail, such as this example:

"Section 5.1 Vacancies: A vacancy occurring in the Executive Board may only be filled by a majority vote of the remaining Board members, though less than a quorum, or by the sole remaining Board member; but a vacancy created by an increase in the authorized number of Board members shall be filled only by election at an Annual or substitute Annual Meeting or at a Special Meeting of Members called for that purpose. As indicated in Section 5.5, the Membership shall have the first right to fill any vacancy created by the Membership's removal of a Board member."

This example of bylaw language is very specific and straightforward. If the bylaws fail to address board vacancies, or the language is ambiguous, the next step is to review the state statutes that address nonprofit corporations.

■ ■ ■

BOARD RESOLUTIONS

Board resolutions are a formal method of recording decisions or actions of an association's board of directors. A resolution can be for just about any subject. Resolutions many times arise when associations take out bank loans or appoint a member to the board of directors. When a resolution is made and adopted during a board meeting, the specifics of the resolution are written down and signed by all directors.

Resolutions serve as a written permanent record of the choices that directors have made. Generally, resolutions do not need to be filed with the association's governing documents. Resolutions should be filed with the association's records and readily available for review in the event that an association member wants to know what actions the board has taken, etc. Resolutions are legally-binding decisions made by the board.

A board resolution is a motion that follows a set format and is formally adopted by the board. Resolutions may enact rules and regulations or formalize other types of board decisions. There are typically four types of resolutions for a community association:

Policy resolutions affect owners' rights and obligations, such as rules for the use of common areas and recreational facilities, architectural guidelines and enforcement procedures.

Administrative resolutions address the internal operations of the community association, such as operating procedures, collection procedures and where board meetings will be held.

Special resolutions document board decisions that apply to a policy or rule or individual situation, such as a decision about an alleged rule violation.

General resolutions involve routine events, such as adopting the annual budget and approving a contract.

■ ■ ■

Membership

■ ■ ■

MEMBERSHIP COMMUNICATIONS

The importance of adhering to the association's governing documents and state statutes regarding notification requirements cannot be stressed enough. Not following the proper procedures and legal requirements can at worst have severe legal consequences and at a minimum cost the association additional expense in correcting the matter.

All association notices in a broad legal sense are used to communicate rights and responsibilities to an interested party. There are different forms of legal notices, with written notices generally required by most associations. The definition of the term "written notice" can vary from state to state and even within different statutes within a state. And what can make written notice requirements more ambiguous are the association's governing documents written by thousands of different attorneys in every state.

Official or required membership notifications are specified in the association's governing documents or state statutes. For association operational issues, such as membership meetings, this information is generally found in the association's bylaws. Notification issues dealing with individual membership architectural violations, if specified, would generally be found in the CC&Rs. If architectural violation notification requirements are not specific in the declarations, state statutes or legal precedent would be relied on for notification requirements.

Generally, the association bylaws are going to specifically outline membership notification requirements for annual meetings and special meetings. Language similar to that below is typical of what would be found in an association's bylaws:

Section 4.6 Notices of Meetings: Written or printed notice stating the time and place of a membership meeting, and the items on the agenda, shall be delivered not less than ten (10) nor more than fifty (50) days before the date of any such membership meeting, either personally or by first class mail, by or at the discretion of the President or the Secretary, to the address of each lot owner. Notice shall be deemed given upon deposit in a US Mail depository.

This again is simply placing the notification in a postage-paid First Class envelope in a US mail box. This is generally the accepted standard of Effective Notice or Effective Delivery and is accepted in a court of law.

An additional method of verification is the affidavit of mailing. An affidavit of mailing is simply a sworn and notarized statement completed by the person who placed the notification in the US mail. For mass membership meeting mailings, an affidavit of mailing can be utilized, as well as on an individual member notification.

All governing documents are different, and there may be exceptions for utilizing First Class mail for effective notice. These alternative notice delivery options, such as posting a sign at the main entrance or physically posting every member's front door with a meeting notice, can create concerns with regard to effective notification of absentee owners or associations with multiple entrances.

■ ■ ■

PRODUCTIVE MEMBERSHIP COMMUNICATIONS

As with any association, there are always issues arising that need membership input and approval. Even when input and approval are not necessarily required for certain issues, membership "buy-in" is a productive community-involvement strategy. Seeking buy-in can settle possible concerns beforehand and help alleviate problems that may arise as the matter moves forward.

- Initial Communication: Share as much information as possible. Most communications should give a detailed account of what is happening or going to be happening. For example, the association's streets are going to be repaved. The most important information to communicate may be the paving schedule, noting the street and the date. Other important information may be to remind members not to park on the street and the cost of the paving to the association. Also include whether or not there will be follow-up communications and when to expect the board of directors to send out this follow-up.

  Another important aspect of the initial communication is how the matter is going to impact the community, either positively or possibly negatively. For example, to communicate that the new mailboxes will improve curb appeal of the entire association.

- Follow-Up Communication(s): Again, share as much information as possible. This follow-up can provide either a current status report or a resolution of the initial matter. If the matter is resolved, state such resolution and the results.

  As with all membership communications, less is more. In a world of texting and Twitter, elaborate multipage communications have a tendency not to be read completely. Main themes and bullet points convey messages much more efficiently.

  Communications of a legal nature should come from the association's attorney or at least be reviewed by the association's attorney.

■ ■ ■

CHALLENGING PERSONALITIES

"People's personalities, like buildings, have various facades, some pleasant to view, some not." - Francois de la Rochefoucauld

Every association membership is different, but there seems to be one constant: there are always members who seem to take a non-positive view on issues that the board addresses within the association. Board members often cite this negativity as one of the most frustrating factors of serving on a board of directors. Avoiding or hiding from these members might be possible, but it may not be a long-term solution to challenging members. Being confrontational with challenging members, in most instances, is not effective either.

POINTS IN DEALING WITH CHALLENGING MEMBERS:

- Always be respectful of the member's concern. No matter how benign or ridiculous the concern may or may not be, no one likes to be treated with disrespect. Generally, if the member's concerns are treated with respect, the respect is reciprocal.
- Seek counsel of others. It is imperative to speak with others who may have had experience dealing with the member or a particular situation. The association manager and other board members can be great resources. Former board members as well can be a great resource. Other parties may provide new perspectives that will aid in a solution.
- Communicate the board's position. Letting the member know the board's intentions will often diffuse the situation. Refusing to discuss the matter or putting them off may be like throwing gasoline on a fire. Before communicating the position, the member may believe that the board is being difficult. Explaining a particular decision and the reasoning behind the decision may allow them to understand the situation.
- Try to comprehend the member's intentions. This may seem like another obvious point, but the member may not have all the facts of the matter. For example, some in the membership may believe they are not receiving anything at all for their dues, and these members may not realize that there are common expenses.
- The past is the past. If a member has had an issue with a prior board, committee, etc., for whatever reason, acknowledging what happened or what the member perceives to

have happened may go a long way in smoothing the issue over. Many times a person will realize that harping on an issue with someone who had nothing to do with the issue will be a waste of time, especially if acknowledged.

- Remain calm at all times. This may seem like another obvious point, and many times it is easier said than done, but losing control and flaring out at the member may lower the discussions for all parties. A confrontational attitude is not conducive to establishing common ground. Anger generally is not effective while a calm persona can be most effective.
- Escalate the matter to third parties. When the above six points have been exhausted, it may be time to rely on third parties, such as the association manager or association attorney. This can come in many forms, such as having the association manager chair the annual meeting or having the association's attorney communicate with the member. Many times fresh blood can defuse difficult situations.
- Last Resort. If all other efforts have been exhausted and the member is still being difficult, as a last resort reiterate the board's position and advise the member that the matter will no longer be addressed further by the board. After all, if the board of directors has worked in good faith to resolve the matter, what else can be done? There may be underlying reasons that are motivating the member to act this way, and if the motivation is not apparent it may be impossible to resolve.

■ ■ ■

THE SLIPPERY SLOPE OF CC&R ENFORCEMENT

There are often complaints from certain association members about restrictions within their association. And there are always certain association members who go further than just grumble and complain loudly about the "unreasonable" restrictions of an association or, "Why do we even need a homeowner's association?" Certainly some members do not see the need for any restrictions, but they may not understand the ramifications of loose or no enforcement of these restrictions. One thing is for certain: an association that has restrictions and that enforces these restrictions increases the overall property values for everyone in the association.

The CC&Rs of an association are legally-binding documents filed with the register of deeds of the county where the association is located. These CC&Rs lay out how the property will be used and maintained—-in other words, how homes look and what can be done within the association.

When someone purchases a home within an association, they are essentially purchasing a code of conduct for their behavior within the community. Generally, homeowners wish for their community, at a minimum, to remain the same after their purchase. Many factors go into purchasing a home, but the old axiom "location, location, location" being the three most important aspects of buying a home ring true — or, more precisely, "neighborhood, neighborhood, neighborhood."

When CC&Rs are not enforced, it is a slippery slope to see how far or how bizarre members' tastes or styles may vary from the CC&Rs. This author has witnessed an array of outrageous infractions of the CC&Rs. In a few instances, the author has been involved alongside boards of directors in cases going to the supreme court in one state and to the appellate courts just below the supreme court a number of times in order to help enforce CC&Rs against noncompliant members.

No association, no matter the price range of homes within, is exempt from serious CC&R violations. Often words will be heard to the effect: "we would never have something like that happen in our homeowners association." Surprisingly, some of the most extreme CC&R violations happen in the nicest communities.

The author was involved with an association that had an association member who began construction of a swimming pool in his front yard. This was going to be a swimming pool costing the member in excess of $75,000. Per the member, the front yard placement for the new pool was due to insufficient space in his backyard. Not only did this member neglect to obtain architectural review committee approval (which he would not have received), but he started this construction project on a Friday afternoon and hoped to be too far along by Monday for anyone to do anything about the situation. The member rationalized that it was better to beg for forgiveness than to ask for permission and get turned down. Unfortunately, this member and the association were forced to resolve this CC&R violation in court at immense expense to everyone involved, with the end result being the front yard being returned to the original condition.

Another extreme example of CC&R violation in a very nice community was a member who had a dilapidated 50-foot sailboat towed to his home and placed in his driveway. This member had purchased this boat to restore, and he chose to do this restoration project in his driveway. As in the example above, this member decided to begin the restoration project on Friday afternoon.

Remarkably, the member and his teenage son by the following Saturday afternoon had taken roughly half the sailboat apart. This could be determined by how they had arranged all the boat's parts on the front lawn. This was in an association that had just spent over $300,000 on upgrading and beautification of their front entrance. Also, this sailboat restoration project was at the second home on the left when entering by the association's beautiful new front entrance.

In both examples above, the overwhelming majority of the membership was upset about these CC&R violations. Some members will baffle the imagination with what they consider perfectly acceptable, which will vary greatly from the CC&Rs and 99% of the rest of the membership. But unless it is an extreme situation such as the examples noted, some in the membership will say, "What is the harm?" Again, it is a slippery slope that begins with small infractions.

Failure to enforce the CC&Rs may seem like a small issue in most instances until the board is faced with a member who wants to build a 400-square-foot air-conditioned tree house for their grandchildren. Enforcing CC&Rs may be a thankless task, but it is crucial to maintaining the property values of the association.

■ ■ ■

GOING ABOVE & BEYOND

Usually when the term "going above and beyond" is used, it is used in a positive and complementary way to apply to someone who has exceeded themselves in helping someone else. Unfortunately, "going above and beyond" within the framework of an association's governing documents is rarely a positive affirmation. From exceeding maintenance responsibilities to becoming entangled in personality conflicts between neighbors, "going above and beyond" what the governing documents specify can be treacherous ground, to say the least.

When "going above and beyond" situations arise, it is usually a result of the board of directors trying to help resolve a situation in good faith. When these situations arise, rarely does everyone realize at the onset the ramifications of exceeding what the governing documents specify.

The CC&Rs are usually the association governing documents exceeded or, more precisely, their scope and authority exceeded. CC&Rs are written regulations, limitations and restrictions on use, mutually agreed to by all owners of homes in an association. CC&Rs are enforced by the homeowners association or by individual owners who can bring lawsuits against violators, and are permanent and "run with the land" so that future owners are bound to the same rules.

Because CC&Rs are legally-binding to the association and individual homeowner, they specify each party's legal obligation. Legal action can be brought against the board of directors or against the individual association member for failing to address issues that are their responsibility. *Vice versa*, each party can also be subject to legal action for exceeding that for which they are responsible. It is also worth noting that a third party such as another member of the association can instigate legal action against the association or another individual association member for failing to act or exceeding the authority as provided for in the governing documents.

There are two examples we are going to reference in this article as "going above and beyond": exceeding maintenance responsibilities, and becoming involved in personal disputes between neighbors.

Maintenance may seem like a clear-cut aspect of a board of directors' decision-making process because this subject is usually covered in detail in the governing documents, but maintenance can be a slippery slope.

For example, there is an erosion issue from storm water running off an association-owned street across a member's property. Is the association responsible for fixing the water runoff issue? Is the association responsible for the damage to the individual's land? What if the water runoff damaged the foundation of the home? Who pays for the repairs? One thing is certain, if the association addresses these items without being required to by the governing documents, be prepared to fix similar problems on other members' property. This often comes up in condominium associations. For example, suppose there is a roof leak, and a piece of furniture is damaged, and per the CC&Rs the association is only required to repair the roof leak and paint the interior wall to remove the water stain. If the board of directors elects to compensate the owner for the damaged furniture because they feel that paying for the damaged furniture is a nominal expense, what does the board of directors do when an expensive piece of artwork is damaged by a roof leak in someone else's condominium in the future?

Another common issue that boards of directors get entangled with is personal conflicts between neighbors. The overwhelming majority of people who decide to serve on their association's board are geared towards helping their association and the membership. Most board members who get involved in resolving personal issues are truly trying to help in a difficult situation. But in almost all cases this board member is drawn into a personal squabble, and both disputing neighbors typically end up being upset with the board member who was trying to help resolve the matter. These disputing neighbors usually just want the board member to take their side, and when that does not happen they assume that the board member is siding with the other party.

The best course of action in these matters is to recommend the name of a third-party mediator to both disputing neighbors with the hope that a trained mediator can broker a peace. Interestingly enough, the author in his years of experience has never had both disputing parties agree to mediation. With such a low number seeking resolution through this method, it truly demonstrates the difficulty in becoming involved in personality conflicts between neighbors. When disputing parties want the board to become involved in the fight, always look for the authority within the association's governing documents to justify the involvement. In the vast majority of situations that arise, there is no such foundation to support the board of directors taking any action.

■ ■ ■

RULES & REGULATIONS

Questions arise when boards of directors initially draft or revise then implement their association's rules and regulations. There are points to consider while going through this process. The board of directors generally has the authority to establish reasonable rules and regulations. While this authority is typically found in the restrictive CC&Rs, in rare instances it may be found in the association's bylaws or in the association's articles of incorporation.

What are rules and regulations? Rules and regulations are legally-enforceable governing documents that, generally speaking, clarify or elaborate upon the other governing documents. For example, the restrictive CC&Rs may state: "trash receptacles must be hidden from view of the street." The rules and regulations could specify: "trash receptacles must be maintained behind the home, out of street view, and returned from the curb within 12 hours." However, the rules and regulations cannot go beyond the authority of the other governing documents and cannot conflict with the other governing documents or any laws.

Most association declarations have rules and regulations language similar to the following:

"Section 9. Rules and Regulations. In addition to the use restrictions set forth in this Declaration, reasonable rules and regulations governing the use of the Property may be made and amended from time to time by the Association. Copies of such regulations and amendments thereto shall be posted prominently prior to their effective date and shall be furnished by the Association to all Owners upon request. Specifically, and not by way of limitation, the Association shall have the right to make reasonable rules and regulations governing the use of the common Amenities and any other Common Elements."

Let's dissect the prior section:

"In addition to the use restrictions set forth in this Declaration..." This language ties the rules and regulations to the declarations, the legally filed governing documents, thus giving the rules and regulations the basis for legal enforcement.

"Copies of such regulations and amendments thereto shall be posted prominently prior to their effective date and shall be furnished by the Association to all Owners upon request."

Membership notification language is a key point of almost all declaration's rules and regulations requirements. Since rules and regulations are usually not filed with the CC&Rs and can generally be changed without membership approval, proper membership notification can be vital for enforcement. A defense of a court action resulting from rules and regulations violations could be that the member was not properly notified of the requirements of the rules and regulations per the posting requirements set forth.

The prior language requires posting or displaying, while other declaration language may require changes or additions to the rules and regulations to be mailed to the membership. Some declarations may have notification language about having to mail rules and regulations to the membership annually—or some other requirement, even if there are no changes—just to keep the membership informed.

"Association shall have the right to make reasonable rules and regulations governing the use of the common Amenities and any other Common Elements."

The word "reasonable" is defined differently by everyone, but a great way of looking at reasonable rules and regulations are that the rules and regulations should be bounded by fairness, consistency and the avoidance of appearing arbitrary or excessive. A good way to consider the reasonableness of any rule or regulation is to imagine standing in court in front of a judge. Will this judge feel the board's rules and regulations are reasonable, especially considering judges will generally give all considerations to the person being held to the standards written by someone else?

KEY POINTS - RULES AND REGULATIONS

- Rules and regulations must be enforced uniformly and equally. For example, restricting children from walking on the grass would be in violation of federal law.
- Only make rules that are necessary. For example, "no gambling in the clubhouse." While listing something such as this under rules and regulations in all likelihood does no harm, gambling is generally a violation of state and federal laws. So if this issue were to come about for enforcement, the illegal activity would be the issue addressed when dealing with the matter. It is best to develop rules only if necessary.
- The rules and regulations must be based upon proper authority. As noted above, do the association's governing documents address developing rules and regulations, or is the association going to have to rely on state statutes, if any, to give authority to develop and enforce?
- Depending upon individual state statutes, or lack thereof, it may be necessary for the rules and regulations to provide for imposition of fines or penalties for the violation of the

governing documents. If there is no provision in the governing documents or state statutes enforcing governing documents, the association may have to seek court actions. For example, a small claims court action may be necessary for someone not rolling their trash can in from the curb if there are no rules or statutes to back up the governing documents.
- Overstepping the authority of all the other governing documents. It occasionally happens that a new rule and regulation is proposed that cannot be enforced without amending the governing documents. For example, putting wording in the rules prohibiting commercial vehicles from the property. Unless there is a provision in the declarations that addresses commercial vehicles to this degree, this topic generally could only be addressed through the amendment process of the CC&Rs.

One final aspect of rules and regulations to consider is that what is set forth is what has to be followed. For example, in an attempt to make everyone aware of the violation process, a board of directors may wish to publish in the rules and regulations a process such as: "A member will receive three (3) warning letters for violating the rules and regulations before being called in front of the board of directors for a hearing." While this may seem informative and good information for every member to have, what if a member does something of such a magnitude to warrant being called immediately before the board of directors? Whatever this may be, the rules and regulations have to be followed, and, until revised, in theory the member could do this two more times before they are called before the board for a hearing. Another item to consider is setting fine amounts for violating certain governing document provisions. What if "disturbing the peace is $20" and a member sets off fireworks for several hours? It may be worth $20 to this member to set off fireworks for this dollar amount. While some governing documents may require specific wording on rules processes or even in order to publish fine amounts, attempting to contemplate what members can do in advance is challenging, to say the least.

In conclusion, make rules in an attempt to ensure that each member can enjoy the community free from the harmful behavior of others. Attempt to make rules that do not necessarily punish, but make rules that encourage understanding and compliance.

■ ■ ■

PETS - RULES & REGULATIONS

Per the American Pet Products Manufacturers Association, there are an estimated 74.8 million dogs and 88.3 million cats in the United States. Additionally, there is an estimated 50 million nontraditional or exotic pets in American homes.

When drafting rules & regulations pertaining to pets, it is more about the owner of the pet than the pet itself. Essentially, the pet owner's behavior is being regulated. A good point to remember is that, when a particular pet is deemed vicious, the pet owner has chosen to have this vicious pet.

DRAFTING & ENFORCING PET RULES

Any rule must be consistent with the association's governing documents. For example, if the governing documents do not restrict certain breeds, this may be difficult to enforce.

These rules & regulations should be publicized and easily disseminated.

Enforcement must be consistent and reasonable.

Rules and regulations drafted around the pet's and owner's behaviors, rather than on the particular breed or size, generally are easier to enforce.

It may be difficult to draft specific language on an exotic or nontraditional pet, but at a minimum the safety and health issues should be noted in the rules, no matter the particular animal.

Rules and regulations must be consistent with state and federal laws.

Federal statutes (Fair Housing Act and, in some instances, Americans with Disabilities Act) exempt and supersede service animals from any rules and regulations or any other association governing documents. Certain states have additional statutes that regulate service animals.

■ ■ ■

ALL BITE, NO BARK

Boards of directors, association members, and association managers are commonly confronted by conflicts, and sometimes those conflicts are on four legs. Firearm safety teaches us that all guns should be assumed to be loaded, and with a dog it may be safest to assume that all dogs bite. When performing property inspections or visiting members' homes, issues with dogs occasionally arise.

While most are familiar with the reputations of dog breeds such as Pit Bulls and Rottweilers, all dogs deserve deference. Conversely, the so-called "dangerous breeds" such as Pit Bulls and Rottweilers are many times very docile creatures, except when abetted by the negative influences of their owners. Fortunately or unfortunately, no matter what breed or size of dog, they are many times reflections of their owners.

The Center for Disease Control (CDC) has reported that while Rottweilers and Pit Bulls are typically not aggressive toward their owners, they generally do exhibit aggression towards strangers. In one CDC study, Rottweilers and Pit Bulls accounted for close to 60% of all fatalities in dog-related attacks, despite both breeds combined representing less than 7% of overall dog ownership.

A number of municipalities and associations have attempted to regulate aggressive or dangerous dog breeds. These regulations usually encompass a handful of particular breeds: Pit Bull, Terrier, Staffordshire Terrier, Staffordshire Bull Terrier, Rottweiler, Mastiff, Doberman Pinchers and Dog-Wolf Hybrid. While these types of measures may be employed with good intentions, actual enforcement is another matter.

There are generally two areas in which issues of enforcement arise: determining breed and the presumption that a dog is vicious based upon their breed.

Determining a particular breed may not appear to be a demanding point, but determining to a legal certainty may be difficult. A legal certainty is a principle in law, which holds that the law must provide those subject to it with the ability to regulate their conduct. In other words, the regulation or law should allow for fair warning and be void of vagueness. With the various breeds and mixed breeds that encompass the canine family, a legal certainty may be a high standard to reach if challenged in court.

The second problem area of enforcement is the predetermination of viciousness of a particular breed. This legal presumption that certain dog breeds are *prima facie* "dangerous" or "vicious" can be another high standard to reach, without specific vicious actions to support the matter.

Interestingly, an Irish research study published in the April 2015 *Veterinary Journal* discovered that dog bite injuries significantly increased with the introduction of legislation regarding "vicious" dog breeds. The study's hypothesis determined that targeting particular breeds contributes to increases in dog bite hospitalizations. The study determined that the legislation-reinforced erroneous stereotypes of risk is determined by breed not individual animals. The result is that people assumed that other dog breeds were safer because those breeds was not legislated or recognized as vicious.

Associations have had limited success with specifically-tailored regulations regarding dogs. These regulations usually revolve around weight or, more precisely, weight restrictions. Pit Bulls, Rottweilers and Mastiffs can weight in excess of 100 pounds. Of course, weight restrictions would need to apply to all breeds. Associations in certain situations have attempted to eliminate all dogs, which is a herculean task, to say the least, and fraught with membership dissension.

While Rottweilers and Pit Bulls are responsible for a large percentage of fatalities despite their relatively lower ownership rate, other dog breeds have a reputation for biting that may surprise many. There are a number of breeds that are much more popular and are considered "family friendly" dogs, such as Poodles, Dalmatians, and Dachshunds to name a few. Again, these breeds are much more prevalent, and their bites are generally much less damaging that a Pit Bull's.

There are five fundamental reasons why dogs bite: fear, territorial encroachment, sexual aggression, training and abuse. When dogs feel threatened, most will instinctively respond by biting. Dogs are very territorial, and thus many will guard their territory furiously. A high percentage of dog bites occur when a dog is eating or tending to her puppies. Sexual aggression can occur when a dog has not been spayed or neutered. The fourth fundamental reason for dog bites is their training as a guard or protection animal. The last reason, abuse, can involve elements of the prior four reasons. It is important to realize that, more often than not, a dog does not bite out of aggression.

Per the CDC, dog bites and other dog-related incidents accounted for more than one-third of all homeowner insurance liability claims in 2015, costing more than $570 million. Approximately 4.5 million people in the United States are bitten by dogs each year, a one-in-50 likelihood of being bitten. Every day, over 1,000 people seek emergency room care for treatment of dog bites.

■ ■ ■

FINES AND THE CONCEPT OF REASONABLENESS

The author has often been asked, "What should we fine for this violation of the CC&Rs?" or "What do other boards fine for this violation?" Notwithstanding state statutes that may limit fines and regulate a fine process, this is not always a cut-and-dried issue. This is where a board embraces the "concept of reasonableness."

This concept of reasonableness, in short, is the use of diligence, prudence and reasonable care in community operations and governance. The concept should be bound by fairness, consistency and the avoidance of appearing arbitrary or excessive.

A good rule of thumb when considering the concept of reasonableness is to imagine being in court in front of a judge. Will this judge feel that the board's decision/action regarding a violation of the governing documents was reasonable?

To this end, if an enforcement matter proceeds to the court system, the judge looks first to whether the board has authority to enforce. The judge will do this by reviewing the community's governing documents and, if any apply, the state statutes. The judge will then look for reasonableness of enforcement. This could involve the court looking for consistency of prior enforcement. The judge may also look at the community's internal due process requirements, as provided for in the community's governing documents. Another and more common point that a judge may consider is how long the particular issue had been in place before the board commenced with enforcement.

The concern is that reasonableness can be decided by the court on a case-by-case basis. So when it comes to reasonableness, a board should go to the extreme in being reasonable whenever a member violates the governing documents. For example, allow a member who must make a repair to their home 30 days rather than 5 days.

However, when violations have occurred and fines determined to be appropriate by the board, the board should remember that a fine is intended to obtain compliance with the governing documents, not to punish a violator. A $5 fine for failing to roll in a trash can would generally not be considered unreasonable, however a $100 fine for failing to pick up after a dog may be deemed unreasonable.

Another point to consider is that the fine must be effective in order to work. A $5 fine per month for an unapproved storage building may be cheaper to pay than to obtain offsite storage. And once a board rules on a violation, the board may be unable to go back and adjust this same violation ruling.

The concept of reasonableness should be the basis upon which any association board uses their elected authority. The board should always ask, "Is the action to be taken reasonably related to the community's purposes?" Also, if action is taken, "Will enforcement be required thereafter, and can that action be appropriately and reasonably enforced?"

Legal

■ ■ ■

STEERING CLEAR OF COURT

There is a great deal of truth to the adage: "the only parties who win a lawsuit are the lawyers." Because of CC&R enforcement issues and collection issues, legal proceedings are a way of life with associations. With all the serious matters facing associations, litigation is obviously not avoidable in all situations, but it is always worth the effort to avoid litigation whenever possible.

There are two common misconceptions of litigation: first, "Our case is a can't–lose;" and second, "We will get a huge settlement." The parties to a court case will many times feel that their case is strong, not only strong, but a "sure thing." No way can they lose. However, a sure thing is hardly ever the reality of a court case. Any experienced lawyer will admit that there are cases that seemed like slam-dunks up until the judge or jury ruled the other way. The best approach for any matter involving litigation is to be prepared to win or lose, no matter the merits of the case.

The large settlement misconception comes from news stories such as the famous *Liebeck v. McDonald's Restaurants* case in

1994, also known as the McDonald's hot coffee case. A jury awarded $2.86 million to plaintiff Stella Liebeck when she accidentally spilled hot coffee in her lap after purchasing it from a McDonald's restaurant. While the jury awarded $2.86 million, the judge reduced the final judgment to $640,000, and both parties agreed to a confidential settlement, for presumably a lower amount, to avoid the appeal litigation.

Per the U.S. Department of Justice report on Civil Jury Cases in Large Counties, the median plaintiff award for all jury cases was $52,000. Jury awards can vary from county to county and state to state, but generally the most generous awards are going to be awarded in the more metropolitan areas of the country. When factoring in legal fees and related court costs, any awards can be reduced significantly. It is important to note here that in this same Department of Justice report, plaintiffs winning cases and receiving awards occurred less than a quarter of the time or exactly 21.2%. These numbers do not factor in how many cases were dropped or settled out of court before a jury verdict was presented, which is usually a substantial percentage of all court cases filed.

There are options to consider in dispute resolution other than full-blown litigation: mediation, arbitration and expert determination.

Mediation is a commonly used form of alternative dispute resolution (ADR) that can resolve disputes between two or more parties. A mediator is a neutral third party who facilitates the mediation and attempts to assist the parties in negotiating a settlement. Mediation is an interactive process with the disputing parties interacting with the mediator and, in certain situations, the parties with one another. One reason the mediation process is so effective is that a well-trained and experienced mediator can guide the process in a constructive manner toward mutual resolution. This is unlike the structured setting of court proceedings, in which the participants are, in essence, along for the ride.

In court proceedings when a ruling is sought, the decision lies in the hands of a judge or jury. These court decisions are not the flexible results that can come from mediation. The nature of a successful mediation is that the results are agreeable to all parties. When all parties are in agreement, compliance with the mediated agreement is estimated to be higher than court rulings. However, a mediated agreement is legally enforceable in court.

The lower cost of mediation, generally under $1,500, is a huge benefit compared to the cost of litigation. Per the National Center for State Courts organization, the typical lawsuit on average will cost between $15,000 and $20,000. Quicker resolution is another benefit of mediation. Court cases can sometimes take years to even reach a courtroom. While court hearings are public, mediation is a confidential proceeding in which all discussions and findings are known only to the parties in dispute and the mediator.

Various organizations offer mediation to interested parties. In the state of North Carolina, the Association Bureau offers mediation specifically to just association boards and association members. The Association Bureau has mediators who have an in-depth understanding of associations and the related legal issues. The Association Bureau is akin to a Better Business Bureau for HOA members and boards.

Arbitration is another commonly-used form of alternative dispute resolution, which can resolve disputes between two or more parties.

Arbitration can be voluntary or mandatory and can be either legally-binding or non-binding. Mediation is similar to non-binding arbitration in that a resolution cannot be forced on the parties. The primary difference between arbitration and mediation is that in mediation the mediator will attempt to negotiate a compromise between the parties. In non-binding arbitration, the arbitrator is an impartial adjudicator who does not participate in the settlement negotiations, only in accessing the liabilities and possible damages of the parties.

As with mediation, arbitration has a lower cost compared to the cost of litigation. Again, as with mediation, arbitration generally has a faster resolution outcome compared to litigation.

While court hearings are public, arbitration is generally a confidential, nonpublic proceeding in which all discussions and findings are known only to the parties in dispute and the arbitrator.

Because of certain state statutes or possible requirements of an association's governing documents, arbitration could be mandatory and binding. By participating in binding arbitration, the parties may waive their rights to seek remedies in court. Generally, there are few, if any, avenues for appealing an arbitration ruling. As in traditional court rulings, arbitration rulings are enforceable.

One final alternative dispute resolution is expert determination. Expert determination has been a long-standing form of dispute resolution, generally called upon before an actual lawsuit is filed. The expert determination approach is utilized when parties have positions that could be mediated or arbitrated, but the parties believe that an independent evaluation by an expert would resolve the matter.

More precisely, expert determination is a process by which parties to the dispute select an independent and neutral expert to determine the dispute. This process is also confidential, in which all discussions and findings are known only to the parties involved. The expert will be an individual with specific knowledge pertinent to the dispute subject matter.

■ ■ ■

LEGAL DISCOVERY & ELECTRONIC COMMUNICATIONS

While steering clear of court may not always be possible, being adequately prepared for the eventuality is possible. One of these preparations is understanding the litigation process and what these processes can entail. One element that boards should be most aware of is their communications with other members and other parties. Communications, even from a board member's personal email to another board member's personal email may be discoverable in a lawsuit.

Any board communications need to always be void of subjective observations. For example; "When I asked Mr. Smith about the matter he acted real strange, I think he has some mental health issues." That would be much better phrased as; "When I asked Mr. Smith about the matter he was unresponsive." Never write anything down that if read back in front of a jury could be construed differently than it was originally intended. In communications, just the facts and nothing more.

Legal discovery, often referred to as disclosure, is a process in which both parties involved in a lawsuit investigate the facts of the lawsuit in order to collect relevant supporting material that can be used in pretrial and trial matters. Both parties are generally obligated to share material with each other. The intended purpose of discovery is to allow both parties access to all relevant case material so that both parties have all the facts. Discovery allows parties to prepare so that they are not caught unprepared in court.

Discovery begins when a lawsuit is filed and attorneys seek to collect as much information as possible to support their cases. The information collected will help determine the structure of the case and how the attorneys prepare their arguments and will be used to help or weaken the arguments of the parties involved.

For example, an architectural violation results in litigation with a member of the association, and before litigation has been instigated, the association member has sent an email to an ARB member stating that they know they are in violation. This email could be used by the association to help with the association's case.

Legal discovery includes collecting documents, physical evidence and depositions from witnesses. Parties to the suit can travel to the site where events took place in order to document aspects. Discovery includes the attorney consulting with and retaining expert witnesses for opinions on materials related to the case.

Attorneys will also file discovery requests with opposing counsel. A discovery request can include an oral or written interview, a request to affirm or deny facts, a request to examine evidence relevant to the case and an opportunity to see which witnesses the opposing counsel intends to call to testify.

In recent years, a more recent discovery issue is electronic discovery or ediscovery. Ediscovery is the process of gathering digital evidence associated with the case. Attorneys may want to review chat logs, stored security footage, emails and other electronic materials. All emails and all other electronic data that a board sends would be subject to discovery.

■ ■ ■

ELEMENTS OF LEGAL DISCOVERY

Fortunately, associations seldom become involved in litigation, other than collection-related litigation involving delinquent members. However, it is beneficial for board members to have an understanding of certain aspects of this legal process. Discovery is one aspect of civil litigation, and it can be one of the most burdensome, given the time involved and the resulting costs.

During litigation, discovery is a pre-trial process through which the plaintiff and defendant can obtain evidence from the other party or parties. Through the law of civil procedure, discovery methods can be interrogatories, document production or request for admissions and depositions. Under the law of civil procedure, discovery can be exceptionally broad and can include any material that is reasonably calculated to lead to admissible evidence.

Interrogatories, one of the most common methods of discovery, are written questions from the opposing party that must be answered in writing. These questions basically establish the particular party's version of the issues surrounding the litigation. These questions can be general or broad: "What happened at the board of directors meeting on September 28, 2016?" Or the questions can be narrow or specific: "Is it the board of director's position that the fence the plaintiff installed at their home on July 7, 2016, is not in compliance with the CC&Rs?" Only the parties to the litigation respond to interrogatories, as opposed to depositions, in which both litigating parties and third parties (witnesses, experts, etc.) are questioned.

Document production, or a request for production, is the requirement that all physical documents, electronic data or other tangible materials be provided to a litigating party. This request for production may not only involve opposing litigating parties, but third parties who may have relative information, such as the management company. For example, an association member's attorney may request copies of all email communications between the association manager and the board of directors regarding the member.

Request for admissions, or a request to admit, are written statements sent from one litigating party to another litigating party to seek either an admission or denial on a specific claim of the lawsuit. A request for admissions, while similar to interrogatories, is different in purpose. This difference is that each admission or question is in a declarative form requiring either admission or denial, or else a detailed explanation of why admission or denial cannot be entered as a response. A request for admissions is generally only answerable in a yes or no format.

A deposition, or examination for discovery, is a sworn oral testimony of a litigating party or witness that is transcribed into written and sometimes audio and video format. Depositions are performed outside of court by the litigating attorneys without a judge being present. This testimony is used for the future trial or possibly for further discovery purposes. The deposition process is ideally intended to provide clear insights into the merits of the litigation for both litigating parties. Many cases are dismissed or settled after depositions.

Not all information is subject to discovery. Information that is deemed to be attorney-client privilege is not subject to discovery. For example, emails between the board of directors and the association's attorney would generally not be subject to discovery. The reason for this protection is so that attorneys and their clients are free to communicate explicitly without hesitation or concern.

■ ■ ■

ELIMINATING OR ADDING AMENITIES

Eliminating or taking on additional association responsibilities may appear to be a straightforward undertaking, but there are a number of considerations. The primary considerations are the requirements of the association's governing documents and the ramifications on the association's budget. A third consideration is the unintended consequences of whatever decision is made.

Boards of directors often grapple with decisions related to the expense of the common elements and, more specifically, the expense of certain amenities. On the flip side of this, occasionally boards will consider "improving" the association by adding amenities or assuming additional expense responsibilities. These matters seem to arise most commonly during the annual budget preparation when all the association's expenses are being reviewed.

There is frequent focus on large association expenses such as the association's swimming pool. For most associations, the swimming pool is usually one of the largest budget items. And, while eliminating an amenity outright may not necessarily be considered, the board might reduce the amenity's related expense. For example, the board might keep the association's pool, but eliminate the heating of said pool or reduce the pool season in order to reduce costs.

Amenities are not always the association's common expense that is being considered for elimination or cost reduction. Other common element responsibilities are often considered.

Because of the maintenance and replacement costs, private streets are one association responsibility that is often discussed for elimination by boards. If the private streets meet municipality or state standards, and a particular government entity is willing to assume the responsibility, this can be an expense-reduction item that can save the association potentially hundreds of thousands of dollars.

The CC&Rs are usually the association governing document that must be evaluated before any common element or amenity is eliminated or added. In certain instances, the association's articles of incorporation may be what must be evaluated. The CC&Rs is the document that is most often reviewed for these types of matters. For example, most CC&Rs will have language similar to the following:

"...In addition, Declarant has deemed it desirable to create a nonprofit, incorporated owners' association, which will be delegated and assigned powers of maintaining, repairing and administering the common areas and facilities on the Property..."

The key words in the example above are: "maintaining, repairing and administering." A cursory interpretation of these four words noting the association's responsibilities fails to address deletions or additions of common elements. The language just addresses maintaining or repairing common elements such as a street or front entrance sign.

How can the association add an amenity or take on additional responsibilities if there is no language in the governing documents authorizing these specific actions? If the governing documents do not provide for the addition of, say, a clubhouse, can the association spend association funds to construct or maintain this new clubhouse? In the declaration wording above, nothing implies the authority to construct or, more importantly, "improve" the common elements of the association. The issue of eliminating an amenity or reducing the expense of a common element brings up the same consideration. The wording in the above declaration language specifically states: "maintaining, repairing and administering." What if the association fails to maintain, let alone eliminate, a common element?

What happens if an association finds it can no longer economically support an amenity? This can easily be the case when association governing documents limit the increase of the membership annual assessment by a certain percentage or a specific dollar amount. For example, say the basic cable television expense is provided for by the association, and the yearly subscription increase has exceeded the amount in which the association is allowed to increase membership assessments. Over time, these higher cable television percentage increases will outpace the percentage rate at which the association is allowed to increase the membership dues.

The unintended consequences of altering any common amenity or adding to the common elements can vary from budget shortfalls to even membership litigation. Potential budget shortfalls occur if an amenity's annual upkeep expense exceeds the budget constraints. For example, in the case of a security gate at the entrance of the association, the initial cost of the security gate may not be much of an issue compared to the annual routine maintenance. In some associations, maintenance on a security gate can exceed $20,000. Membership lawsuits regarding these matters are not all that common, but there is still litigation risk.

Another unintended consequence of adding an amenity is the additional insurance that may have to be purchased. For example, adding a slide to a swimming pool may substantially increase the association's insurance premiums.

Drawing people from outside the membership to the association property is a very common unintended consequence. This is most prevalent with walking trails and, in some instances, sports amenities. While it may not seem that non-members using the association's amenities would be an issue, it can be an issue in certain instances. Amenities that attract non-members to the association property have the potential of increasing criminal activity, and, at the minimum, the association takes on additional liability from these non-members on association common property.

Temporarily suspending an amenity is a more straightforward proposition than eliminating an amenity. This can occur due to an unrelated unexpected association expense that has taxed the association's financial resources or because of a needed repair to the amenity that is not economically feasible until the next budget year. If pure economics is the primary culprit of temporarily suspending an amenity or common element, it would generally be considered reasonable for the association board of directors to suspend it. Another suspension consideration is: if the amenity or common element is not maintained, would there be any potential long-term damage from not maintaining it or any possible safety issues?

Beyond a temporary suspension of an amenity or common element responsibility, the association's attorney should be consulted for legal guidance on eliminations or additions. The association's attorney can provide the proper steps involved in this process. This guidance sometimes provides that a board of directors only has to formally act at a regular board meeting in order to accomplish this process. At other times, this legal guidance may call for an amendment to the governing documents, which is a much more drawn-out process. And at other times, the legal guidance may be that whatever the board is wishing to do is not possible within the constraints of the governing documents.

Along with working with the association's attorney on these types of matters, the board of directors should communicate with the membership and seek membership input. Obtaining membership input is always productive in these matters. Hopefully, this input leads to membership buy-in, and buy-in is crucial for the ultimate success of any undertaking. This buy-in can also reduce the likelihood of hard feelings or even litigation from the membership.

■ ■ ■

Vendors

■ ■ ■

HIRING A CONTRACTOR

Hiring a bad contractor is akin to marrying the wrong person. A board of directors' due diligence applies to all contractors, from the professional association management company to the association's attorney to the vendor who cleans the clubhouse. If the association is under professional management, hopefully the management company has a deep bench of competent vendors that can be recommended. With this being said, hopefully some of the ground work of the vendor's competency has been verified by the management company from prior experience.

Everyone is aware of the obvious consequences of a poor contractor being hired: additional and unnecessary expenses, longer project completion time and poor work quality, but one of the most under-looked consequences at the onset is how it appears to the membership when a poorly-performing contractor is selected. Boards of directors are elected by the membership to spend associations funds in the most effective and efficient manner. The membership can be unrelenting in their vocal protests when a poorly-performing contractor is hired and association funds are expended with poor results.

So how does a board of directors get a foolproof guarantee of job performance from a contractor? The unfortunate truth is that there are no guarantees. However, with reasonable due diligence of the contractors and with process planning, the likelihood of success improves drastically. And in the unlikely event of an unsuccessful contractor experience, the board of directors can fall back on the due diligence process when discussing any contractor shortfalls with the membership. The membership then has to accept the fact that reasonable due diligence was performed and that the board made every attempt to hire the best contractor.

Depending upon the size of the project, a formalized bid may or may not be needed. The dollar amount or the project size that warrants a formalized bid is up to interpretation and geographic location. Finding good, "reasonable" contractors can be serendipitous at times. Ideally, an association is looking for a happy medium between price and quality of service.

If the project is of a size or type to warrant a formal bid and the association is under professional management, the management company should have standardized bid forms for most projects. The benefit of having a standardize bid is the ability to make apples-to-apples comparisons. In the Appendix there are sample standardized bids.

Looking solely at the price can be fraught with risk not offset by the lower price. The quality of the service desired for the funds expended is the key factor to consider. For example, there are landscaping companies that have botanists on staff who will know the Latin names of every bush and flower around an association's clubhouse and can provide a detailed care regiment. While this may be a great service and may come in handy in certain communities, a majority of associations are not willing to pay substantially extra for this benefit. The flipside of this is a contractor who does not have insurance, but works really cheaply.

The author is aware of a tree-trimming contractor who worked for an association managed by a management company that was considered to be the lowest-price service provider in that particular market. The tree-trimming contractor was removing a substantial tree when a bracing rope broke, allowing the tree in question to fall backwards onto a home and causing over $20,000 in damages. This contractor's immediate response was to not say a word to anyone, but to gather his chainsaw, get in his truck and drive off. Not only did this contractor not have insurance, he had no assets that could be attached in a lawsuit. The author is unaware of what this tree-trimming contractor was charging for his services, but it is doubtful that his low price was offset by the $20,000 plus the association had to pay to have the damaged home repaired. These funds had to come from the association's operating account because the association's insurance carrier denied coverage.

Finding the right contractor begins with defining the scope of the work to be performed. Large project or small, does a formalized bid need to be developed? Are there sufficient funds in the association's accounts to accomplish the project? It may seem obvious, but it is the association's responsibility to have the work in question performed. Is the association membership in favor of the project being done and their dues being spent on the project? Even though the prior sentence may have no bearing on the project being done, perhaps because the project is 100% necessary, membership buy-in may be required for association political reasons.

Is the project of a nature that requires a general contractor to handle a multitude of job tasks, such as a structural reconstruction? If a board is contemplating managing the general contractor role in hopes of saving the 10% contracting fee, this savings is rarely if ever obtained due to a multitude of issues, primarily the difficulty of achieving the expertise and efficiencies of a qualified general contractor.

The benefit of a qualified general contractor is that they will manage the many different aspects of a project, engaging and overseeing subcontractors, obtaining building permits and oversight of the related inspections.

FINDING VENDORS

Generally, the first place to look for a qualified vendor is the management company. Many times there are contractors who will only work with management companies' clients. This could be due to several factors relating to the efficiency of receiving their payment and the steady work that this business model offers. The benefit to the association is, hopefully, more competitive vendor pricing and better quality of work. If a contractor does a great deal of work for a management company, the association client should have influence over making sure the work is done properly. The contractor will be concerned about losing future potential business with the management company's other clients.

Other sources of vendors can come from other association boards of directors or from other vendors who work for the association. Angie's List is also a great source for maintenance vendors. The Better Business Bureau is an excellent source for vendors. And both Angie's List and the Better Business Bureau have ranking scales, as well.

Websites that offer reviews of businesses need to be taken with a grain of salt. Most of the online reviews are anonymous and impossible to verify. The company itself could have left the positive reviews, or a competitor could have left the negative reviews. For example, management companies generally get hammered by online reviews, where delinquent members or members who have received CC&R warning letters are prone to leave negative reviews. The best place to evaluate any company or organization is the Better Business Bureau and their rating system. The Better Business Bureau reviews cannot be anonymous, and there is a dispute resolution process for complaints.

POINTS TO LOOK FOR IN SELECTION ANY VENDOR

How long the company has been in business should have a bearing on the selection process. Of course there is the old analogy about a doctor who has been practicing medicine for 30 years and a recent medical school graduate knowing the latest medical practices: who should be chosen? However, when it comes to most professions, experience matters. An experienced attorney and a management company with broad experience are vital to most associations.

Does the particular profession require licensing or certifications? Most states require most trade professions such as electricians and HVAC contractors to hold trade licenses. Licensing can range from basic registration to a comprehensive qualification process. Many licensing boards maintain websites where these licenses can be verified and complaints or disciplinary actions can be reviewed.

Be leery of awards or certifications that can be purchased. There are a number of awards that are marketed to businesses that require the business to purchase the award plaque. One of the larger award companies awards "The Best of [insert city where business is located]" in which the business pays $80.00 for the plaque to hang in their lobby.

Be leery of certifications as well. There are instances of businesses claiming to have "A+" accreditation from the Better Business Bureau and actually being found to be on the Bureau's Scam Tracker index. There are dishonest businesses that either pay for certifications from bogus organizations or fraudulent claim certifications from legitimate organizations. Unfortunately, some of these "legitimate" organizations have very low or no standards other than that the organization's members paying an annual membership fee.

INTERVIEWING VENDORS

Reviewing the bid of a vendor is a great place to start when interviewing a potential vendor. This process can help determine a number of factors: primarily, how has the vendor approached the bidding process? and, basically, does the vendor show the competence to complete the project successfully? This interview process should allow the board of directors a level of comfort with the vendor.

Questions to ask potential association vendors:

How many projects has the vendor completed that are similar to the proposed project in question?

For example, if the project is installing a new membrane flat roof, and the roofing vendor has only installed asphalt shingles or never installed a flat roof before, because of the intricate installation requirements of a flat roof, utilizing a vendor who has never performed this work can be risky, at best. It goes without saying that it is not a good idea to let vendors still learning their trade to do the work on the association's project.

References of the vendor can be checked, but most vendors do not put bad references on their reference list. The author is aware of one association management company that actually paid people to provide glowing recommendations of their services.

Ask responsibility questions such as: "Who will obtain, if necessary, the municipalities' work permit for the project?" or, "Who will contact 811?" (811 is Call Before You Dig, a service set up by utilities to prevent third parties from breaking utility lines.) If the vendor is relying upon the board of directors or the association's management company to perform either of these important tasks, this vendor should not be used. The vendor who is doing the actual work is better suited to handle those details.

If the project does require a permit, that expense and any related work it entails should be included in the bid. Most municipalities require permits for certain projects, and surprisingly even small projects may have such requirements. A competent vendor will know what is required and will obtain all the necessary permits before beginning the project.

Asking about the vendor's insurance coverage is very important. Does the vendor have general liability and workers compensation?

While general liability insurance is relatively inexpensive, workers compensation can be astronomical for certain professions. Roofers' and landscapers' workers compensation coverage can be a huge operating expense for those types of vendors.

Different states have different requirements for workers compensation, usually based on the number of employees. Some vendors will claim that they are exempt from having to carry workers compensation because of the number of employees or that they will sign a waiver of liability in the event of a claim. However, generally, neither of these arguments negates the association's liability in the event of a claim. So it is always best to require the vendor to carry such coverage.

Liability insurance, also known as Commercial General Business Liability, provides coverage for damages or injuries caused by the vendor or the vendor's employees. The coverage needed depends upon the type of business insured and the related risk that the business entails. For example, an electrician would usually need more liability coverage than the association's management company.

Obtain copies of the vendor's insurance certificate or COI directly from the vendor's insurance company. Obtaining it directly from the insurance provider helps assure that the vendor is current with the policy and that the COI has not been altered by the vendor to reflect nonexistence coverage.

Ask about the project start time and the completion timeframe, even if this topic was addressed in a formal bid. It is always a good to discuss this topic in person in order to confirm or verify everyone's expectations. Vendors can at times be overly optimist on start and finish times. Scheduling can be a major challenge with some vendors and particularly with vendors in high demand. While the vendor may not be exact on start dates and completion dates, a rough idea of what to expect is important if communicating and/or scheduling with the membership is necessary.

Will subcontractors be used on this project? This is an important question to ask for two primary reasons: first, the vendor must verify that their subcontractors have the proper licenses and insurance; second, the subcontractors must get paid for their work. There is always a chance when using vendors who subcontract out parts of the project that if the vendor fails to pay the subcontractor, the subcontractor can make a claim for payment against the association. This could happen even if the association has paid the general contractor in full.

PAYMENT TERMS

If the association is being managed by a professional management company, generally speaking the vendor essentially "knows the association is good for payment," since the vendor has a working relationship with the management company. Notwithstanding the prior sentence, avoid paying a down payment, and never pay for the project up-front. If the situation arises in which the vendor needs payment or payments as the project progresses, payment should be made only when certain predetermined points in completion have been met. By doing this, if the project is not progressing according to schedule the vendor payments can be deferred.

It is always best to have a written agreement detailing the project and each party's expectations. Depending upon the size and scope of the project, the association's attorney should draft the agreement. This agreement should address the following points:

- Total cost of project
- Start date and completion date estimate
- Cancelation clause for non-performance
- Warranties covering materials and workmanship and the length of the warranty with any limitations
- What the vendor will not handle or repair
- Primary vendor, subcontractor and possibly supplier payment schedules
- The vendor obtaining all permits
- List of materials to be used
- Every party to the agreements' name, address and any license numbers if applicable

The Cash Discount. For numerous and valid reasons, an association should never pay a vendor in cash. The two primary reasons are: first, this is an obvious attempt by the vendor to evade paying income taxes for work performed, as corporations, for-profit and nonprofit, are required by IRS regulations 114-113, Div. Q, Sec. 201, to report third-party vendor payments in excess of $600 on Form 1099 each year; second, the lack of proper accounting controls.

Verification that subcontractors and suppliers have been paid generally comes into play on major projects. While it can be difficult to be certain that all vested parties in a project have been paid in full, it is a good idea to ask for a lien waiver or a lien release before making a final payment. State statutes can vary from one state to another, but in many states, if a party provided materials or performed work, these parties have the right to file mechanic's liens against the property in question. Obtaining a lien release is not a guarantee that every potential claim has been satisfied, because it can be difficult to determine who all provided supplies and work for a project.

■ ■ ■

WARNING SIGNS OF AN UNSCRUPULOUS CONTRACTOR

Be leery of:

- A vendor who continuously boasts of their abilities or discusses topics such as how honest they are.
- A vendor who claims that their competitors are all dishonest. This can be a telltale sign of their own dishonesty.
- A vendor who has materials leftover from a previous job and can do a special deal.
- A vendor who has to be paid up front.
- A vendor who has to be paid upfront in cash.
- A high-pressure sales pitch to make a decision or sign a contract.
- A vendor who states they do not need insurance for some absurd reason.
- A vendor who offers to do the work as a "demonstration" for the cost of supplies or wants to do the work in order to provide a reference on future projects.

- A vendor who has only been in business a relatively short amount of time as compared to what the vendor claims in years of experience.
- A vendor who changes company name and/or phone number frequently.
- A situation in which the vendor's background cannot be verified, such as: business address, prior customers or suppliers.
- A limited-time offer in which the bid is good only for today.
- A warranty as an extra charge.

■ ■ ■

BID FATIGUE

Complications can arise in obtaining bids if the dollar amount of the bid or the number of bids being sought discourages contractors from participating, meaning that the potential dollar amount of the potential project is not substantial enough for the contractor to participate. For example, if the project is in the $500 range, by the time the contractor drives to the potential project, discusses the project with all interested parties and then writes up the bid for consideration, the contractor has expended 3 or 4 hours of their time. Most contractors realize that there are at least two more bids being obtained, so they have a 1 in 3 chance of being awarded the business. Factoring up all these points can make obtaining bids challenging unless economic times are difficult and contractors are desperate for work. Which brings up another interesting point: if economic times are good, what is the quality of a contractor who has the free time to spend on preparing nominal bids?

■ ■ ■

THE DOUBLE CHECK
It is a good idea for a board to occasionally double-check the contractors that the management company is recommending by going out and obtaining additional proposals. Like any other profession, there are very good association managers, and some that are not so good. Association managers may be recommending a particular vendor because obtaining a quote from that vendor takes the least effort, and this vendor may not be the most competent or best value, as a result. Unfortunately, there may be other alternative motives, such as an improper business relationship, so again it never hurts to keep everyone on their toes. However, obtaining additional bids alone is not a fool proof method of verifying competitive work or pricing. Other work or price factors may have not been taken into consideration. When it comes to a lower price bid, it is always possible to find parties who will perform work cheaper and this risk/reward needs to be accounted for accordingly.

What to do after the presentation

For general maintenance items of a non-bid nature, finding a "reasonable" vendor may be a hit–or-miss affair, but fortunately it is obtainable.

The benefit of a qualified contractor is that they will manage the many different aspects of a project, engaging and overseeing subcontractors, obtaining building permits and the overseeing of the related inspections.

■ ■ ■

WHEN A VENDOR RELATIONSHIP HAS PROBLEMS

Performance issues with vendors do arise. Some issues are resolvable, and others are not. Whether the issue is resolvable or not, review the agreement and see if the area of performance is addressed. If the issue is addressed in the agreement, determine the steps to correct. If the issue is not addressed specifically, keep a log of telephone calls, conversations and other related activities. If applicable, take photographs of the problem issue or issues. These types of records help build the case and serve as the foundation of resolving the problem issue.

■ ■ ■

A PROJECT CHECKLIST

Surgeons and airline pilots use checklists, so it is also a good idea for an association to use a checklist when reviewing and tracking a project. Checklists can be either broad or very detailed, but at a minimum a checklist needs to be used to measure project progress and completion. The board should ask the vendor to develop the project checklist, and the list can be fine-tuned from that point if necessary. Depending upon the project, a third party such as an engineer or architect may need to be hired in order to develop a checklist or even to oversee the completion of the project using the developed checklist.

A great book on the topic of checklists *is The Checklist Manifesto: How to Get Things Right,* by Atul Gawande.

■ ■ ■

INTERVIEW A POTENTIAL VENDOR

To maximize efficiency, do an initial telephone interview of potential vendors and ask:

- How long have they been in business?
- What is the size of their typical project?
- Can they provide supplier or bank references?
- Can they provide references who have had similar projects?
- Typically, how many projects do they have going at one time?
- Do they subcontract out work?

FACE-TO-FACE VENDOR MEETING

Narrow down the vendors from the telephone interviews. In the face-to-face meeting, notice: Is the vendor on time? Does the vendor carry themselves professionally? In carrying themselves professionally, does the vendor come across as honest and trustworthy, or not so much? Since the vendor has passed the telephone interview, ask or verify some of the same questions asked during the phone interview. Make sure that the same answer that was given on the telephone is given in person.

BACKGROUND CHECK

Rarely does any vendor give bad references, and some vendors even pay for the good references. The Internet has a number of review websites, but the problem with these sites is that they can be anonymous or, as in the case of property management companies, reviews many times derive from members who have been placed for collections or have received CC&R violation letters.

■ ■ ■

VENDOR PAYMENT SCHEDULE

Typical payment schedules can vary from one part of the country to another and from profession to profession. The payment schedules can also be a revealing indicator of a vendor's financial stability and, in certain instances, the vendor's quality of work to be performed. When vendors want to be paid in full upfront or even half upfront, this could be an indication of financial difficulties. When a vendor is experiencing financial issues or is concerned about being paid on small projects, find another vendor.

If an upfront payment is required, upfront payments typically start at 5% to 10% and should only be paid the day the vendor shows up to work, not when the contract is signed or at any other point before the vendor shows up to begin the project. Typically, from that point forward payments of 20% to 25% correlating to the percentage of satisfactory completion of the project are paid, with a final payment of 15% or 20% upon satisfactory completion.

■ ■ ■

PRICE, PRICE, AND PRICE

If price is the roadmap, make sure that the association is driving a four-wheel drive. Price is always a consideration, be it high or low. One common bidding practice is to not consider the lowest or highest proposal, but to look at every proposal in between. While this sounds good in theory, it is best to dig deeper and look at every proposal and try to determine why the vendor bid at the price they did.

The vendor might have left out a critical aspect of the project. For example, a landscaper may have figured on putting out a 1,000 bales of pine straw when the other landscapers thought the project needed 2,000 bales. Did the other landscapers figure wrong, or did this landscaper not realize that more bales are needed? This leads to wondering about the competence of all parties bidding. Are the other vendors wrong, or is this vendor right? Does the vendor know that they can reduce the number of bales by reducing the size of the beds and thus make the beds look better, etc.? Price always needs to be analyzed.

Analyze in a way that helps determine how the bid price was derived. For example, a landscape vendor may be more competitive on doing the association's landscaping because the vendor has a contract on the adjacent association property and already has a crew in the area. The vendor may be trying to build up business in a particular area and want to be as competitive as possible.

The flipside of a lower price may be that the vendor is going to make up the difference in other fees. Charging additional fees is standard practice in certain industries. For example, an association management company may offer the association a low management fee and charge members high transfer fees when members sell their homes. Under normal business conditions, additional fees may not be an issue if those additional fees are for services that are not needed. Unfortunately, in the case of members selling their homes, the member has no other option but to pay the management company fee in order to obtain the needed paperwork for closing.

Looking past the particular vendor's ability to perform the job, how the vendor comes across is an important factor to consider before hiring. Does the vendor come across as being straightforward and truthful? If there is ever any doubt or just a gut feeling about a vendor, find another vendor.

■ ■ ■

THE ASSOCIATION & THE 1099 CONTRACTOR

Most associations utilize 1099 contractors instead of hiring full- or part-time employees. The primary benefits are the flexibility and cost savings. A 1099 contractor is a legal and tax-related term used to refer to the type of worker who contracts their services out to an association or any other type of business. The 1099 refers to the Internal Revenue Service (IRS) form that an independent contractor receives stating their income from a given party during a given tax year. A 1099 contractor is not an employee of the association for which they perform work; instead they are an independent contractor who is considered to be self-employed. Like most self-employed workers, they do not receive employee benefits such as health insurance or retirement benefits.

When balancing the tradeoffs between a 1099 contractor and hiring an employee, the largest consideration should be the way in which the worker is compensated for their services. In a typical scenario, independent contractors are not paid until the service is fully completed, and they are not offered any type of employment benefits. As a result, the payment scheme for most such workers requires more independence and responsibility, as things such as medical and dental benefits and savings to cover future sick and vacation days, as well as tax obligations, fall solely within the purview of the worker.

Those 1099 contractors are issued 1099 forms from the party who paid them. Regular employees must pay income and Social Security taxes on their income, and independent contractors are responsible for these taxes.

The difference is that employers generally withhold taxes on the employee's behalf, while 1099 contractors are responsible for their own payments. Additionally, employers generally cover half of the total Social Security and Medicare taxes, which is a 15% tax of net income in 2012, meaning that the employer covers 7.5% on behalf of the employee, while independent contractors are typically responsible for the entire amount.

Since an independent contractor is considered self-employed, they are essentially the employer and employee. Therefore, they are responsible for withholding their own taxes and paying the total amount of the Social Security and Medicare taxes. Regular employees usually have estimated tax liabilities withheld from each paycheck, but this is not done for a 1099 contractor. Self-employed individuals may be required to make quarterly installments against their projected tax responsibilities for the year.

The independent contractor generally has scheduling advantages over the employee. Often, they are not restricted to the typical nine-to-five workday and Monday-through-Friday work week like an employee. Deadlines, of course, may confine the independent contractor's work schedule. On the other hand, they generally don't get the benefits that employees often do, such as time off with pay due to illness or leisure.

Further, there are different legal implications for an independent contractor than an employee, and these implications can vary greatly based upon the specific contract terms between the contractor and customer. In most cases, the 1099 contractor can be discharged at will, with or without cause. Additionally, they are usually responsible for their own health insurance and retirement benefits, as the companies for which they perform work are under no obligation to provide benefits.

■ ■ ■

Selecting an Association Management Company

■ ■ ■

SELECTING AN ASSOCIATION MANAGEMENT COMPANY

The right association management company to manage the day-to-day operations of the association is, without a doubt, the most important vendor that a board will select. This is because of the extreme benefit of a good management company or extreme damage caused by selecting the wrong management company. Selecting a management company should be a thorough process because of the difficulty involved with changing to another management company, compared to the selection of most other association vendors.

The association management industry is made up of various-sized companies with various levels of competence. There are management companies in the marketplace with as few as one employee, and those with many hundreds of employees, with a few having thousands of employees. While the size of the association management company may be important in order to ensure stability of the company, core business competence is just as important.

While looking at the varying sizes of management companies, many boards of directors may believe that they would receive better services from a larger or smaller company. The small company may give the impression of personalized service, while possibly not being able to handle major operational issues that could arise. Or *vice versa*, the larger company may have experience in almost any issue that arises, while not being flexible enough to offer certain personalized services. It is difficult to draw conclusions just from the size of a management company.

When selecting a management company, which factors should be used: depth of operational experience, services offered or cost of services? In determining any of these factors, let us expand upon each of these three points:

Depth of Operational Experience. When interviewing management companies, a board of directors would be hard-pressed to find one that would not claim they could handle any situation that arises. A number of factors can help determine operational experience, such as length of time that the company has been in the association management business, size of association portfolio under management and types of associations under management.

Determining how long a company has been in business can be obtained by asking for a detailed company history outlining the founding and ownership or management structure. When interviewing the prospective management company, take the company history and ask basic questions such as length of time at their current location. Ask: How long were they at their last location before the present location? Does their company history make sense when it is explained to the board during a one-on-one presentation?

Management company competence is another area that may be difficult to determine. From outside the industry, it may appear that if a management company can manage one type of association they can manage them all. However, this is definitely not the case. A single-family homeowner association with five sub-associations with complicated financial reporting requirements has entirely different needs from a 25-story high-rise with backup generators and fire-control systems that require regular maintenance. Even basic functions such as annual meetings might require different levels of experience. An association with 4,000 members requires a different annual meeting sign-in process from an association with a 100 members.

For this book, we are going to separate management companies into three categories: small, midsize and national.

Small Companies - Commonly referred to as mom-and-pop operations, these generally have under 20 employees, the majority having fewer than 10 employees in one office location. There are many operations with one, two or three employees that may or may not have a physical office location. This size of company comprises roughly 95% of the industry.

The primary benefit of these smaller companies is sometimes they have a lower cost and can many times offer more personalized services. The main drawback is that the small size may limit the number of accounts that they can properly handle. For example, when an employee is out sick or leaves the company, how is this situation handled without disrupting service with a small staff?

Regional Midsized Companies – These larger management companies have more than 50 employees and may have over 100 employees. They might have multiple offices in multiple states. This size of company comprises roughly 4% of the industry.

The primary benefit of midsized companies is that they generally have experience and can handle associations of any size or home style. Also, because of their size many times they are more technology-driven operations. Drawbacks can be that they have less ability to tailor their services to an individual association. With certain companies and in certain markets, employee turnover may be higher than with the smaller management company operators.

National Companies - There are two national association management companies that cover the majority of the country. They have hundreds, if not thousands, of employees and many dozens of offices. These two companies comprise well under 1% of the industry.

The primary benefit of these two companies is that they have experience and can handle associations of any size or home style, but they primarily focus upon larger communities. Also, because they may specialize in niche markets such as high-rise condominiums, they offer additional services such as concierge, security, maintenance, etc. Drawbacks can be no flexibility in individual account services such as additional or custom financials that are not standard. Employee turnover may be much higher than with the smaller and midsized management company operators.

FINDING A MANAGEMENT COMPANY THAT IS A FIT FOR YOUR COMMUNITY

STEP ONE

Finding a management company that meets an association's needs may at first seem to be a daunting task, however with a little research and footwork it can be a straightforward process. First, a professional management company will understand the association's needs and strive to fit those needs. Second, a professional management company will understand the transition process from the association's current provider and ensure a successful transition to their company.

Where to start the search?

One great source can be real estate professionals, such as real estate agents, appraisers and real estate closing attorneys who interact with management companies on a daily basis. These individuals are a great resource for information, as they are on the receiving end of the unvarnished customer service from the management companies — good, bad or indifferent.

- The best agents to speak with about this topic are the one-person real estate operations. The large-volume real estate agents many times will have people working for them who handle much of the interaction with the management companies. A one-person operation will be talking and

communicating with the management company directly and thus should have firsthand experience.
- Most cities have law firms that handle large volumes of real estate closings. These firms can be found by asking the real estate agent above. When contacting the law firm, ask for the person who coordinates the real estate closings. This person may not wish to discuss bad management companies, but usually they will not hesitate to say who the good companies are and who provides them with needed information promptly.

Good sources that may or may not be biased are vendors that associations commonly use, such as attorneys, landscapers, etc. Sometimes these sources may not be exactly impartial, as they may only work with certain management companies and would not recommend the ones with whom they do not work.

PLACES TO CHECK OUT POTENTIAL MANAGEMENT COMPANIES

Better Business Bureau. A management company may not necessarily be a member of the BBB, but checking for complaints and whether or not consumer complaints are addressed is a good starting point. Even if a management company is not a BBB member, it is still given the opportunity to address complaints in attempts to resolve the matter. This can provide a good indicator of how the management company addresses client concerns.

Complaints to the BBB are one of the few complaint forums that can be judged with any level of objectiveness. Complaint forums such as Yelp, Yahoo Reviews and the like allow anonymous and unsubstantiated complaints. In the association management industry, any management company of size will have these types of complaints. Association management companies are as unpopular as the Internal Revenue Service because of the matters that they deal with on a daily basis, such as collections, CC&R enforcement, etc.

IT MUST BE TRUE BECAUSE I READ IT ON THE INTERNET

There are Internet businesses that specialize in posting fake complementary reviews and burying negative consumer reviews. So Internet research can be misleading at best.

QUESTIONS TO ASK ON THE INITIAL PHONE CONVERSATION:

- "Do you manage associations such as ours?"
- "Roughly how many associations like ours?"
- "Can we receive additional information about your company? Also, can we get a copy of your standard management agreement and your fidelity bond?"

THE IDEAL RESPONSES:

- "Do you manage associations such as ours?"
- "Roughly how many like ours?"

Ideally, the response should be: "Yes, we have around a dozen 500-plus single-family home associations under management," or "Yes, we have 6 associations that have onsite personnel." The reason for these types of questions can easily be summed up as: does this management company have the needed experience and resources to handle the association? For example, high-rise condominiums have backup electrical generators and plumbing systems unlike 99.9% of most other associations, so experience with high-rises is beneficial.

If the association has specific financial situations, such as rebilling neighboring associations for shared amenities or membership collection issues, these would be good questions to ask about in order to gauge their experience.

- "Can we receive additional information about your company? Also, can we get a copy of your standard management contract and your fidelity bond?"

Asking for additional information allows the management company to put their best foot forward and demonstrate their customer service. When the requested information is received, this should represent what the management company has to offer and provide a guideline for additional follow-up.

Once the company's information is received, first note the timeliness of receiving. Was the material received in a reasonable amount of time? Did they send everything that was requested? Is the material professional and informative, and does it answer potential questions? These factors can be indications of the management company's level of customer service and core competence. If the management company does not follow-up to make sure that their information was received or whether there are any additional questions, this can be an indicator of their customer service philosophy.

Was the management company's material informative or lacking? A management company should be putting their best foot forward with this initial material. However, even if the initial impressions were lacking, this should not be an automatic disqualification from consideration, only primary observations to consider.

■ ■ ■

During this initial evaluation period, do not ask for a proposal or pricing from the management company. It is too soon to begin excluding management companies. Any initial price proposed may exclude certain services, and there may be hidden fees. A management company's fees may appear to be high as compared to another prospective management company, but once the additional fees or costs are calculated in, the first management company may include all those fees within their basic management package.

■ ■ ■

In reviewing the management company's information, decide what can be easily determined. Is the material brief? Is there a great deal of detail? Is their material emphasizing their company's sales position: price, service or quality? Are they promoting that they are a low-cost provider? Are they selling high service standards? Are they selling high-quality systems and personnel? There is a place for each type of sales position in every marketplace, but no company can sell all three. No management company can offer the lowest price, highest service and highest quality. Really good companies can offer two of the three, but no company can offer all three and stay in business. To confirm this compare and contrast, look at Wal-Mart and Nordstrom. Both companies sell quality product. Nordstrom also sells service, and Wal-Mart also sells price. Nordstrom's service cannot be compared to Wal-Mart's service, and *vice versa* with the lower prices obtained at Wal-Mart.

REVIEWING THE MANAGEMENT COMPANY CONTRACT:

When reviewing a management company contract, there are two areas that need close review: termination provisions and additional fees. The following is typical association management contract term-of-agreement language.

"Term of Agreement - The term of this agreement shall be for a period of 12 months beginning on November 1, 2017, and ending on October 31, 2018. Upon the expiration of the initial term of this Agreement, it shall be extended for successive one-year periods. If neither party has given the other party 90 days' written notice of its desire to terminate this Agreement at the end of any given term, then the term shall automatically renew for an additional one-year term and such renewals shall continue on a year-to-year basis unless terminated."

Automatic renewals of management contracts are standard within the industry, and this is primarily due to continuity of service. However, note that this language does not allow for early termination. So if the management company is doing a "crummy" job, the association is stuck with them for at least a year. Also, the "90 days' written notice" means that 90 days before the end of the first year, or for that fact, any renewed contract year, the association would have to provide 90 days' written notice so that it does not automatically renew. It is important to remember that this "90 days" does not mean "89 days" or "30 days," it means 90 days. So if this notification requirement is not met, the association is automatically renewed or else has to pay a penalty of up to a year's management fee in order to get released from the contract. It is not uncommon in the industry that, if a notification requirement is not met and before the management company turns over the funds and records to the new management company, the prior management company deducts a year's worth of management fees or whatever happens to be the early termination penalty.

Management contracts that do have provisions for termination will normally have some type of non-performance language. This language will generally be conditioned on the management company having a minimum of 30 days' notice to appear before the board of directors and then at least 30 more days to remedy the non-performance. Then the board of directors and management company many times will have to mutually agree upon the non-performance being corrected or not corrected. If the board of directors and the management company can come to terms on the "mutually agree" and wish to terminate, a 60-day termination period is standard. If nothing else, the association is stuck with a bad situation for at least 120 days.

These types of contract provisions scream the obvious question: "If you guys are going to do such a great job for us, why is it so hard to fire you?"

THE ESCAPE HATCH

In the contract negotiations, it is advisable to make sure that there is a way out of the management contract in the event that the relationship turns negative. When management companies push multiple-year contracts, these are usually difficult to exit without penalty. It is worth noting that some association governing documents require that all contracts have 30-day termination clauses in order to ensure that the association can exit a negative business relationship.

The second area in a management contract that needs extra consideration is the additional fees. Additional fees are a huge driver of revenue for management companies. In the Atlanta market, there is a management company for which management fees account for only 42% of their overall revenue. While a low management fee may be what an association is looking for, looking beyond the management fee can many times save an association money. While the costs for ordinary office supplies and expenses such as copies and postage are standard management company reimbursements, some charges may not seem standard and may require further review. A lower management fee with high ancillary charges may work for some associations. The board just needs to be aware of the true cost.

THE FIDELITY BOND

A fidelity bond, while called a bond, is not actually a bond. It is an insurance policy. This insurance policy provides coverage for losses resulting from fraudulent acts. It is most commonly used for fraudulent acts of a management company employee or agent. A fidelity bond protects the association's funds and other valuables from acts of fraud, dishonesty, forgery, theft, larceny, embezzlement, wrongful abstraction, willful misapplication, misappropriation or criminal acts from guilty parties. Because insurance companies have varying underwriting guidelines for fidelity bonds, it is difficult to address specific coverage requirements and the various situations in which coverage would apply.

The key point regarding fidelity bonds is that the management company should have a fidelity bond, without exception. While some state statutes and some association governing documents require the management company or managing agent to carry a fidelity bond, this may not always be the case. If a management company does not have a fidelity bond or tries to say that they have a crime provision in the company insurance policy, find another management company. If a management company corporate policy has a crime provision or crime rider, this in most circumstances only protects the management company's funds, not their association client's funds.

An association can have their own individual fidelity bond as well, and it is highly advisable to have this double coverage. It is important to make certain that the association's fidelity bond provides coverage for wrongdoing not only by members of the board/association, but also by contractors or agents of the association. Agents and contractor coverage may need to be added to the association's fidelity bond, because the bond may not automatically include non-association members.

Another issue is the amount of coverage. Even if a management company has a fidelity bond, there may be insufficient coverage because these bonds provide coverage to all their accounts. Because of the expense, many management companies carry coverage well under $250,000, with some larger management companies having a million-dollar bond. Determining the fidelity bond coverage amount will vary from association to association, but a rule of thumb is two times the association's annual assessment.

▪ ▪ ▪

To obtain a fidelity bond, insurance companies require the applying party to complete an application. This application generally addresses the accounting controls and fraud deterrents of the company, in order to help the insurance company determine the potential loss risk. There have been incidences in which the person completing and signing the fidelity bond application was also the same person committing the fraud, and insurance companies have been known to deny coverage. The reasoning is that the initial application was fraudulently completed. A person cannot take out fire insurance, burn down their house and expect the insurance company to pay the claim. This is another argument for the association to maintain their own separate fidelity bond as a safeguard.

▪ ▪ ▪

STEP TWO

After narrowing down the management company candidates, possibly to 3 or 5 companies based on the initial contact, schedule face-to-face presentations with the top candidates. Ideally, presentations should take 45 minutes to an hour-and-a–half, leaving time for questions and answers afterwards. This is the opportunity for the management company to put on its best efforts to be awarded the association's business. This process is essentially a job interview, and the management company should be prepared to answer tough questions to the board's satisfaction. Obviously, another great source of questions is the items not being addressed by the current management company and how this prospective management company would address them differently.

Do not send these questions out beforehand. This prevents the management company from formulating a rehearsed response. An honest, unrehearsed response is always best. If the management company presenter becomes defensive, ask yourself: Why are they being defensive? Unless it is politics, religion or sex, there is no reason for them to be defensive. This is a job interview, where tough questions need to be asked. The association is potentially turning the association's operations and related funds over to their company.

RECOMMENDED QUESTIONS TO ASK DURING THE PRESENTATION

A management company representative should be able to answer these questions spontaneously and without preparation:

- "What are your accounting controls?"
- "How are membership collections handled?"
- "Does your company have an ownership interest in any of the vendors that you recommend to your clients?"
- "Does your company have an In-House Maintenance Department?"
- "Does your company also manage rentals or sell real estate?"
- "What type of management software does your company utilize?"
- "How many accounts do your managers have?"
- "Who will be our primary contact?"
- "Can you tell us about your company's technology?"
- "What are the transfer fees or estoppel certificate cost to a member who is selling or buying into the association?"
- "Can you tell us about board and membership communication policies, procedures and tracking?"
- "When mistakes happen, how does your company address those mistakes?"
- "What is the chain of command at your company?"

- "What employee training do you have at your company?"
- "When you hire a new employee, what is your process?"
- "Do you perform pre-employee background checks on employees, credit and criminal?"
- "Do *any* of your employees or principal owners have a criminal record, and if so what was the nature of the crime?"
- "Will we have Internet access to our association's data?"
- "Can you tell us about a problem that an association client had and how your company helped solved the problem?"
- "What would you like to ask us or tell us about your company and why we should select you?"

QUESTIONS AND ANSWERS IN DEPTH

- "What are your accounting controls?"

Ideally, the management company will have a substantial accounting department, meaning that there is segregation of duties. Segregation of duties is paramount for the safeguarding of an association's funds, which is also referred to as internal controls.

Another great control is for the management company's software to allow for remote Internet access for the board of directors.

Q – "How are membership collections handled?"

Ideally, the management company will have an accounting department big enough for a sub-department dedicated solely to collections. While having a full-time collections department is not always possible for a management company, what should be avoided if possible is having the association manager handling collections. Collections being such an unpleasant aspect of the industry, companies that rely on their managers to perform this task often find that the manager puts these collection efforts on the back burner.

Ideally there will be a formalized collection process in which late notices are mailed, demand letters and coordination with the association's attorney in the event these more forceful collection efforts become necessary and, basically, that collection matters are handled in a proficient and professional manner.

Q – "Does your company have an ownership interest in any of the vendors that you recommend to your clients?"

It is not uncommon for management companies to have an ownership interest in a variety of service and maintenance-related businesses. Landscaping, handyman, plumbing and pool management companies seem to be the most common. In recent years, management companies have been known to own collection agencies and insurance agencies as well. While these ownership interests are not necessarily good or bad, these conflicting relationships should be disclosed to the clients or potential clients. A good question to ask is: "How does the management company ensure that the business in which they have an ownership interest gives their clients a competitive price compared to nonrelated businesses?"

Arm's length relationship with third-party vendors is the best option. The association management industry has had issues with management companies and vendors having less than arm's length relationships. Any prospective management company should be asked about their internal written policies in order to guard against improper relationships. Ask for a copy of this for the association's records.

Q - "Does your company have an In-House Maintenance Department?"

It is also not uncommon for management companies to have in-house maintenance departments. While this is neither necessarily good nor bad, there needs to be a mechanism to ensure that the management company is not unnecessarily sending maintenance personnel to the association to just find work and to ensure the association receives competitive vendor pricing.

A common concern is how the management company writing up the work-order and then writing up the invoice and then cutting the check avoids conflicts of interest.

Q – "Does your company also manage rentals or sell real estate?"

While there are many companies that specialize in managing associations, there are many companies that both manage rentals and sell real estate. There needs to be an understanding of how conflicts of interest will be prevented with regard to these other two real estate-related activities. For example, if the company is going to manage rentals within the association, how will the management company deal with their owners and tenants violating the CC&Rs?

Q – "What type of management software does your company utilize?"

Ideally, the management company is using management software with integrated accounting and operations in one system. It is very common for smaller management companies to utilize QuickBooks accounting software because of the lower expense. While QuickBooks does fine producing financials, the integration function of financials and association operations on one software platform is a large benefit to management companies and boards of directors.

Q – "How many accounts do your managers have?"

A common question to ask management companies is how many associations each manager has. While this may seem like a straight-forward question, it is akin to defining love. No matter what response is received, determining what any individual association manager can handle is impossible from simply looking at their total number of accounts. The reason is that every manager will have their own ability level, and every association has a different workload requirement. Some associations meet every month, while others meet once a year. Single-family home associations are generally less work than condominium associations, and a manager should be able to handle more single-family home associations. There are many more determining factors that can't be qualified in a simple ratio of manager to number of accounts.

A great customer service test is to ask the presenter who would be the association manager, then wait several days and call the management company and ask to speak with the manager. If switched into voicemail, just leave the following message: "My name is Jane Doe and my number is 555-555-1234. Please give me a call." See how long it takes to receive a returned call.

Q - "Who will be our primary contact?"

Many management companies utilize manager assistants as a way of putting more properties on their association managers. If the representative explains that there are different "team members" responsible for this and responsible for that, this essentially means that no one is going to be responsible if balls are dropped. With the exception of the accounting functions, the association's manager should be able to be stay on top of any issues that arise. If this association manager cannot stay on top of the association's issues, unfortunately, the association manager is not competent or has too many accounts to manage.

Q – "Can you tell us about your company's technology?"

As with most industries, technology over the past 20 years has had a major impact on association management companies. Most association management software should have the following abilities:

- Association members: ability to pay dues online
- Association members: ability to view their account online
- Association members: ability to submit work orders online
- Association members: ability to submit ARC requests online
- Association members: ability to download governing documents online
- Board of directors: ability to review financial statements online
- Board of directors: ability to review operational reports online

Many management company software programs allow for complete board of directors access, which in essence is the ability to see everything that is happening in real-time within their association, from who was mailed a CC&R violation letter that day to how much money is in the operating account.

> Q – "What are the transfer fees or estoppel certificate costs to a member who is selling or buying into the association?"

While these fees will not be a direct cost to the association, the members selling or buying will bear the cost. Transfer fees and estoppel certificates are the paperwork that real estate closing attorneys request from management companies. They basically state what is owed by the member and whether there are any pending association legal matters.

Most management companies charge in the neighborhood of $100 to $150 for this paperwork to be completed. However, there are management companies that charge $300, $400 and up for this needed paperwork. Some management companies attempt to justify this practice by pointing to their lower management fees.

> Q – "Can you tell us about board and membership communication policies, procedures, and tracking?"

Communications, or lack thereof, are one of the biggest complaints that boards and membership have about management companies. Does the management company have a policy on returning phone calls and emails? The response should be that there is a standard policy about returning all telephone calls and emails before the end of the business day when the manager is in the office or within 24 hours if the manager is out of the office. Tracking ideally would be electronic phone logs noting the date and time that a member calls and a brief summary of the call.

Q – "When mistakes happen, how does your company address those mistakes?"

Ensure that the association management company has policies and procedures on learning from mistakes and that attempts are made to avoid the same mistakes again. How companies deal with their own mistakes speaks volumes about the entire organization.

Q – "What is the chain of command at your company?"

Ideally, the association manager reports to a manager who will come and meet with the board at their first board meeting after being hired. This manager should be checking in on a frequent basis either by phone, email or possibly performance surveys.

Q – "What employee training do you have at your company?"

The company should have an initial extensive formalized training period before a new manager is assigned accounts, even if the manager has 20 years of industry experience. The company should have formalized ongoing training in the form of manuals extolling best practices and case studies.

Is the association manager trained to chair the association's annual meeting if need be? Does the association manager have routine training in problem-solving?

Q – "When you hire a new employee, what is your process?"

The response is, hopefully, that there is an extensive hiring process with testing and background checks (criminal & credit). Not only is prior job experience important when hiring, but additional intelligence and personality testing is important as well.

It is not uncommon for some management companies to have the new association manager sit with the leaving manager for two weeks as the extent of the new person's training. Hopefully this will not be the response.

Q - "Do you perform pre-employee background checks on employees, credit and criminal?

While again this can be an uncomfortable question, it is a necessary question. The author is aware of a management company at which one of their accounting employees is on federal probation. Not only are criminal background checks necessary, but credit checks are important as well, especially with accounting employees or potential employees.

Q - "Do <u>any</u> of your employees or principal owners have a criminal record, and if so what was the nature of the crime?

The question above can be an uncomfortable question, but it is a necessary question. These people will be handling the association's funds. Owners or employees having criminal records can make obtaining a fidelity bond problematic.

Q – "Will we have Internet access to our association's data?"

Most association management software provides remote Internet access for board members. This remote access ability is not vital, but is a great accounting control feature and operationally assists the board with association information 24/7.

Q – "Can you tell us about a problem that an association client had and how your company helped solved the problem?"

Ideally, the response is an association problem that arose that shows the management company was resourceful and used their experience to help resolve the problem.

Q – "What would you like to ask us or tell us about your company and why we should select you?"

Many times the response to this question will be very interesting.

Some of these are tough questions or uncomfortable questions; however, the board of directors has a fiduciary responsibility to perform due diligence on a potential vendor. In the event that the management company does not work out after they are selected, the board of directors has used reasonable care and due diligence in their selection process. If a management company presenter becomes defensive with these questions, this speaks volumes about the management company.

Whether it is the person who owns the company or a higher-level person who does the presentation, they are usually a reflection of the people below them. If this presenter is not impressive, or if there are other questions about them, it usually does not get any better when meeting the rest of the organization.

■ ■ ■

> If the management company presenter inquires about other management companies doing presentations, always take any negative competitor comments with a grain of salt. Obviously, it is unprofessional to bad-mouth a competitor, but this is a tactic of some management companies in attempts to bolster their own images by running others' down.

What to do after the presentation.

STEP THREE
An unannounced visit to the management company office

The last step of the meeting and evaluation part of the process is the unannounced or surprise visit to the management company office. These visits need to be unannounced so that an honest and realistic view of the management company is obtained. It is best to do these visits Monday through Thursday, because of casual-dress Friday and the fact that some management companies traditionally close earlier on Fridays.

How was the unexpected visit received? Are the management company personnel friendly? Were the employees annoyed by the unannounced visit? If a management company is not flexible enough to deal with a prospective client dropping by unannounced, they may not be the right company for the association.

Is the office clean and orderly? Maybe not new or in an expensive office space, but clean and orderly? If their office space is junky or in disrepair, is this how they manage associations? The author remembers a management company that had a large sign in their waiting area that read: "Be Nice or Leave." Do they have to "buzz" visitors in through a security door? Does the lobby have bulletproof glass and give the appearance of a check-cashing business rather than an office? Is the office situated in a bad part of town? Are association members going to be worried about coming into this part of town to pay their dues because of where the management company is located?

How is the office laid out, and does it appear to be well-organized? Are there file boxes stacked everywhere? Does the management company have the proper facilities? Does the management company even have a mail postage meter, or are they using postage stamps? This is a concern because how the management company handles the association's annual meeting notices can be a problem when two other associations have mailings on the same day.

Are the management company employees professional, intelligent, high caliber?

Was everyone friendly or annoyed by the surprise visit?

Note: Try and avoid Friday visits because many management companies traditionally close early on Friday or have casual Fridays. Also, Fridays are when many people take days off.

■ ■ ■

HOW MANAGEMENT COMPANIES DETERMINE THEIR MANAGEMENT FEE

(The following is based on the South Atlantic Region of the United States.)

While every association situation is different, the following is generally how management fees are calculated.

Style of home plays a large factor in the fee.

Single-family home communities generally do not have the same issues that arise when member homes are connected. Maintenance issues are generally limited to common expenses such as roads, clubhouse, pool, tennis courts, etc.

Townhome communities, like condominiums, have members living in close proximity, but have fewer moving parts. Townhomes traditionally will have their own parking situation, and there are no members living above or below a townhome. Townhomes generally have fewer maintenance requirements than do condominiums.

Condominium communities have a great many moving parts, from maintenance to parking. Condominiums are generally the most labor-intensive communities for a management company.

Mixed-use communities and mixed-use buildings have a number of issues that never even occur with the first three types of communities. If the community is mixed-home style or a mix of residential and commercial, keeping up with all the moving parts takes an experienced management company. Maintenance alone on these types of communities can be much more involved than other types of communities.

SIZE OF COMMUNITY

The size of a community factors in as the basis of the management fee as a rate "per door." "Per door" is used in the industry to denote a home. The management fee would be a dollar amount per door, per month. For example, a rate per door of $7.00 on a 100-home community equals a fee of $700 per month.

The actual number of homes in a community also factors into the management fee, in that an association can obtain a type of economics of scale. The more homes an association has, the more management expenses decrease. Conversely, fewer homes in association can result in a minimum monthly management fee that can range between $500 and $750.

AMENITIES

Amenities are a significant driver of management fees, especially swimming pools. Swimming pools can add $0.50 to $2.50 per home, per month to the total management fee. Other amenities, depending upon what involvement is needed from the management company, could increase the management fee as well.

NUMBER OF INSPECTIONS

Property inspections factor in to the management cost. For certain sizes of associations, a monthly inspection would generally be factored into the management fee. The cost for associations wanting additional inspections could be between $100 to $300 additional per month, depending upon location and size of the community (the drive time and time that it takes to drive/walk a community) and the related follow-up.

NUMBER OF BOARD & MEMBERSHIP MEETINGS

The number and time involved for association board/membership meetings can vary from one association to another. A good rule of thumb is that a management fee between $525 to $750 equates to four board meetings per year and one annual meeting. Likewise, $751 to $1,100 equates to 6 board meetings and one annual meeting. Above $1,101 per month can equate to ten to thirteen meetings per year. Meetings lasting more than 2 hours and beyond 9:00 PM can incur an additional hourly fee of $60 to $125 an hour for the association manager.

LOCATION OF THE ASSOCIATION

If an association is adjacent to or near other associations, this can reduce a management company's operational costs and thus help reduce the management fee. Conversely, if an association is in a more remote area, those additional costs of travel would normally have to be factored in, unless possibly the management company is expanding into that area.

OTHER FACTORS THAT INFLUENCE MANAGEMENT FEES

There are, on occasion, special situations or nonstandard issues that can increase a management fee. For example, associations that are near universities and are predominately student-occupied create an additional workload with student housing that the management fee usually has to reflect. Another example would be an association that, because of property age or other maintenance-related matters, would require above-average work by the association manager. These factors have to be reflected in the management fee.

GENERAL MANAGEMENT FEE RANGES (BASED ON THE SOUTHERN ATLANTIC STATES IN 2017)

Condominium pricing can generally range from $14.00 to $25.00 per unit, per month. High-rise and midrise condominiums can be higher than these amounts because of additional services or other special requirements.

Townhome pricing generally ranges from $11.00 to $18.00 per home, per month.

Single-family home pricing generally ranges from $4.00 to $9.00 per home, per month.

PARTICULAR POINTS REGARDING MANAGEMENT COMPANIES

Management companies should have an arm's length relationship with the vendors that they recommend to their association clients. With this being said, it is very common for management companies to have internal maintenance departments and ownership interest in everything from plumbing companies to pool management companies. There can be conflict of interest considerations, so good questions to ask when interviewing management are:

> "Does your management company have a written policy for employees regarding conflicts of interest with third-party vendors?"

"Do any of your company owners or employees have an ownership interest in any vendors that your management company recommends to your clients?"

"Does your company have a maintenance department, and if so, how do you ensure that your clients receive the best quality for the price?"

There is a common practice with certain management companies that tout "preferred vendors." Sometimes these "preferred vendors" are paying the management company a percentage of their maintenance billing and/or a monthly fee to be on a "preferred vendor" list. Any time that there are these types of questionable relationships, vendors often mark up the maintenance billing to compensate for the fee that they have to pay to the management company.

Now, this is not to say that every management company that utilizes certain vendors is doing anything improper. The majority of the time, repeated use of a particular vendor is an indication that the association manager has found a good and dependable vendor and that this vendor does what they say they are going to do for a reasonable price. However, if the vendor does a poor job and charges a high price, and the association manager defends the vendor's job performance, this can be an indicator of an improper relationship. Because why would the association manager defend poor vendor performance?

Certain management companies will attempt to change an association's vendors after they take over management. This can be anything from the landscaping vendor to the insurance carrier.

There may be valid reasons that a management company would recommend changing vendors, such as that the vendor does not have proper insurance coverage. However, what benefit does the management company gain from switching out a vendor with which the board of directors is happy? It is important for the board to remember that the vendors are their vendors and not the management company's vendors.

An important point to consider is that, if an association's current vendor will not work with a certain management company, this may be a point of concern. This vendor needs to be asked for particulars. Many times, the vendor will be very blunt about the issue or issues with the management company in question.

■ ■ ■

CONTACTING REFERENCES

Contact their references, if possible by telephone. It is always best to try and schedule with the reference an ideal time to call them because the telephone call should take 15 to 20 minutes. Below is a typical list of questions:

How long has your association been with Acme Management?
What do you think of their management services?
What do you think of their association manager?
How does the association manager interact with the board of the directors?
How does the association manager interact with the general membership?
Does your association manager attend and participate in your board meetings?

Does your association manager chair your annual meeting?
Does your association manager perform property inspections?
Does your association manager return telephone calls in a timely manner?
Would you consider the association manager a problem-solver, or do they need board instruction?
Does your association manager efficiently handle their duties, or does the board have to follow up to make sure everything is completed?
In what one area does the association manager excel?
In what one area does the association manager need improvement?
Are you satisfied with administration functions such as accounting?
Are association invoices paid in a timely manner?
Are financial statements prepared in a timely manner?
Is there any area in which their accounting department could improve?
Are they providing all the services that you and your board need?

■ ■ ■

Other Association Vendors

■ ■ ■

SELECTING AN ATTORNEY

Most major cities in the United States have at least one law firm that has a major portion of their practice specializing in homeowner association law. As in any profession, all attorneys are not the same. One attorney may be an excellent litigator, while another attorney may excel at collections. Attorney hourly rates vary. Hiring an attorney who has a lower hourly rate may not be a savings, if the attorney, through lack of specific experience, takes twice the time to answer or resolve a legal matter.

Attorneys who specialize in association law should have a deep knowledge of the state statutes and governing documents. The secondary benefit of an experienced association attorney is that they should have experience with the inner-workings of associations and be able to offer a great deal of problem-avoidance guidance. For example, many governing documents have provisions allowing the board of directors or their agent to enter a member's land or home in order to rectify a member's architectural violation. While this may be a provision of the governing documents, an experienced association lawyer will generally advise against this form of legal "self-help" to resolve matters, primarily because of safety concerns and because judges usually frown upon self-help to resolve legal matters.

The association's attorney provides legal opinions on topics that affect the association. This can include reviewing contracts and other documents such as governing documents, to provide a legal perspective, and attending board meetings and membership meetings to answer questions, explain concepts or documents and provide information to homeowners or board members. The association's attorney will assist in the enforcement of the CC&Rs, including writing and sending demand letters in the collection of delinquent member assessments if the association management company does not offer this service. Attorneys file liens for delinquent accounts and proceed with foreclosure when necessary. Attorneys also defend the association and/or board of directors in the event of litigation.

Just like any other vendor, an attorney should be held accountable for their collection efforts. To do this, the board of directors should request a process map of the collection efforts that they can expect from their attorney. This process map should give a rough idea of legal filings, court dates and the steps to ultimate foreclosure if necessary. There will always be mitigating factors that a board of directors will need to take into account, which can alter the standard collection process, such as a delinquent member fighting the collection efforts. However, the process map should be in the ballpark. An association board wants to avoid an attorney who is not efficiently proceeding with collection efforts. Some attorneys are known to file liens and not move forward with foreclosures.

If the association is under professional management, the management company should be able to recommend several law firms that work with the management company and have good track records with other association clients.

MEETING WITH THE ASSOCIATION'S ATTORNEY

All association boards of directors at one time or another must meet with the association's attorney. These meetings assist the board through the legal mazes that every association encounters. To reduce legal expenses, there are some simple steps that should reduce legal fees and improve the efficiency of everyone involved.

Preparation before the meeting is critical to maximizing the time with the attorney. Provide the following to the attorney before the meeting so that they can prepare:

- Agenda of what needs to be discussed (prioritize, if multiple issues, and try to limit to 3 issues or less)
- List of questions to which the board wants answers
- Documents that need to be reviewed beforehand by the attorney (i.e. association's governing documents if not already on file with the attorney, contracts, relevant board meeting minutes and correspondences)
- List of everyone who will be in attendance and their relationships to the issue

It will generally save the association money if this meeting can be scheduled during regular business hours at the attorney's office. The board should bring the following to the meeting:

- Final agenda
- List of any additional questions
- Physical exhibits (i.e. photographs, notes, etc.)

During the meeting:

- Avoid bringing up issues that are not on the agenda
- Obtain a timeline on how further issues will proceed
- Have the attorney follow up in writing with the issue(s) discussed, for association's records
- If the issue discussed is of a sensitive nature, board members should seek clarification from the attorney on what can be discussed regarding the issue at a meeting with non-board members
- If it is determined that additional meetings are needed, try to schedule those at end of this meeting

Whatever the nature of the meeting, being organized and maximizing everyone's efficiency can save the association money and the board members time

■ ■ ■

COLLECTION COMPANIES

It is a common trend for management companies to utilize collection companies and even have ownership interests in collection companies. Because federal statutes and, in many instances, states statutes for violating collection statutes are extremely harsh, make certain that the association's attorney reviews any collections company's agreement and make certain that the association is indemnified for the collection company violating any statutes. Fines for violating federal collection statutes cap out at $500,000 per violation, so it is imperative that the association is indemnified for any and all issues regarding collection statutes.

Another common trend is for management companies to have an attorney on their payroll to represent association clients, charging legal fees back to the association. In almost all situations, it is advisable to maintain the association's legal counsel separate from the management company. Notwithstanding the obvious potential conflicts of interest of whomever the attorney actually works for, the association or the management company attorneys, like most professionals, have specializations. If the management company's attorney is great at collections, are they also great at document interpretation or litigation? The essential consideration here, is the association obtaining the best legal counsel, or is the attorney a revenue center for the management company?

Another point to consider with a management company is their collection practices and procedures. Do they have a full-time collections department, or are collections part of the association manager's responsibilities? Because of the unpleasant nature of this job, it is always best to have employees solely dedicated to this job function. If the collections function is just a part of the association manager's responsibility, or a part-time responsibility of another employee's job, many times these unpleasant work functions end up taking a backseat to more enjoyable job activities.

Management companies also sometimes charge for legal work or collection fees to individual members. There are management companies in the marketplace that charge delinquent members collection fees or other similar types of "legal" fees. These fees to members are many times in violation of federal and state statutes, and the association's attorney should review and approve any such fee to make certain that the association is not liable for the violations. Remember that the association and board of directors are ultimately responsible for collection actions taken by the management company. The author has even encountered management companies that file liens on delinquent members' homes without the legal authority to do so. Filing a lien and charging the association to do so is, in most states, practicing law without a license.

■ ■ ■

SELECTING A BANK

Selecting a bank for the homeowners association involves much more than opening a checking account at any local bank or choosing the bank branch most convenient to the community. A bank should to be chosen by what services the association currently needs and by what services could be needed in the future. Finding a bank and building a banking relationship is best done early, or, more precisely, before there is a need for a loan. As in many professions and businesses, there are banks that specialize in managing homeowner association accounts.

There is a vast difference between banks when it comes to homeowner associations, as compared to the traditional bank customer. For example, most traditional banks derive very little business from associations. Thus, the lack of a homeowner association account base—and the inexperience coming from this—can have a negative effect upon an association obtaining loans and filling other banking needs.

Lending services for an association typically tend to be term loans and lines of credit. In selected instances, even equipment-leasing can arise from lending services. Equipment-leasing is normally found in large associations that have on-site staff who require leased vehicles or copiers.

When it comes to deciding on a bank for an association, lending services are often not thought of or—if thought of at all—not considered important. While, in most instances, associations normally would not need to obtain a bank loan, lending needs do arise on occasion. These occasions normally revolve around emergency situations and, more often than not, situations where membership special assessments are not practical or even possible.

Lending to a homeowner association is one area in which most traditional banks have the most difficulty. This lending difficulty normally revolves around the collateral or lack thereof. Traditional banks are accustomed to making loans secured by assets, and most associations generally do not have these types of assets. If lending can be offered through a traditional bank, in many cases the bank may require the association board of directors to personally guarantee the loan. These personal guarantees can be problematic, not least because the loan maturity date may exceed the member's board term.

There are around a dozen or so banks in the United States that specialize in managing the funds of homeowner associations. Thus, it is much easier for associations to borrow from specialty banks than traditional banks. Instead of attempting to secure a loan to an association's assets, these specialty banks will usually secure the receivables of the association or, in other words, the membership dues that are being collected.

Banks that provide cash management options for homeowner associations tend to offer lockbox services and merchant services (credit card transactions). Traditional banks may offer a wholesale lockbox service to an association, but usually the related bank fees make it costly and thus unfeasible. It can be beneficial for an association to utilize a lockbox, because this process saves the expense of receiving membership dues payments directly and makes funds available sooner. The association specialty banks, depending upon the association account size, many times will reduce these lockbox fees and, in some cases, waive them altogether.

Merchant services, or credit card processing, can be a huge help in reducing association delinquencies. The membership often appreciates another payment option, even if there are related credit card transaction fees charged to the member. Credit card companies charge between 2% and 2.50% to the merchant for using the card. In most cases, credit card companies will allow a convenience fee to be charged back to the member. This eliminates that cost to the homeowners association.

Generally speaking, what these specialty banks look for when lending money to homeowner associations is: first, does the association have the ability to pay the loan back with the current operating cash flow? The specialty bank verifies this by reviewing the income statement and delinquencies report. High delinquencies can negatively affect a loan request, and if there is no effective collection effort taking place, the loan may be difficult to obtain. Second, are the funds just going to be used to pay budgeted operating expenses and why? If budgeted expenses are not being met with the cash flow, how will the loan be paid back?

When it comes to an association specialty bank, here are a few important aspects to consider:

Always consider a bank relationship a long-term partnership. Look past immediate needs, and try to anticipate needs down the relationship road.

■ ■ ■

SELECTING A LANDSCAPER

The process of selecting a landscaping company generally begins with whatever the board of directors feels the current landscaper is not doing correctly. While this may seem to be the analytical approach, there are a number of factors that the landscaper has no control over, such as a drought or a municipality issuing watering restrictions. However, if the board determines that the current landscaping vendor is not meeting the needs of the association, great care should be used in selecting a new vendor. The primary reason for this is that landscaping is front-and-center in the membership's minds every time they enter or leave the association. Landscaping can be one of the leading generators of membership complaints.

Selecting a new landscaper should begin with a clear understanding of what the board of directors and overall membership are looking to achieve. There are obviously budget constraints and possibly environmental conditions such as water restrictions, but a starting point is the formalized bid process. (There is a sample association landscaping bid in the Appendix that can either be used as-is or tailored to individual association needs.)

If beginning the written bid process from scratch, write down what landscaping services are presently being provided by the current landscaper. In describing these services, be clear and as brief as possible.

After getting the basic services outlined, the next step is taking a map of the association that shows the areas to be addressed. The map, at a minimum, should indicate the property boundaries and common areas that need to be addressed. This map should indicate not only areas where grass needs to be trimmed, but also flowerbeds and even doggie-waste stations that need to be emptied. The more detailed the map, the less likelihood of the bidding landscapers missing anything.

There are generally four areas of primary focus when constructing a landscaping bid: lawn or turf maintenance, bed maintenance (mulch, pine needles, pine bark, stone, etc.), perennial and annuals (flower plantings) and pruning. Depending upon other factors relating specifically to the association, other landscaping needs such as seasonal leaf removal, snow removal, pond maintenance, retention pond maintenance, doggie-waste station emptying and other association-specific landscaping needs may need to be addressed in the formal bid.

Lawn or turf maintenance of the common area lawn is usually the most costly area to address in a landscape bid, primarily because lawn maintenance is more labor-intensive and needs to be performed more often. First, determine how many times per year the lawn will need to trimmed. Depending upon region and climate, this can vary drastically, especially in the warmer climates and where common areas have sprinklers. Are there any restrictions on when mowing crews can start, or times when crews have to be finished?

A great question to ask any landscaper under consideration is: "If the association's normal lawn-cutting day is, for example, Monday, and it rains that day, how does the landscaper make up for that lost rain day? Or, if it rains two or three days in a row, how does the landscaper cover all their accounts?" The landscaper should give a detailed game-plan on how they manage rainy-day situations. Rain situations and how they are addressed by the vendor is where the professional landscapers are distinguished from everyone else.

Bed maintenance (mulch, pine needles, pine bark, stone, etc.) comes in different variations, depending upon the area of the country. No matter what material is used to layer or cover flower beds, the process dresses up the beds and helps prevent weeds. Considering the expense of manual hand-weeding or spraying herbicides, bed maintenance is generally a cost-saving procedure. However, while adding additional layers of cover may be beneficial, it is not uncommon to have too much bed cover. If this is the case, the association may be able to cut back on adding cover for a season in order to save association funds.

Pruning or trimming should only be undertaken by landscapers who have the training and experience on how and when to properly prune. Improper trimming of trees and shrubs can result in the premature deaths of those trees or shrubs. And *vice versa*, failure to prune can result in the premature death of foliage or the association looking unkempt if the foliage is allowed to grow unchecked. If the local municipality regulates tree trimming, the landscaper should have a good understanding of this process in order to avoid issues with code enforcement. The bid should address the pruning requirements and whether or not the association has already determined the frequency and time of year.

If the association has a planting maintenance schedule for perennials and annuals, those requirements need to be addressed in the bid. A perennial is a plant that lives for more than two years. An annual is a plant that completes its lifecycle, from germination to the production of seed, within one year and then dies. Summer annuals germinate during spring or early summer and mature by autumn of the same year. Winter annuals germinate during the autumn and mature during the spring or summer of the following year. The bid map should indicate the bed locations, along with the types of flowers, etc.

Other landscaping needs such as seasonal leaf-removal or snow-removal need to be addressed in the bid as well. Determine how to dispose of leaves. Will leaves need to be hauled away, or will they be mulched and used around the property? If the leaves will not be mulched, will they be hauled off or disposed of in another way? Depending upon the number and types of trees in an association, leaf-removal can be a major undertaking.

Besides normal seasonal landscaping issues, does the landscaper have the experience and necessary licenses or certifications for dealing with a pond? There are a number of companies who specialize in just pond maintenance and subcontract through the landscaper.

Most landscapers will price emptying doggie-waste stations and restocking the bags when necessary. Having the landscaper perform this function can be a huge cost-savings for the association over hiring a specialized contractor. There are vendors who specialize in managing pet issues such as this, but utilizing the landscaper saves the association funds.

■ ■ ■

SELECTING AN INSURANCE AGENT

An insurance agent, similar to a great many professions, can have a broad range of specialties and areas of expertise. Insurance agents specializing in homeowner association coverage should have in-depth knowledge of what particular coverage is needed. If an agent is writing automobile policies, life insurance policies, selling annuities, etc., what percentage of their business is homeowner associations? This is not to say, physicians who are general practitioners should be underappreciated, but most people would elect to use a heart surgeon for heart surgery.

The association's insurance agent should have experience reviewing association governing documents and recommending the appropriate insurance coverage requirements for an association to maintain. The insurance agent should also be able to recommend additional coverage if needed, based on prior experience from other homeowner association clients.

Another important aspect of an insurance agent writing homeowner association insurance is their understanding of claims and the implications of filing claims. An experienced agent will advise the board of directors about claims that can result in the association's policy being canceled. And, more importantly, an agent can possibly recommend a strategy to prevent this cancellation. The insurance agent should also be able to inspect the community and identify potential claim exposures that can be addressed.

The association's insurance agent should be able to establish valuations and reconstruction costs of the association's common elements, or what the association is responsible for insuring. It goes without saying how important it is for the association to have adequate insurance coverage. One aspect of reviewing insurance proposals (see the Appendix for a sample Insurance Bid) is the valuation that is given to structures and other common elements. What may seem like an obvious way of reducing the premium is to affix a lower valuation on what is insured. This is where the standard bid form, when used, makes these valuations on which the proposed premium is based more prominent. The author has seen insurance proposals where the insured valuations are not easily determinable by reviewing the proposal.

The last responsibility of the association's insurance agent is insurance education: educating the board of directors about coverage, exclusions and any limitations of the policy, and educating the membership about the association's policy, where the association's coverage ends and where the membership's responsibilities start.

The association's insurance agency is also tasked with providing certificates of insurance or proof of coverage to mortgage lenders.

■ ■ ■

SELECTING A POOL COMPANY

It is not uncommon for the single largest expense for an association to be the operation and maintenance of the swimming pool. The association swimming pool, aside from being a huge operating expense, is also one of the largest areas of liability with or without lifeguards. The fundamental role of the pool management company is opening the association pool, maintaining pool chemicals, testing the pool water and closing the pool.

The pool management company has the primary function of operating the association swimming pool according to federal, state and local regulations or statutes. These functions involve cleaning the pool and testing the pool water to ensure legal compliance. These responsibilities may also involve staffing and supervision of lifeguards or pool attendants.

However, some basic operational questions need to be answered. If lifeguards are to be used, does the pool management company have the staffing ability to properly schedule for the association's pool needs? Are there backup lifeguards when a lifeguard calls in sick or does not show-up? Generally, if lifeguards are scheduled to be on duty at a certain time and are not, the pool may need to be closed. If the municipality health department shuts the pool down, for whatever reason, does the pool company have the staff to immediately address the issue to get the pool reopened?

A professionally-managed pool company, no matter the company size, will have the experience and ability to solve problems to prevent the pool from being closed unnecessarily and, if the pool is closed, to help get it reopened as soon as possible.

Pool management companies should include in their service a detailed weekly inspection report along with onsite inspections. These inspections will revolve around multiple inspections in order to review safety and health department compliance. These compliance issues are, primarily, lifeguard duty performance and pool water testing.

Opening the pool - The pool management company is responsible for the filling or draining of the pool, removal of any debris and any cleaning that is needed. The opening process includes an inspection of the safety equipment, check for warning signs, a first-aid kit, and making sure that these items are in compliance with all regulations.

Chemical supplies - In most circumstances, the pool management company includes supplying the pool chemicals as part of the service. The pool management company is thus also responsible for keeping the water chemistry at acceptable compliance levels.

Water testing - Testing pool water is the responsibility of the pool management company. Most municipalities require pool water to be tested at least daily so that, if needed, chemical adjustments can be made to keep the water in compliance. A log of these daily tests must be maintained and available for inspection by the department of the local municipality that regulates pools. Most municipalities require weekly advanced testing for other issues, primarily dealing with potential health risks.

Closing the pool - The pool management company is responsible for winterizing the association swimming pool. Depending upon the area of the country, winterizing means different aspects of protecting the swimming pool and swimming pool facilities. Generally, all water lines and filters need to be drained to prevent freezing. In certain instances, antifreeze is placed in water lines and pool bathroom fixtures to prevent freezing. If the pool has a cover, this will be installed, along with removing ladders, rope floats, etc.

The pool management company should maintain liability insurance coverage and workers compensation coverage. It is advisable that the homeowners association be named as an additional insured on the pool management company's policy.

The pool maintenance vendor will also include in their services a preopening health department inspection and a closing inspection regarding repairs and possible compliance issues that need to be addressed for the following pool season.

■ ■ ■

HOW TO HIRE A PLUMBING COMPANY

Once a leading surgeon called a plumber to unstop a clogged toilet. The plumber arrived and spent 20 minutes unclogging the toilet and then handed the surgeon a bill for $250. The surgeon was shocked and said, "I am a surgeon, and I don't charge that much." The plumber smiled and said, "When I was a surgeon, I could not get that rate either."

It is an old joke, but to a certain extent close to reality. Paradoxically, a skilled plumber is not that dissimilar to a surgeon. Good experienced plumbers can pay for themselves by quickly and efficiently correcting plumbing problems, whereas some plumbers can cost the association money due to lack of experience. For example, plumbing works basically on the old saying, "it rolls downhill," but there are many finer points in plumbing that come only from experience. For example, plumbing in a condominium high-rise, or in any multilevel structure, for that matter, can have plumbing considerations different from the plumbing in a typical single-family structure.

Selecting the right plumbing company for the right job will save association funds and accomplish the task efficiently. Whether the plumbing company is large or small, the required knowledge base is the most important factor in the selection decision.

Several key points to consider are: How long has the plumbing company been in business? What is the scope of the business? Scope of business means: is their company a dripping-faucets and clogged-toilets kind of company, or do they have backhoes to dig and repair broken water lines? Or are they somewhere between light plumbing-repair and major plumbing-repair types of companies? Besides being a competent plumber — which is the most important aspect — does the plumber handle 24/7 emergency calls? If the plumber is just a regular business-hours type of plumber, pass on that type of plumber and find a plumber who will answer the telephone at 2 AM in the morning.

■ ■ ■

HIRING A ROOFER

Roofing can be one of the most underappreciated trades. What could be simpler than installing a roof? Well, there is a great deal that goes into properly installing a roof.

Whatever the roofing material the association structure requires, make sure that the roofing contractor has been approved by the roofing material manufacturer to install or repair the roofing material in question.

Many types of roofing materials may require roofing contractors to have special training, certifications or licenses to ensure proper installation.

In the Appendix there is a sample roofing bid for a typical asphalt shingle roof. No matter the roofing material, a detailed bid or detailed proposal in writing from the roofing contractor should provide clear and thorough specifications regarding the association project.

Besides basic information, such as the project start-time and duration and roofing materials used, insurance needs to be verified for liability coverage and, especially, workers compensation coverage. There is a reason workers compensation coverage is so expensive for roofing contractors, and this coverage needs to be in place.

■ ■ ■

STORM CHASERS - ROOFERS

There is only one group of people who watch the Weather Channel more than farmers: Storm Chasing Roofers. These "roofers" travel around the country following storms, usually hail or high winds, looking for unsuspecting customers. They realize that these types of storms generate enormous amounts of insurance claims.

Storm chasers will normally focus on one particular area of town and go door-to-door soliciting. As part of their sales process, they will offer to perform free roof inspections. They will also offer advice on filing the insurance claim. Chasers have a great deal of experience in dealing with insurance companies and understand how the roof claims process works. They will provide an estimate, and they will agree to absorb or rebate the insurance policy's deductible if they are hired.

The core of the problem is that there is no incentive for the storm chaser to do a good job. The chaser will be gone by the time any possible problems arise. What can also happen, as a consequence, is that if the roof was not installed properly the manufactures' warranty may not be honored.

As an added risk, in many instances, storm chasers will not have liability insurance or workers compensation coverage. As a result, if someone is injured the injured worker will usually have legal recourse against the hiring property owner if the vendor does not have coverage. And, in certain instances, even if the vendor does have insurance there may be recourse against the hiring party or property owner. Unfortunately, with the nature of storm chasers and these types of vendors, employee safety may not be a high priority, so injuries could be more prevalent.

Hiring established roofing companies that have good reputations is worth more than any potential initial savings that could be realized by utilizing storm chasers. Red flags for storm chasers are: door-to-door soliciting, out-of-state license plates, no local office address and no workers compensation insurance. Another red flag can be the inability to provide references for prior local work dating back for any extended period of time in order to gauge the quality of work performed.

■ ■ ■

HIRING A PUBLIC INSURANCE ADJUSTER

When disaster strikes an association such as fire, flood, hail damage etc., and a claim needs to be filed, a public insurance adjuster is the association's advocate and can usually save an association thousands of dollars and, in some instances, hundreds of thousands of dollars. A public insurance adjuster is an insurance claims adjuster who represents the association in appraising and negotiating the claim. A public adjuster principally appraises the damage claim, prepares an estimate and other claims documentation, reviews the insurance policy to determine coverage and negotiates with the insurance company to maximize the association's coverage.

Typically, the board of directors retains a public adjuster to document and expedite their claims, obtain a more satisfactory claim recovery faster and restore the damaged property more promptly. Another huge benefit of utilizing a public adjuster is that the board of directors insulates itself from negotiating an insurance claim in the event that they are not proficient in the complicated claims process.

Legally, only a public adjuster — aside from attorneys and the insurance broker — can represent the rights of the insured during an insurance claim process. A public adjuster is most beneficial during an insurance claim when loss-valuations or supplementary issues arise. A supplementary issue would be asbestos being discovered or building codes requiring additional modifications not in the original construction. Generally, public adjusters charge a percentage of the settlement, and generally, these funds come from the insurance claim settlement.

- A public adjuster's main responsibilities are to:
- Evaluate the insurance policies in order to determine what coverage may be applicable to a claim
- Research and confirm damage to buildings and contents and any supplementary expenses
- Determine values for settling the claim
- Prepare, document and support the claim on behalf of the association that they represent
- Negotiate a settlement with the insurance company on behalf of the association
- Re-open a claim and negotiate for more money if a discrepancy is found after the claim has been settled

Most public adjusters are paid based upon a percentage of the total settlement. Fees range from 5% to 10%, based upon the type and amount of the claim. Some public adjusters charge a flat percentage, while others use a regressive scale such as 15% of the first $100,000, 10% between $100,000 and $200,000, etc. regardless of the fee structure, it is important to consider that the fee is generally offset, either partially or totally, by an increase in the settlement amount negotiated by the public adjuster.

A public adjuster is best retained as soon as possible after a claim occurs, and while it may not always be clear when an association may benefit from hiring a public adjuster, the most benefit is likely to be realized if they are engaged immediately in case of a loss. However, in the vast majority of instances, a public adjuster can come to the assistance of a board of directors whenever issues arise that require an expert on the process.

It is important to consider that shortly after the insurance carrier receives notice of a loss, a claims adjuster representing the insurance company's best interests will be dispatched. The claims adjuster will visit the association to gather facts about how the loss occurred, the magnitude of the loss, etc. During this initial investigative phase, incorrect, incomplete or inadequately-expressed answers to the adjuster's questions may reduce the amount that can be claimed. A public adjuster engaged early in the process will have more opportunity to help the association receive a fair claims settlement under the insurance policy. However, at any time during negotiations with the insurance company and even after a settlement has been received by an insured, a public adjuster may be able to negotiate for a higher amount to cover a supplementary issue that arises.

■ ■ ■

HIRING CIVIL ENGINEERS

Civil engineers or civil engineering firms are routinely used by associations for the purposes of reviewing structural defects or construction projects. Civil engineers generally provide guidance, along with solutions to construction defects. These construction defects usually relate to initial construction for most associations. Civil engineers are also used to review and sign-off on projects such as replacements roofs and paving projects.

When selecting a civil engineering firm ensure the firm has broad experience in the particular area of concern. For example, if the association clubhouse has foundation issues, a civil engineering firm that predominately works on roads and bridges may not be the ideal firm for the association. It is always best to seek out either engineering firms that are large enough to have a broad experience base or smaller firms that specialize in projects of the nature that the association faces.

■ ■ ■

HIRING A SECURITY COMPANY

A great deal of consideration goes into selecting the right security company for an association. Communities with manned security gates or roving patrol cars have different requirements. Armed or unarmed guards have liability issues, along with higher insurance premiums.

Look for a security company that has other homeowner association clients. With this homeowner association experience, hopefully the security company will have an understanding of what level of service will be needed. Security for a construction site or shopping mall has different requirements from security for an association with its members coming and going.

If the state regulates security companies or individual security guards, only hire a licensed and bonded security company. Require liability insurance of at least five million dollars in coverage with the association listed on the policy as "additional insured." If utilizing armed security guards, five million dollars may not be sufficient coverage in the event of a shooting.

■ ■ ■

SELECTING A CERTIFIED PUBLIC ACCOUNT (CPA) FIRM

A board of directors should seek out a CPA or CPA firm with experience working with homeowner associations. As with an attorney with homeowner association experience, there is a benefit in having a CPA who has worked with other associations. This experience should also save the association in tax preparation costs and the cost of other financial reporting because there should not be a learning curve. The experienced CPA should be more able to spot issues or problems during audits or reviews.

In addition to an association's CPA performing the annual tax returns, the CPA should have the ability to perform other financial reporting. It is a good practice for every association to have a financial audit or, at a minimum, a financial review performed every year. One consideration is that not all CPAs or CPA firms have the ability to perform audits.

There are three levels of accounting evaluations: audits, reviews, and compilations. Audits are the most thorough and thus the most expensive of the three. Compilations are the least thorough and are not recommended for general association reporting needs.

Accountants can charge a set rate for a financial task, such as preparing the association's annual tax returns or preparing the association's financial statements. As with attorneys, some CPAs will charge an hourly rate, which can be beneficial for specific matters. One consideration of a CPA firm or, especially, a single practitioner CPA is that access or availability may be an issue during tax-filing periods.

■ ■ ■

CAVEAT EMPTOR (BUYER BEWARE)

Ongoing maintenance is a fact of life for associations. As every board of directors realizes, finding and selecting the right vendor is 90% of the process. While potential vendors come from many sources (management companies, association members and other parties) selecting the wrong vendor can be expensive and many times, disastrous. Below are five red flags in the vendor selection process:

- "Money up front or a deposit." Vendors who require money up front to pay for materials (or for any other reason) should be a huge warning sign. What can happen once a vendor has money in hand is that the project is no longer a priority and thus takes forever to complete. Or, worst case scenario, the vendor just disappears completely without doing anything. Another common scenario is that they perform poor quality work, and, because they have already been paid, the customer has less leverage to have the vendor resolve problem issues.

- "Material left over." This scam usually comes in the form of paving contractors who approach a "mark" with a pitch of leftover product from a recent job. The scammers offer to fill potholes at a "low" price. At best, the potholes are filled with cold patch at triple what a legitimate contractor would charge, and at worst, the potholes are filled with something that lasts only until the first rain.
- "Let us show you what we can do for free at no obligation." This scam comes in many varieties of trades. A common trade is pressure-washing. "Let us pressure-wash a portion of the siding to show how good job we do." The scammer then pressure-washes half the siding, leaving one side untouched that looks terrible compared to the just pressure-washed portion. Because the pressure-washer is already there, the mark pays them to finish pressure-washing the entire home, usually at 3 to 4 times what a legitimate contractor would charge.
- "God's honest truth." These scammers play on the mark's trust and make all kinds of promises. These promises are never in writing, and it really does not matter if they are in writing or not because the scammer is not going to honor them anyway. When a vendor talks about how honest they are, they bear watching.
- "Unexpected problems." The scammer discovers additional maintenance problems that escalate the cost. These

discovered problems can be design changes or code upgrades that are not required. In some instances, these unexpected problems can be legitimate, but a common tactic for scammers is to underbid the work required and then jack up the price.

■ ■ ■

HIRING MEMBERS TO PERFORM WORK FOR THE ASSOCIATION

At times, finding the ideal maintenance vendor for the association can be challenging. This is especially the case when it comes to long term contracts such as landscaping and pool maintenance. Finding and selecting the right vendor begins with not selecting the inappropriate vendor. Inappropriate means not necessarily the wrong or a bad vendor, just not appropriate for the association.

There will be, on occasion, association members who own businesses or are employed in the various maintenance trades. While many times these members and their related companies are outstanding at what they do, whether they would be a proper fit for the association is another question. At first thought, it may seem convenient to have a vendor so close and hopefully "invested" in the well-being of the association.

The consideration may be true that a vender who resides in the community will be handy to deal with issues that arise. However, the old saying "The shoemaker's son always goes barefoot" could be the case as well. Unfortunately, there is no way to determine either possible situation beforehand.

While it may be convenient, the real issue is not whether to hire an association member. The real issue may be whether to fire the member if the work relationship needs to be terminated, for whatever reason. The termination of the work relationship may be difficult in and of itself, and it can be very awkward for the member and board of directors moving forward. Terminating the vendor relationship with the member may cause resentment that continues long after the actual firing. Seeing this former vendor at the swimming pool or at the annual meeting can lead to uncomfortable situations for the board and the member.

Another point that may need consideration is the fairness to the member of essentially being on-call around the clock. The membership may have an issue with a member working for the association. There are concerns with potential conflicts of interest that could arise with a vendor being a member of the association. The member would probably do a good job, but the risk of poor performance and dealing with that situation should be weighed against any possible benefit.

■ ■ ■

Common Association Issues

■ ■ ■

BACKFLOW PREVENTION

Backflow prevention, also commonly referred to by the device itself, backflow preventer, is the process used to protect potable drinking water from being contaminated or polluted. As the word implies, this contamination comes from water back flowing into the water supply lines. Per the Environmental Protection Agency (EPA) potable water system requirements, water providers are mandated to require backflow prevention mechanisms from end-users of their services. As part of these requirements, water providers may require backflow preventers to be inspected at least annually in order to ensure proper operation.

A backflow preventer is basically a mechanism to prevent backflow. This mechanism provides a physical barrier to backflow. There are a number of backflow prevention devices or styles. Basically, the backflow preventer device is composed of seals, springs and other moving parts. From continual use, all of these parts are subject to normal wear and tear and thus either hinder the backflow preventer from working altogether or, at a minimum, impair its effectiveness.

Cross connections are points at which potable water systems connect with non-potable water systems.

Backflow preventers are commonly located at fire sprinkler systems where they connect to a main water line. Another common application for backflow preventers are lawn sprinkler systems.

Questions often arise of: "How can backflow happen on pressurized water supply lines?" This is because municipal or county water is delivered via pressurized water lines to residences and businesses. This is unlike sewer lines, which primarily rely upon gravity to function properly. What can happen is that water pressure is interrupted by a broken water line or exceptionally high water use, which drains the lines. This reduced pressure in the water lines can, in fact, suction contaminated water back into the fresh water supply. This is known as back siphonage. For example, fertilizer could have contaminated a lawn sprinkler water supply line through the sprinkler heads.

Backflow risks are categorized into five different levels, with each level representing a higher level of health risk. For example, a Category 1 backflow is pure potable drinking water and poses no risk. A Category 5 backflow could be polluted with sewage and is thus a very serious health risk.

■ ■ ■

ASPHALT PREVENTIVE MAINTENANCE

Boards of directors spend a great deal of time and funds on preventive maintenance and understand the long-term savings benefits of such energies. While painting, gutter cleaning and other preventive maintenance items are annual events, asphalt many times goes unnoticed. Because asphalt – or more precisely, replacing asphalt — is such a large expenditure, preventive maintenance to extend the useful life is usually association funds well spent.

Asphalt cement or asphalt binder is a petroleum-based product that is used to bond together aggregates, stone, sand and gravel to form asphalt pavement. The asphalt binder is created from the refinement process of crude oil. Maintaining the asphalt binder is paramount in the long-term preservation of asphalt pavement. The everyday environment of water and sunlight will break down the binder and begin the deterioration of asphalt.

The life cycle of asphalt can vary greatly, depending upon a number of factors such as degree of use and geographic location. An industry standard life cycle can range from 25 to 35 years. Again, this is depending upon use. For example, a clubhouse parking lot that is driven on by less than a few dozen cars a day can well exceed the upper limits of this life cycle. Conversely, a street located at the front entrance of an association that has several hundred cars a day entering and leaving may have a much shorter life cycle.

Geographic location has an enormous influence on the life cycle of asphalt. Asphalt is susceptible to both cold and hot temperatures. In winter months, freezing occurs both below and above the asphalt, which can cause cracks. Water penetrates these cracks, and when this water freezes it expands, causing the asphalt to split further. This is the genesis of a pothole. Just as cold affects asphalt, heat can cause asphalt cracks as well, which again causes water intrusion. While this water may not freeze, it does break down the subsurface of the asphalt, eventually causing potholes.

Because the condition of asphalt can vary with use and climate, preventive maintenance schedules can vary. However, sealing asphalt cracks every 3 to 5 years is a good standard. Sealing cracks helps prevent water from penetrating the asphalt and thus prevents more serious and expensive damage from occurring.

"Crack-filling" is the process of cleaning out cracks prior to inserting crack-filling material. When properly done, crack-filling reduces the infiltration of water into the asphalt and lasts 3 to 5 years. There are basically three crack-filling materials in use today: asphalt cements, fibered asphalt and polymer-modified.

After crack–filling, the next step is the "crack-sealing" process, and this involves grinding out the cracks to half an inch or wider in order to provide a reservoir for the rubberized crack-sealing material. Rubberized asphalt is the material used for crack-sealing. Rubberized asphalt materials are use- or performance-graded, meaning that they are designed for specific uses and variables. For example, some crack-sealing materials will be labeled specific road-grade or parking lot-grade material.

The final step is sealing the asphalt, or sealcoating. Sealcoating is an asphalt surface application. There are primarily three types of asphalt sealers: coal tar, asphalt emulsions and acrylics. Sealers are primarily applied utilizing three methods: manually by hand with a squeegee, with a self-propelled squeegee machine, or pressurized spray equipment. The sealcoat process is typically done with two coats, which require 24 to 48 hours of curing before use.

Preventive maintenance on asphalt pavement should generally be performed in 3-to-5-year cycles. Performing preventive maintenance with this frequency will generally be more cost-effective and extend the overall life cycle. While the natural environment effects and vehicle use on asphalt paving can vary, extending the life cycle 10 years or more is obtainable.

■ ■ ■

THE IMPORTANCE OF GUTTER CLEANING

While it may not seem to be a serious matter, stopped-up gutters are much more than just an eyesore. Clogged gutters restrict rainwater flow and can cause water damage to the interior and exterior of a home. The water from clogged gutters routinely rots the fascia board and soffit board, along with elements of the roof structure.

Gutters, downspouts and splash blocks are all fundamental components of a home's ability to prevent water intrusion, from the roof to the foundation.

The species and number of trees in the surrounding area helps determine how often gutter-cleaning is necessary. Many associations have common gutters routinely selected to be cleaned twice a year, or more frequently if conditions require. Other associations have their gutters cleaned on an as-needed basis.

Gutter covers or other leaf-blocking devices may prevent leaves or the majority of leaves from traveling into gutters, but none of these devices prevent 100% of the debris. Gutter covers, at best, reduce the number of gutter cleanings down to once a year or possibly once every two years. Even considering the expense, gutter-covering devices are well-suited for high or difficult-to-reach places. Reducing difficult gutter-cleaning locations or situations can pay for gutter covers, considering the higher maintenance costs for cleaning.

Not only do clogged gutters restrict the flow of water and cause wood rot, a clogged gutter can become home to mosquitoes and other pests. Mosquitoes need standing water in which to lay their eggs, so they find clogged gutters a great habitat for this activity. The wet, decaying leaves provide the nourishment that these eggs and mosquito larvae need for development.

■ ■ ■

FLASHING OR WEATHERPROOFING

Association boards are often faced with maintenance issues revolving around water intrusion. A majority of the time, this water intrusion is the result of failing flashing or improperly installed flashing. Flashing refers to material placed in a joint — such as where a chimney meets a roofline — to prevent water intrusion. Depending upon specific material or joint requirements, flashing can be either exposed or concealed. Concealed flashing can be either rigid metal or flexible material, while exposed flashing is generally metal.

The most common metal materials for flashing are aluminum, galvanized steel and copper. Flexible flashing can be any number of materials, the most popular being vinyl and rubberized asphalt. The different materials vary in use for climate, temperature ranges, compatibility adhesion, chemical compatibility and resistance to ultraviolet light. Unlike metal flashing, flexible flashing materials are generally not well-suited for direct exposure to the elements.

In the construction and repair of roofing systems, roof flashing is installed around distinct breaks in the physical continuity of the roofing system. Valleys and items that extend beyond the roof system must have flashing to deflect water. Roofing system flashing falls into two categories: valley flashing and roof-penetration flashing. Valley flashing is used in the valleys of intersecting roof planes. Roof-penetrating flashing is used for waterproofing pipes, supports and all other roof protrusions. Pipe flashing for plumbing pipes and vents is called boots, and it falls into the roof-penetrating category.

Wall flashing is used in the installation of windows, doors and other wall joints that are susceptible to water intrusion. The installation of flashing around windows and doors creates a water barrier between the joint and siding. Wall flashing can be placed within the wall to redirect penetrating water back outside, such as sill flashing (commonly referred to as a sill pan), which is flashing installed under windows or door frames. Or flashing can be installed to prevent initial water intrusion altogether, such as channel flashing (commonly referred to as a "J" channel), which prevents water intrusion by having a small channel that directs water away from wall joints.

The damage when flashing fails or is not installed properly can amount to many thousands of dollars. The resulting damage could lead to more than just rotting wood. Insect infestations such as termites thrive on decaying wood and moisture. Faulty flashing or improperly installed flashing can not only fail to prevent water intrusion, but can actually direct water into the structure.

■ ■ ■

FRENCH DRAIN

A French drain is basically a ditch lined with rocks or gravel that helps drain water away from an area. It is used to protect the foundation of a house or structure from ground and surface water. French drains are also used in areas with standing water problems to help drain water away.

A French drain works on the principle of gravity, being slightly sloped down from the area to be drained toward the area where the water is to be redirected. It is typically lined with perforated pipe and surrounded with landscaping matting in order to prevent dirt or plant roots from clogging the system. Excess ground and surface water percolates into the French drain and is directed away.

■ ■ ■

TREES

A Poem Lovely as a Tree

I think that I shall never see
A poem lovely as a tree.

This is the first part of the wonderful poem "Trees" by Joyce Kilmer, which praises the virtues of all trees. However, Joyce Kilmer may not have resided within an association and, therefore, probably did not deal with the issues that arise with certain trees. Some of these particular issues could be minor in nature — such as attracting annoying insects — but more major issues could be the continuing or long-term maintenance consequences.

Trees do bring splendor and beauty to any landscape, but trees serve many practical purposes as well. Properly-placed trees can provide shade to a home and improve efficiency of air conditioning systems during summer months. Trees can also improve heating efficiency during the winter months by breaking winter winds.

Rarely do association governing documents specifically restrict particular tree species. Governing documents will many times broadly restrict placement or location via the architectural review provisions, but most governing documents do not specifically address this matter, leaving the details up to the architectural review process.

Utilizing the architectural review process provided in most governing documents is generally where boards of directors and architectural review committees establish the maintenance and planting guidelines, establishing guidelines about the species of trees and where each species can and cannot be planted.

One element that is commonly not taken into consideration is the future growth of the tree as it reaches maturity. For example, a white oak grows up to 50 to 80 feet in height and has an eventual circumference limb spread of 50 to 80 feet. Even considering that a white oak can take over 40 years to grow to maturity, it still should not be planted ten feet from a home.

Another consideration is what is not visible: the tree's root system. Certain tree root systems can extend 40 to 50 feet down, with an average tree root system growing 10 to 20 feet down. Considering the possible damage to foundations and plumbing lines near these root systems, the wrong tree could result in thousands of dollars in future damages. Conversely, a shallow root system is generally more likely to topple during extreme weather situations than a deep-rooted elm tree.

Generally speaking, the best tree species to plant around structures are those that have shallow roots systems and are less than 25 feet high at maturity. These trees are often referred to as ornamental or decorative trees. Keep these types of trees at least 7 to 10 feet from sidewalks and foundations, because roots may eventually grow and cause damage. A rule of thumb is not to plant any tree closer to a structure than half the circumference at maturity. This should keep the foliage, as well as the root system, from the structure.

Ornamental trees typically fall into four categories: evergreens, deciduous, flower and fruit.

Evergreens generally provide year-round benefits such as shade and color. Certain evergreen trees grow tall but have a small circumference spread. Popular evergreens are varieties of spruce, holly and cedar. Arborvitae or cypresses are also popular evergreen trees.

Deciduous means "falling off at maturity" and is typically used to refer to trees or shrubs that lose their leaves seasonally. This seasonal loss generally happens in the fall of each year. Common deciduous trees are varieties of chestnut, ash and maple.

Flowering trees are sometimes confused with large shrubs or plants. These types of trees can enhance or contrast with other landscaping features. Popular flowering trees are dogwoods, smoketrees, magnolias, tulips, crepe myrtles and maidenhair trees.

Fruit trees can be well suited for planting near structures, particularly dwarf varieties of pear, apple, plum and cherry. However, because of these trees' fruit falling to the ground, and because some governing documents may limit fruit trees, these types of ornamental trees are generally not ideal for associations.

SIX TREES TO AVOID

- Silverleaf maple tree – This is a beautiful fast-growing shade tree that grows in colder climates as well as warmer climates such as Florida. Unfortunately, the silverleaf maple has a reputation for having weak limbs that can easily break during storms. The most problematic issue is the shallow root system. Silverleaf roots attack plumbing lines and crack sidewalks and driveways.
- Black walnut - While great for furniture-making and shade, black walnuts produce large amounts of pollen. And what can be most troubling is that the tree puts off toxins that kill nearby plants and flowers.
- Elm tree – This is a common and majestic tree with a very deep root system that breaks plumbing lines.
- Willow tree - The beautiful willow tree is very distinctive with its low, drooping branches. The willow tree has an expansive root system that can wreak havoc on plumbing lines.
- Bradford pear tree – This is very common in many associations, with its spring blossoms that have a strong aroma.

Unfortunately, Bradford pear limbs are prone to break or split from as little as 30-mile-an-hour winds.
- Mulberry tree – This has a shallow root system and is a large producer of pollen. Another concern is that its berries will stain sidewalks and driveways.

■ ■ ■

TREE TRIMMING

Trees are one of the many landscaping factors that make an association beautiful. And, like many or most association elements, some trees require routine maintenance. Routine maintenance can many times extend the life of a tree, but routine maintenance also protects other association elements that are affected by the tree. For example, trees planted near the clubhouse may have branches touching the roof that are causing damage. Trimming back these branches at the cost of hundreds of dollars may increase the life of the roof, thus saving thousands of dollars.

The Department of Agriculture suggests pruning or trimming trees only during the dormant season. Trees go dormant every autumn and wake up every spring. This sleep — technically called dormancy — enables trees to survive harsh winter periods. Of course, unforeseen events can prompt an immediate trimming. If possible, this should be done under the supervision of a professional arborist.

The US Department of Agriculture gives the following guidelines for choosing if and when to trim a tree:

1 - Prune first for safety, next for the tree's health and finally for aesthetics.

2 - Trees near utility lines should be trimmed by the utility company or a professional arborist.
3 - The following size guide should be used when trimming tree branches:
   - Under 2 inches in diameter, generally no problem with trimming
   - Between 2 and 4 inches diameter, make sure trimming is needed
   - Greater than 4 inches, have good reason and consider an arborist to perform the trimming

While trimming may be done solely for aesthetics or safety, removing dead or diseased branches will benefit the overall health of the tree. In addition, trimming can encourage trees to develop stronger core structures to withstand the elements. Trimming trees will many times improve flower/fruit production.

■ ■ ■

THE COST TO THE ASSOCIATION OF OVERWATERING

Water rates between 2010 & 2015 increased by 41%, according to circleofblue.org. Reasons for this increase vary from the replacement costs of the aging water infrastructure to the theory that it is less controversial to raise water rates than property taxes. Interestingly enough, another theory for increases is reportedly the reduction in water consumption by the government-mandated water-reduction regulations. The lower demand has forced municipalities to make up the lost revenue by increasing rates.

No matter the cause of the higher water rates, water, like any other association expense, should be contained wherever possible.

However, overwatering or wasted water may cost more than the actual water cost, environmental damage and possible legal issues.

The environmental damage primarily comes from overwatering plants and trees, which leads to various problems. The various types of soils beneath grass and other plants have porous spaces filled with oxygen. When watering, water fills those porous spaces and pushes out the oxygen. Continually overwatering keeps those pores constantly filled with water instead of with the oxygen that plants need for growth. This excessive water literally suffocates the roots and kills the plant.

If this overwatering does not kill the plant outright, at a minimum, limiting oxygen in the soil will put the plant under stress. This stress makes plants more prone to disease and insect damage. Many plants, including grass, go dormant in dry periods and do not necessarily need additional watering. As long as the correct plants are placed in the ground — correct being the amount appropriate for the area's normal environment — additional water may not be necessary. Interestingly, overwatered lawns can lead to more weeds, and these weeds are typically more difficult to control.

Additionally, when fertilizer is applied to overwatered lawns and other plants, it has a propensity to wash through the soil before it can be absorbed by the plants' roots. Unfortunately, a common response to this non-absorption is to apply more fertilizer. Even more impactful is that, when fertilizer is not absorbed by the plant, it can contaminate groundwater or turn into runoff.

Surface water runoff — caused by storm water or overwatering — is another issue that can cost an association in fines. Runoff most often occurs when there is more water than the soil can absorb. Fineable runoff is polluted water that has drained into streams, storm drains or other water sources. Runoff pollutants can include debris, chemicals and other deemed pollutants that have drained from surface land. Fines from the EPA and other local agencies can lead to many thousands of dollars.

Overwatering also leads to faster deterioration of association hardscaping. Hardscaping items such as fences and retaining walls constructed of wood tend to deteriorate or rot much sooner. Walls and front entrance signs — or any association improvement constructed on a foundation — can be undermined by excess water. Walks and streets are negatively affected by excess watering, no matter the construction material used, because of the potential for erosion and soil consolidation. Soil consolidation is a process by which soil decreases in volume when the oxygen is forced from the soil by water and not replenished.

■ ■ ■

SEARCHING FOR UNSEEN WATER LEAKS

Concealed water leaks can go undetected for extended periods of time, even many years. There can be various reasons for this delay in detection, but most commonly it is because these leaks are small in nature and cause no obvious damage or noticeable water consumption. Unfortunately, when the damage appears, it can appear in elevated water bills or, in extreme situations, sinkholes.

A yearly estimate, per the American Water Works Association Research Foundation, is that almost 14% of all drinking water in the United States is lost due to leaks. These losses are understandable, considering that a broken one-inch diameter irrigation line can leak up to 648,000 gallons in a single month. A single running toilet can waste up to 21,600 gallons a month.

The fundamental cause of these leaks can vary as well, from environmental factors to aging water supply systems. In recently-formed or -constructed associations, improper original installation is a common culprit. While there is not a great deal that can be done to prevent these types of leaks beforehand — other than, in many cases, digging up and replacing all the water lines — there are some simple methods to try to discover leaks.

In order to check individual homes or structures, the first place to begin a leak search is the water meter providing service. Water meters are usually found near the curb in the front of the structure that the meter services. The actual meter will normally be housed in a steel, concrete or fiberglass-type box at grade with a removable cover. The meter face will generally have a mechanical or digital readout.

If all the water using apparatuses are not in use within the structure, the meter readouts should not be moving or indicating water consumption. If the meter is actively measuring water use, there is a leak somewhere within the structure or possibly between the meter and the structure.

To isolate the leak between the structure and the water supply line between the meter and structure, find the primary water shutoff within the structure and shut the water off at that point. The primary water shutoff can be found in various locations, including the basement, garage, utility room, next to the water heater and in the crawlspace. This water shutoff – or, more precisely, valve — can be turned clockwise to stop the flow of water.

If the meter keeps indicating water usage after the structure's primary water shutoff is turned off, the leak is in the yard between the meter and the primary water shutoff. If the shutoff valve is shut off at the structure, and the water meter stops, then there is a leak within the structure.

If the leak is between the meter and the primary shutoff, determining the exact location may be either quite simple or very difficult, without possibly digging up the entire water line. The water lines between the meter and the primary shutoff are usually laid in a straight line. Roughly determining the lay of the lines and looking for a wet spot or mud on the surface can pinpoint the location. Roughly determining the lay of the water line can be done by standing on the meter and looking towards the structure to the nearest bathroom or major plumbing source within the structure. Although not always a certainty, plumbing lines generally run to the nearest need. Another common indicator can be greener grass then surrounding grass due to the additional water. A slump or possibly a swell in the ground can be an indicator as well. These are the types of leaks that can lead to sinkholes.

If the leak has been isolated to be beyond the primary shutoff, typically finding the leak should be much more straightforward than a leak from a buried pipe. Leaking pipes past the primary shutoff are usually very obvious because of the interior damage done and thus much easier to discern, so this potential issue can be eliminated. The exception could be a leaking pipe in a basement or crawlspace that has gone unnoticed. These areas can be inspected visually or by the use of moisture meters. If the structure is constructed on a slab or constructed of concrete, moisture meters can be used, along with looking for signs of wet spots or seepage.

If there are no indications of a leak in the basement, crawlspace or slab, there are three other likely culprits: a leaking toilet, a leaking water heater or a dripping faucet or faucets. While these three possible culprits can be checked initially, eliminating the other leak possibilities can be beneficial in helping to make certain of the origins of a leak. If the leak is originating from a faulty toilet, that only leaks intermittently, so the only true way to make sure that the problem has been corrected is by waiting for the next water bill to see if there is a drop in usage.

A toilet can be checked by lifting the tank cover behind the toilet seat and listening for a hiss or the sound of escaping air. Another test is to put several drops of food coloring in the tank itself and wait at least ten minutes to see if the food coloring appears in the bowl. (Flush the toilet after ten minutes to prevent the food coloring from possibly staining the bowl.) If food coloring appears in the bowl, this is caused by a defective flapper, and this is the source of the leak. One problem, as mentioned previously, is that toilets can leak intermittently and not indicate leaks in certain circumstances. Since the cost of "toilet repair kits" are very reasonable and they easily installed, it is usually more productive to replace the interworkings of the toilet than to wait.

The next likely culprit is the water heater. If there is a drain pan under the water heater, it may be capturing water and draining it away, so a leak may not be overly obvious. Also, all water heaters have a pressure relief valve, and this is where many leaks originate. It is common for pressure relief valves to be plumbed directly into a drain line, and there will be no way of determining whether the valve is leaking without removing the drain line itself.

The last of the three potential culprits — and probably the most common — are dripping faucets. While dripping faucets are usually obvious, the amount of water loss can be surprising. Per the EPA, a leaky faucet that drips at the rate of one drip per second can waste more than 3,000 gallons per year. When checking faucets, remember to check the outside spigots or foundation faucets. Leaking faucets, in most instances, are the simplest of all leaks to eliminate.

Annualized, one dripping faucet is equivalent to 180 showers. Per the EPA, just correcting common water leaks such as faucets and toilets could save 10% on water bills.

If all else fails in locating a leak, there are companies that specialize in leak detection. These companies usually have the latest in leak-detecting technologies and can many times find the most difficult of leaks.

■ ■ ■

PREVENTING WATER DAMAGE

Water damage can be caused by a multitude of events, from rain to frozen pipes bursting. However, no matter the cause, most water damage is expensive. According to the Insurance Information Institute, the average insurance water damage claim was $7,479 in 2013. Fortunately, regular inspections and preventive maintenance can help prevent water damage in many situations. The following guidelines can help identify potential problems and help avoid water damage altogether:

KNOW THE WATER SUPPLY

- Water Shutoff Valves. Know where all the water shutoff valves are located throughout the structure, especially the main water supply. In the event of a leak, this will enable the water to be shut off quickly. The best time to locate all these shutoffs is before it's necessary.

MAINTAINING MAJOR APPLIANCES

- Water Heater. The average lifespan of a water heater is 7-10 years. Make sure that there is an overflow pan under the water heater. If water is collecting, it is generally time to replace the water heater.
- Appliance Water Hoses. Washing machines, dishwashers, icemakers, air conditioners and garbage disposals all use water to operate, and all either have hoses or gaskets that can leak. Inspect these appliances for leaks, and periodically replace hoses. Washing machine hoses are a large percentage of all water claims. It is a good idea to shut off the washing machine water supply before leaving for an extended period of time.
- Sump Pumps. Sump pumps are located wherever water has a tendency to accumulate, such as basements and crawlspaces. Generally, sump pumps last around 10 years, and it is important to keep them well-maintained and tested regularly. Besides regular testing, the most important thing to do is keep the area around the sump pump clear

of debris. In certain instances, if power outages are common, a battery backup is recommended to ensure proper operation.

- Air Conditioner. Drain pans and pan drain lines need to be inspected annually for standing water and in order to make sure that the drain lines are clear and flowing properly.
- Basement. Periodically inspect foundation walls and floors for cracks that might allow water seepage, especially in older structures or in areas with poor soil drainage.
- Roof. Missing, worn or broken roofing materials may allow water to penetrate and deteriorate the roof structure. Inspect roofs periodically, especially after severe storms.
- Roof Flashing. Flashing is located at the intersection of all roof and wall lines, as well as along chimneys and roof valleys. Flashing may separate from adjacent surfaces and allow water to leak inside.
- Gutters/Downspouts. Clogged gutters can lead to water backup that can damage exterior siding.
- Grade of Property. Soil should be graded from the foundation so that water flows away from the house during rain storms.
- Outdoor Hoses. Turn off exterior hose bibs during the winter, or insulate to prevent frozen pipes.
- Exterior Drains. Regularly remove all leaves and other debris from exterior patio, sidewalks and driveway drains.

Water detection devices can detect even small amounts of water. These systems can either shut down appliances or be wired into an alarm system that will notify in the event of a leak. Such alarm systems may allow for insurance discounts as well. There are a variety of water detection systems.

- Leak Detection Systems. These systems can not only detect leaks, but can also be electronically tied to the shutoff valve on the water lines. When one of these sensors is activated due to a leaking pipe or appliance overflow, the shut-off valve closes and prevents additional water flow.
- Water Flow Sensors. A broken water line or frozen pipe could result in water flowing — sometimes unnoticed — for a long period of time. A flow sensor can be installed on the main water line. These sensors are programmed to allow continuous water flow based on water needs during a given timeframe. If the flow of water exceeds this preprogrammed amount of time, a valve will automatically close to stop the flow of water. These sensors can be programmed for varying times, depending upon the structure's occupancy.

■ ■ ■

TERMITES

Termites swarming from wood or soil often are the first sign of a termite colony. Subterranean termites are the most common and thus the most destructive wood-destroying insects in the United States. Termites feed on cellulose, primarily dead wood and wood by-products.

TYPES OF TERMITES

Subterranean termites live in below-ground colonies that can contain hundreds of thousands of termites. Termite colonies have tunnels that can extend hundreds of feet in all directions. Soldiers, reproductives and workers are the three types of termites found in a termite colony.

Soldiers are creamy-white to grayish-white in color, wingless and soft-bodied. They have large, rectangular, yellowish-brown heads with large jaws. The soldiers' primary responsibility is the defense of the colony.

Reproductives can be male or female, winged or wingless. Both male and female reproductives produce offspring. Reproductives are black and about 0.4 inch long, with pale or grayish translucent wings. A king and queen of primary reproductives head a colony.

Workers are creamy-white to grayish-white with round heads about 1/8 inch long. They are blind, soft-bodied and wingless. Workers are the most prevalent in a termite colony, and they are the termites that eat wood. Workers search for food and water, build and repair shelter tubes, feed and groom other termites, care for eggs and young and participate in colony defense.

Detection of Termites - Subterranean termites may be detected by wood damage, the presence of mud tubes or the sudden appearance of winged termites.

Winged Termites - A "swarm" is a group of adult male and female reproductives that leave their colony in an attempt to pair and initiate new colonies. Swarming is triggered when temperature and moisture conditions are favorable, usually on warm days following rainfall during March and April. Swarming occurs in mature colonies that typically contain at least several hundred thousand termites.

Termite swarmers have two pair of long, equal-length wings that break off easily and straight antennae with thick waists. Winged termites can be differentiated from winged ants, which have elbowed antennae, small waists and two pair of unequal-length wings that are not easily detached. Ants are generally harder-bodied than termites.

Mud Tubes - Other signs of termite presence include mud tubes and mud protruding from cracks. Subterranean termites transport soil and water above ground to construct mud tubes that allow them to tunnel across exposed areas to reach wood.

Wood Damage - Termite damage to the wood's surface often is not self-evident because termites tunnel within the wood as they feed. Wood damaged by subterranean termites generally has a honeycombed appearance because termites feed along the softer grains, not on the entire wood.

TERMITE PREVENTION

Prevention of subterranean termite infestation of wooden structures centers upon disrupting their ability to locate moisture, wood and shelter. Moisture accumulation near foundations and crawlspaces should be avoided. Termites must have water to survive. Diverting water away from foundations with properly-functioning gutters, downspouts and splash blocks are vital to preventing termites. Soil needs to be sloped away from the foundation in order for surface water to drain away from the building.

Wood, mulch, paper, etc., that is in contact with soil provides termites with ready and unobservable access to food. It is very important to eliminate any contact between the wooden parts of the house foundation and soil. Maintain at least 10 inches between the soil and porch steps, lattice work, door or window frames or any other wooden materials. On a structure, wood below 18 inches of grade must be treated.

CONTROL & PREVENTION MEASURES

Soil Barrier Termiticides - Conventional soil treatment methods rely on creating chemical barriers in the soil, which are toxic to termites. Many of these treatments also have repellent characteristics causing termites to avoid treated soil. To obtain termite control for extended periods of time, such termiticides must be applied as a continuous barrier in the soil next to the structure's foundation. If there are untreated areas in the soil, termites may circumvent the chemical treatment.

Baits - Bait technology uses wood or a cellulose material favored by termites that is impregnated with a slow-acting toxic chemical. Termite workers feed upon the bait and transfer it to other colony members, eventually reducing or eliminating the entire colony.

In-ground bait stations are inserted in the soil next to structures and near known or suspected sites of termite activity. In-ground bait stations often initially contain untreated wood that serves as a monitoring method. The monitoring wood is replaced with the toxicant once termites have been detected feeding on the untreated wood. Bait systems must be serviced at regular monthly intervals to function properly.

PREVENTION TIPS

Borates and pressure-treatments protect wood against termites. However, even creosote-treated railroad ties over time can be damaged by termites.

Never store firewood, lumber, newspapers or other wood products against the foundation or within the crawl space.

Avoid or minimize the use of wood mulch next to foundations.

Seal cracks in foundation to prevent termite access.

Make sure that downspouts and splash blocks are diverting water away from the foundation.

Cut back shrubs from siding and foundations in order to allow air and light around foundation.

■ ■ ■

WINTER PLANNING FOR THE ASSOCIATION LANDSCAPE

Winter is the appropriate time to plan the landscaping for the coming spring. Even considering that vegetation can be dormant during the winter, preplanning for spring can save the association time and money.

Many boards of directors and landscaping committees schedule a walk-through or property inspection with the landscaper midwinter. At this time of year, landscapers are generally more accessible and can devote more time to this inspection. A knowledgeable and experienced landscaper can suggest many ideas and strategies that can benefit an association. For example, they might suggest vegetation placement for maximum aesthetics and long-term sustainability. A landscaper should have an idea of how a particular planting will look at full maturity and whether it is even viable.

Another benefit of a winter walk-through is addressing possible additional landscaping needs. If the board wants additional items added to the association's contract, winter is the best time to negotiate these contract add-ons. Pricing during the slow winter months will always be more competitive than during a landscaper's busy summer months.

An added benefit with this early walk-through is the additional time that it allows the landscaper to plan their schedule for the coming summer busy season. Unpredictable or unplanned landscaping needs can play havoc with landscapers, who are many times dealing with unpredictable weather. If the landscaper has a clear idea of what the board of directors is expecting in the coming months, meeting these expectations will be much easier.

■ ■ ■

PONDS

Many associations have ponds that were in place before the association was formed, and others have ponds that were created by the developer for fishing, irrigation, wildlife and water runoff. What all ponds have in common is that they almost all require regular maintenance, even if the pond is doing no more than enhancing the appearance of the association. Pond monitoring or maintenance can involve inspecting different areas of the pond on a routine basis for drainage, erosion, water quality decline, weed control and possible wildlife damage.

One of the most vital aspects of any pond is the drain or spillway. The spillway allows excess water to exit the pond in a controlled manner, which prevents damage to the pond and surrounding property. Most ponds require some type of spillway, yet many ponds have blocked or insufficient spillways. In some ponds, the spillway could be just a grassy dip in one corner of the pond. Relatively recently-constructed ponds can use pipes to collect and drain water to the base of a dam or drain the water into a catch basin. Spillways and emergency spillways must be kept clear and free of water-restricting vegetation.

Erosion around a pond can be a very serious matter for an association as well as for the properties bordering the association. A heavy rain or flash flood can magnify a small erosion problem into a large problem. Pond shorelines void of vegetation can erode to cause muddy water and silt buildup. The dam or catch basin and the shoreline should be inspected at least once a year. Soggy ground around the bottom of the dam, muddy water seeping through the dam, soil eroding off the dam and washouts should be looked for and are indicators of issues that need to be addressed.

Grass is an effective and permanent solution to most erosion. If eroded areas are discovered, these areas should be filled and reseeded or resodded. The roots of the grass, once established, will help stabilize the soil and prevent further erosion. If it is not clear where the eroded soil is coming from, this may be a job for a professional pond maintenance company. If dam stability is in question, an engineer needs to be consulted to find a solution to the erosion.

A pond's water clarity is measured by using a black-and-white disk called a Secchi disk. The Secchi disk is lowered into the pond until it disappears from view, and the depth of disappearance is a measure of water clarity. Several feet of visibility is generally reasonable and an indication of a healthy and balanced pond. Healthy pond water will have color variations from light green to a dark brown color.

Shore erosion, algae, plankton and silty runoff entering the pond are the major causes of poor pond water clarity. To possibly help determine the cause of poor water clarity, fill a clear glass jar with pond water and view it under a bright light. Algae or plankton will appear as green flecks or tiny moving organisms. A siltation problem is present when, after 48 hours, all the matter settles in the bottom of the jar.

Clarity issues can also result from the breakdown of vegetation or algal blooms, sometimes referred to as red tides, which are caused by nutrient runoff. These problem nutrients are usually nitrogen and phosphorus, which can come from fertilizer, septic systems and animal waste. All attempts should be made to prevent these types of nutrients from entering a pond. If this runoff cannot be avoided, a settling pond may be the solution. A settling pond is an area upstream from the pond that catches, retains and produces a controlled breakdown of nutrients. A settling pond is generally constructed as a shallow point or swale with thick grass or even reeds to capture as much nutrient runoff as possible. Settling pond areas are generally 5% to 15% of the size of the entire main pond in order to accommodate the runoff. If a settling pond area does not resolve the clarity issues, there are chemical solutions that can be utilized.

Wildlife such as muskrats and beavers can do damage and cause other issues that negatively affect a pond. Muskrats can create stability problems by burrowing holes into pond dams and burrowing holes elsewhere around the pond, resulting in erosion. When muskrats are burrowing into a dam, the affected area on the pond dam needs to be covered above and below the shoreline with rocks or metal fencing mesh.

Beavers can block pond spillways and pipes with limbs and mud. These blockages can result in pond levels rising and flooding the areas around the pond. Beavers are so proficient at blocking spillways that many times explosives have to be used to remove these blockages.

Dealing with or removing muskrats or beavers generally requires a licensed contractor who specializes in wildlife control.

Pond plants/weeds provide a great many benefits to a pond. Plants can promote fish habitats, oxygenation and, most importantly, erosion control. If excessive plant growth begins to interfere with the operation of the pond, it must be dealt with before it causes damage. Familiarity with the various plants in a pond and determination of the issues at hand, many times, are best accomplished by pond maintenance contractors.

There are various methods used for pond weed control. However, before any of these methods are employed it must be determined whether excess nutrients such as nitrogen and phosphorus are entering the pond and whether this is a factor that must be controlled before implementing weed control. These excessive nutrients may be the cause of the undue plant growth.

Once the cause is determined, the treatment could be as simple as raking algae off the surface or adding a new breed of fish to consume excess weed matter. Surface-floating weeds and floating algae masses can be removed with a skimmer or rake. Issues below the surface can be dealt with by physically removing plants by hand or possibly by introducing a fish called a Grass Carp — also known as a White Amour — which consumes aquatic plants. In winter months, ponds can also be partially drained without negatively affecting wildlife.

Seeking quick remedies for pond plant problems is never advisable. Aquatic herbicides are available, but should only be used in extreme situations. The disadvantages of chemical treatment options are the higher cost, higher risks of deoxygenating, possible need for permits and, in certain cases, the need to obtain permission from multiple government agencies.

▪ ▪ ▪

RETENTION PONDS

A retention pond is a human-made pond or reservoir constructed to catch runoff water from higher elevations or improved surfaces. Retention ponds can be either temporary or permanent, depending upon the circumstances and the volume of water to be contained. Most are built to be sloped basins that capitalize on gravity and the natural flow of water down hills and inclines. Keeping runoff away from homes and other structures can keep the ground from growing soggy, prevent erosion and foundational problems and drastically reduce the risk of flooding during heavy rains or significant snow melt. Building a pond like this is more than just digging a hole. The structures usually have to be engineered specifically for the circumstances. For instance, most have overflow pipes that can help control water levels and disperse water evenly. Precautions against contaminants and pollutants are also necessary in order to protect both the nearby environment and the greater public health.

Most ponds are built in areas that have surrounding land capable of accommodating high water during rainy periods. Allowing for excess surrounding land is usually considered essential for proper function and safety.

Ponds are often built in lower land areas that tend to accumulate excess amounts of water. Retention ponds often actually aid in the removal of pollutants, as trash and debris typically run into such ponds after heavy rains. The basins also catch runoff containing petroleum, fertilizers, sediments, bacteria and other harmful substances that may have negative impacts on overall water quality.

As pollutants enter such a pond during heavy rain, the basin works to slow water movement. Stagnant water allows heavier contaminants such as solids or metals to sink to the bottom of the pond and eventually become bottom-layer sediments. The retained water naturally filters contaminants and returns clean water to nearby streams or wetlands.

Ponds often need regular maintenance in order to function properly. Adding features like waterfalls or aerators may help keep mosquitoes and other pests from breeding excessively around the pond. A pest control specialist may also alleviate insect issues by adding a natural larvacide to a pond. Algae overgrowth is another potential concern, and it may be necessary to contact an aquatic management specialist to provide the proper bacteria and microbes.

■ ■ ■

WATER EVAPORATION OR POOL LEAK

With water being such a large part of a homeowners association annual budget, watching for pool leaks is always prudent. However, it is very common for normal everyday water evaporation to be mistaken for a pool leak. Determining the evaporation rate is the first step in determining whether the water disappearance is due to evaporation or a leak.

Geography and environment determine the rate of evaporation. Due to evaporation, swimming pools lose about a quarter of an inch of water each day on average. However, environmental issues such as sunlight, humidity and wind intensity can significantly affect evaporation rate.

The humidity of the southern United States has a positive effect in that a dryer environment pulls more water out of a pool. Thus, humidity keeps more water in a pool because humid air is already heavy with moisture. The sun also has a major impact upon evaporation by heating the pool water and turning water molecules into air molecules. Interestingly, wind plays a large part in water evaporation by blowing away water particles.

Non-environmental issues such as the level of activity in the pool also affects water levels. While it may seem insignificant, pool users continually getting out of the pool does have an effect. Normal splashing and playing will also reduce the water levels.

A simple and effective test to determine whether the association pool has a leak or the water loss is due to normal evaporation is the Bucket Test. The Bucket Test:

- Fill the pool to the normal level
- Fill a 5-gallon plastic bucket with pool water to within 2 inches of the top of the bucket
- Place the bucket on the steps of the pool at least 6 inches submerged in the pool water
- Mark the level of the water within the bucket
- Temporarily turn off the pool pump and autofill. Then mark the pool water level on the outside of the bucket. Turn the pump and autofill back on.
- Measure the distance between the marks
- Allow for 24 hours and compare the two water levels

If the water levels are the same distance apart, it is usually an indication that only evaporation has occurred. If the pool water goes down more than the bucket's water level, more than likely there is a leak. At this point it would be advisable to retain the services of a company that specializes in finding leaks and have the leak fixed.

If there is a leak, continuing to fill the pool may seem like a viable option, but pool leaks can be very serious. If a pool leak is not addressed, there is potential for severe damage. Over time, leaks can damage the structural integrity of the pool, resulting in thousands of dollars in repair costs.

■ ■ ■

DRAINAGE ISSUES

Proper drainage is the removal of surface and sub-surface water from an area. Drainage issues in homeowner associations usually revolve around foundations and common areas where water stands for an extended period of time after it has stopped raining. Poor drainage is routinely caused by construction and planting practices. Nonetheless, some areas are just naturally predisposed to saturated soil because of soil type, heavy rains, flooding, high water tables or the lay of the land. For example, soils with elevated levels of clay have a tendency to have drainage problems because clay is easily compacted compared to soils composed of higher levels of sand, which drain quickly.

THE FIVE WARNING SIGNS OF POOR DRAINAGE

Standing Water - Rainwater standing for more than 48 to 72 hours after a rain may be an indication of drainage problems.

Excessive Water Flow - Large levels of water surging over an area without soil absorption can be an indication of poor drainage.

Erosion - Excessive levels of erosion can be an indication of a drainage problem.

Soil - The type of soil is a large factor in drainage issues. Sandy soils generally have high penetration rates with excellent water flow. Clay soils are completely the opposite of sandy soils and tend to restrict water penetration.

Root Decay Causing Dying Trees and Shrubs - Soil that drains poorly can cause root decay and slowly kill trees and shrubs. Leaf edges turning brown can be an indication of excessive water in the soil.

GENERAL CAUSES OF POOR DRAINAGE

Construction Practices - Grading and other earth-disturbing activities can alter established drainage patterns or water flows. During any construction or landscaping project, land should be graded so that no low spots are left without effective drainage. Maintaining the prior flow of the land as much as possible so that drainage is not disturbed is ideal. During grading or other soil excavations, soils should be segregated in order to avoid the poorer subsoil being mixed with the more fertile top soil. In order to avoid soil compaction, limit as much as possible heavy equipment use and parking on sensitive drainage areas. When backfilling soil into drainage-sensitive areas, eliminate as much as possible rocks, large roots and any other material that could impede the flow or absorption of water.

Hardpan - Hardpan is the hardened impervious layer, typically clay, occurring in or below the soil, which impairs drainage and plant growth. Hardpan soil is generally found below the uppermost topsoil layer and is generally remediated with one of two methods: first, mechanical remediation with digging or plowing to disrupt and improve the absorption of water; second, soil modification that alters the soil structure and promotes the breakdown of the hardpan. Soil modification is typically the introduction of organic materials such as manure, compost or peat onto or into the hardpan. In extreme hardpan situations, lime and gypsum can be introduced in order to increase the pH level. Both methods, mechanical and soil modification, can be used in combination with each other as well as separately very effectively. The largest drawback with utilizing only soil modification is the amount of time that the modification takes to work, which can typically be years.

Irrigation or Sprinkler System - Often overlooked but probably the most obvious source of poor drainage is the irrigation system and its settings. Improperly-set irrigation systems or overused irrigation are a cause of many drainage issues, which are fortunately easily solved. Irrigation needs to be set to water only when necessary, instead of on a particular set schedule. There are many technological innovations with irrigation systems that eliminate overwatering. These technologies can be set up to water only when necessary.

■ ■ ■

FOUNDATIONS - DRAINAGE ISSUES

Drainage issues affecting foundations around the association can pose various problems that, at times, can be difficult to resolve. These difficult resolution options are typically due to the association's budget constraints and the feasibility of access to repair. While standing water or water-soaked areas may not be aesthetically pleasing, drainage issues affecting foundations are much more serious and must be addressed in order to avoid more expense to the association in the future.

Water properly draining from the foundation is vital to the integrity of any structure. No matter what type of drainage has been initially installed or any additional waterproofing that has been applied, water or moisture problems can damage the integrity of a foundation. Initial indicators of problems can be damp crawlspaces or basements and mold or moisture on interior walls. Extreme indicators of foundation problems can be sinkholes and outright foundation failures.

While direct rain is many times the primary factor of drainage issues, there are two other water sources that cause problems: underground water and an inadequate gutter system. Underground water, be it a high water table or an intermediate wet spring, seeps into the foundation's footer and undermines the integrity from below. More common than underground water intrusion is roof runoff that attacks the foundation from the surface.

The primary purpose of gutters is to collect rainwater and distribute it away from the structure. How water runs off any roof depends upon the gutter system or lack thereof and how it travels to the ground below. And even more important is what the water does when it reaches the ground and how it disperses. The unassuming and under-appreciated splash block has a major impact upon moving water away from the foundation. If a splash block is not sufficient, there are two common options for utilizing the gutter system: first, an "extension" attached to the bottom of the gutter downspout can push water further away from the foundation; second, a small catch basin can be installed at the base of the gutter downspout. A catch basin is essentially a box buried just below the surface with an attached drainpipe that moves water away from the structure and foundation. Generally, the most economical of the two options is the downspout extension.

If there is not a gutter system, and even if there is, a gutter system adding a slope to the ground around the structure is beneficial for drainage. Sloping the ground away from the structure and compacting the soil so that water is not easily absorbed is another effective method for removing water from the foundation. Gravity will naturally pull the water away from the structure with as little as half an inch drop per foot.

The soil around the foundation needs to be compacted to prevent excess water absorption. If the soil is not properly compacted, the soil will absorb water and be more prone to erosion and settling. These compacted areas should be evaluated in 3 to 4 years in order to gauge settling and whether additional maintenance is needed.

■ ■ ■

Insurance

■ ■ ■

THE BASICS OF INSURANCE AND THE HOMEOWNERS ASSOCIATION

Insurance is one of the funny things in life — as in, funny strange. It is strange in the fact that one pays premiums faithfully in order to have insurance coverage, while filing an insurance claim can result in premiums rising or, in the worst-case scenario, the insurance policy being canceled altogether. Understanding more about the insurance policies that homeowners associations have to maintain will help board members make reasonable and prudent decisions about insurance coverage and hopefully help them continue with appropriate and affordable coverage.

With regard to insurance coverage, what to do, and sometimes more importantly what not to do, can many times be beneficial to board members. Anything written in this section regarding insurance is by no means a substitute for speaking with and obtaining guidance from a licensed insurance agent.

THE INSURANCE PROFESSIONALS

Also known as an insurance company, the insurance carrier is the producer of insurance products. Insurance policies are originated and administered and any claims paid by the insurance carrier. Since the insurance carrier has originated the policy, the insurance carrier is the party that assumes the risk of the policy.

An insurance agency is the storefront for the insurance carrier. The storefront sells and services the policy originated by the insurance carrier. This agency can sell products exclusively for one insurance carrier or offer insurance products from multiple insurance carriers. An insurance agent or retail insurance agent acts as an intermediary between an insurance company and the marketplace. Insurance agents are not insurance companies, and no coverage liabilities are taken on by the agents. Risks are transferred 100% to the insurance carrier in insurance transactions.

Insurance underwriters have the responsibility of making decisions regarding the acceptability of a particular policy submission and of determining the amount, price and conditions under which the policy submission is acceptable. On existing policies, an insurance underwriter's job is to evaluate the past performance of a particular policy and the likelihood that losses could occur on renewal. Any factor that causes a greater likelihood of loss is generally charged a higher rate.

The adjuster, or claims adjuster, is basically the party who settles insurance claims. This settlement involves the investigation of the loss and a determination of the extent of coverage. In the context of property insurance, the adjuster negotiates a settlement with the policyholder. In liability insurance, the adjuster coordinates the insured's defense and participates in settlement negotiations. Adjusters may be employees of the insurance company, or they could be independent adjusters who represent insurance companies.

Public adjusters are consultants who specialize primarily in assisting policyholders in presenting claims to insurance companies in a manner that will maximize recovery to the policyholders.

Actuaries are professionals who analyze the financial consequences of risk. Actuaries use mathematics, statistics and financial theory to study uncertain future events.

Independent third-party insurance administrators can include underwriters, claims adjusters and claims administrators. These parties can work on a contract basis with insurance companies. Insurance companies often utilize these companies for their special expertise, for operational efficiency.

■ ■ ■

OVERVIEW OF TYPICAL ASSOCIATION INSURANCE COVERAGE

What follows is typical of the different types of insurance available to associations. An association does not necessarily need all of these types of coverage. The board and the association's insurance agent should work closely in reviewing the association's governing documents in order to obtain the proper coverage required for the association. The association's insurance agent is an industry professional and should understand the association's unique needs.

Property Insurance or Master Hazard Insurance: This type of insurance generally covers all buildings, structures and personal property owned by the association, including common property and other real property. This coverage is often called Business Owners Policy or BOP, even though it is for an association's coverage. For example, if the association's clubhouse burns down, this is the insurance that provides coverage.

General Liability: In addition to coverage protecting physical property, associations should have commercial liability insurance. Unlike property damage, which often can be measured in dollar amounts, liability claims can have no limits other than those imposed by courts. This is the type of insurance that comes into play if someone is injured on the property.

Directors & Officers Liability Insurance: This provides coverage for the directors and officers of an association, in the event that they are sued in conjunction with the performance of their duties on the board of directors.

Auto: (owned, non-owned and hired): Associations with employees who drive cars, trucks or maintenance vehicles on association property, or elsewhere while carrying out association business, need auto insurance. This can provide coverage to board members performing association-related activities on behalf of the association.

Worker Compensation Insurance: This is insurance that provides wage replacement and medical benefits to employees injured in the course of employment, in exchange for mandatory relinquishment of the employee's right to sue their employer for the tort of negligence. If an association does not have payroll employees, this coverage may still be necessary per state statues to cover subcontractors working for the association. Even association volunteers may have to have coverage, in the event that they are injured while on association property performing volunteer activities.

WHAT IS INSURANCE COVERAGE & WHAT IS NOT INSURANCE COVERAGE

What is not insurance coverage, or, more accurately, what does insurance not cover? Insurance is not a maintenance program. A leaking roof that should have been replaced would fall under neglected maintenance and would usually be excluded from insurance coverage. However, if a storm comes along and blows the roof off, that generally would qualify as an insurable event and would be covered. Typically, an insurance loss must be unexpected, sudden and accidental.

Insurance is coverage by contract in which one party undertakes to indemnify or guarantee another against loss by a specified contingency or peril. It is a form of risk management primarily used to hedge against the risk of a contingent, uncertain loss. How insurance basically works is that the insurance carrier collects premiums from multiple policyholders and pools these funds in order to pay for the losses that some policyholders may incur. The policyholder is therefore protected from risk by paying a premium, with the premium dependent upon the likelihood of a loss occurring.

WHAT ARE INSURABLE RISKS

Insurable risks typically share seven common characteristics:

A large number of uniform exposure units: The existence of a large number of homogeneous exposure units allows insurers to benefit from the so-called "law of large numbers," which in effect states that, as the number of exposure units increases, the actual results are increasingly likely to become close to expected results.

The exception to the large number of uniform exposure units criterion lies with Lloyd's of London. Lloyd's of London is a secondary-market insurance provider that insures high-risk exposures such as associations that have been canceled in the primary market because of claims issues.

Definite Loss: The event that gives rise to the loss that is subject to insurance should, at least in principle, take place at a known time, in a known place and from a known cause. An example of definite loss is a fire that burns down the association's clubhouse.

Accidental Loss: The incident that constitutes filing a claim should be unexpected and not preventable or at least outside the control of the beneficiary of the insurance.

Significant Loss: The magnitude of the potential loss must be significant and worthy of insurance.

Affordable Premium: If the possibility of a claim is so high, or if the premium cost to insure is so high that the insurance expense is higher relative to the amount of protection offered, it is unlikely that anyone will purchase insurance coverage.

Calculable loss: Probability of loss and a reasonable estimate of cost of the loss must be at least estimable, if not fully calculable. Probability of loss is generally an experiential exercise, while cost has more to do with the ability of a reasonable person to make a reasonably definite and objective evaluation of the amount of the loss as a result of a claim.

Limited risk of catastrophically large losses: Insurable losses generally do not happen all at once, and individual losses are not severe enough to bankrupt the insurance carrier.

■ ■ ■

INSURANCE CANCELLATION

One important factor to consider about an association's insurance policy is that it is not like obtaining personal insurance. If an association's policy is canceled, primary market insurance companies will usually not insure that association, and the secondary insurance market may have to be utilized. The secondary insurance market is dominated by Lloyd's of London, and premiums will generally be three times or more from the primary insurance market premiums. In addition, Lloyd's of London, at a minimum, writes association policies with $25,000 deductibles or higher. These policies will many times exclude policy coverage on problem areas on which the association has had poor claims experience. For example, if the association was canceled by their insurance carrier because of three sewer backups within a 12-month period, Lloyd's commonly writes policies excluding coverage for the claims area that resulted in the association losing primary-market coverage in the first place. It is not uncommon for an association to be forced into this secondary insurance market in order to find coverage that only covers fire claims. And this limited fire-claims policy still may have a $100,000 deductible and premiums costing three times or more the prior insurance carrier's premiums.

Association Insurance is generally canceled for three primary reasons:

1. Excessive claims in a policy period - In most instances, an association would not have its insurance canceled for an occasional claim over a period of years, even if one claim is major. However, if there are excessive claims during a policy term, an insurance carrier may cancel the insurance policy. Repetitive claims of a similar nature, especially water damage claims, are very concerning to an insurance carrier because they indicate a much higher probability of additional claims in the future. This is why it is important to know the policy's deductible and, in certain situations, possibly self-insure for some claims. A rule of thumb on filing a claim is the claim should be twice the amount of the deductible in order to financially justify filing.
2. Large claims and fire claims – Large claims and fire claims are costly and, for lack of a better word, hit the underwriter's radar. If a fire or large claim happens, this is one of the times that it pays to have a long and good claims history with an insurance company. If the association has been with an insurance carrier for an extended period of time (multiple policy years) the underwriter hopefully will take this into account, and it can help the association renew its policy with the carrier. Generally speaking, cost savings must be substantial in order to change from one insurance carrier to another. If the association is hit with a large claim in a policy's first year, the policy may be canceled and the association forced to seek coverage in the secondary market.
3. Unacceptable risks found on the property – Associations being in disrepair or potential disrepair can result in policies

being canceled. At the time of an insurance policy's renewal, the underwriter may perform a property inspection. Sometimes this is done to spot-check the condition and safety of a property, which may result in the policy being canceled. Issues that are potential risks, like leaky or old roofs, outdated plumbing, high crime areas, etc., can result in an insurance cancellation. If the issues are fixable, what can be done— is to correct the condition or make the repairs as soon as possible and ask the insurance underwriter to re-inspect and reconsider the cancellation.

■ ■ ■

CLAIMS AND A PLAN OF ACTION

Most boards of directors understand how insurance basically works and what happens when claims are filed. What boards may not realize is the severe ramifications of being canceled by a primary-market insurance carrier. Primary carriers Nationwide, State Farm, Travelers, etc., are considered primary insurance carriers because they seek out and underwrite stable and predictable lines of insurance. These stable and predictable markets are fairly competitive and offer affordable premiums.

The secondary insurance market is not a competitive market, because it is dominated by just a few insurance providers. When associations end up in this market, premiums can be expected to at least triple and offer limited coverage. The goal should always be to stay in the primary market, and there are steps that can be taken to help stave off the secondary market even if an excessive number of claims has occurred.

The association plan of action should revolve first around the insurance agent, who should be an experienced writer of association insurance. The association's insurance should be consulted on the likelihood of cancelation or significantly higher premiums at renewal. Not surprisingly, depending upon the size of the insurance agency, the insurance agent may not be aware of the claims, meaning that it is never too early to get the agent involved if a problem is perceived.

Hopefully, the agent will have suggestions that will help stave off a cancelation. The agent communicating the board's concerns with the insurance carrier's underwriter can be very productive. Underwriters take agent and board interest as a positive step towards reducing future claims.

Steps that are usually taken are increasing the deductible to an amount that reduces the number of claims filed. For example, on a condominium property there might have been three frozen pipe claims filed in the past 12 months, each averaging $7,000. Increasing the deductible to $10,000 would prevent this type of claim being filed. Of course, the governing documents should be reviewed in order to ensure that the new deductible will be in compliance with these documents. In certain cases, this review should be completed by the association's attorney, and the membership should also be notified if their individual policies are going to have to make up the difference in the deductible.

if the origin of the claim is one common denominator such as fire sprinkler systems rupturing or leaking water heaters in multi-family structures, another avenue that sometimes comes into play is— letting the underwriter know that an organized effort is being taken to repair or replace these defective elements. This should reduce the claims frequency or eliminate these claims altogether.

One of the basic points to try to stress to the underwriter is how long the association has been with the insurance carrier. Again, this may not count for anything, but the author has experience with an association that had an $850,000 claim with their carrier. The only thing that kept this association from being canceled was the fact that they had been with the same carrier for over 20 years and had had a low claims experience. It is standard in the insurance industry for claims histories to be reviewed only for the prior 2 to 3 years, the underwriter making a renewal determination from that timeframe. Now, this association's insurance premiums went up significantly at renewal, but nothing like what would have happened if they had been forced to seek coverage from Lloyd's of London.

■ ■ ■

ANNUAL INSURANCE REVIEW

It is a good practice for boards of directors to review the association's insurance policy at least once a year with the association's insurance agent. This is best accomplished by having the insurance agent come to a board meeting and go through the current policy. The items that need to be discussed include coverage amounts, what is covered and what is not. Most importantly, review the valuation of the property insured and whether there is sufficient coverage in the event of a claim. The association's insurance agent is an expert in this area and can usually provide key insights into the insurance needs of the association.

COMMUNICATION WITH MEMBERSHIP INSURANCE
When there are changes in the insurance coverage of the association, it is advisable to notify the entire membership of these changes. If necessary, this will allow the membership an opportunity to seek adequate insurance as it relates to the common insurance of the association. For example, the association's insurance carrier might decide to increase the claims deductible, letting the membership know this and advising them to make sure that they review their own individual polices with their insurance agent.

■ ■ ■

MORE ON DIRECTORS & OFFICERS INSURANCE

Directors and Officers (D&O) liability insurance provides coverage in the event of a lawsuit over some board or individual director's act or omission. D&O insurance does not protect the association when a claim is made for personal injury or property damage as a result of negligent actions of the board of directors. Personal injury and property damage claims generally fall under the general liability policy of the association.

However, if a board or individual director knowingly violates the association's governing documents or applicable law, D&O insurance will not generally provide coverage. Each board member is expected to act in good faith and in the best interests of the association. A board member is obligated to apply diligence, obedience and loyalty in the exercise of their authority. With this authority come these possible grounds for a lawsuit in which D&O coverage may not apply:

Conflicts of interest
Mismanagement of funds
Irregular attendance at board meetings
Unwarranted salaries
Misrepresentation
Misstatement of financial condition
Misleading statements
Discretionary practices
Self-dealing
Actions beyond granted authority
Theft and other criminal activities

■ ■ ■

THE ASSOCIATION'S INSURANCE AGENT

Insurance agents, like doctors, have a broad range of specialties and areas of expertise. Homeowner associations have unique needs and exposures. An association should try to work only with insurance agents who have a great deal of experience writing association policies. There are too many fine points of this particular line of insurance that an inexperienced insurance agent could overlook or not realize.

The association's insurance agent should review the association's governing documents, recommending the correct and minimum insurance required and additional insurance coverage if necessary. Along with the insurance carrier's underwriter, the insurance agent should inspect association property and identify potential claims exposures that need to be addressed. The agent should review and verify the property values for replacement costs as compared to coverage and make adjustments as necessary.

The agent has a responsibility to educate the board about coverage, exclusions and limitations. The agent should also assist in educating the membership about the association's insurance policy, where the association's responsibilities end and the member's responsibilities begin. The agent provides insurance certificates or evidence of coverage to mortgage lenders. The insurance agent should provide guidance in how claims and deductibles are processed. Most importantly, the agent should help review the association's claims each year and recommend ways to reduce future claims if possible.

The agent should also provide additional insurance quotes from other carriers if better coverage becomes available.

■ ■ ■

FILING AN INSURANCE CLAIM

If the need arises to file a claim with the association's insurance carrier, certain factors need to be taken into account.

First: Is the potential claim amount more than the insurance deductible? The rule of thumb on filing claims is that the claim is double the deductible amount.

Second: How many claims have been filed this year, and is this claim a recurring item such as a leaking water heater? Insurance underwriters typically look at a number of factors when determining whether to raise the insurance premiums or cancel coverage altogether because of excessive claims. However, one factor that tends to negatively affect renewals is claim frequency of a particular faulty element. For example, if lightning has struck the clubhouse, what are the odds of that happening again? Probably not that high.

However, if a condominium property is ten years old and, in the course of a year, has four leaking water heater claims in excess of $5,000, considering the age of the property and life expectancy of water heaters there are more claims on the horizon. So instead of filing a claim in this situation, it may make economic sense to not file a claim and instead work on a program to encourage members to inspect and replace their aging water heaters.

Third: Obtain input from the association insurance agent about whether or not to file a claim. Insurance agents do receive reduced commissions because of claims, but they receive even larger reductions when a policy is not renewed.

FILING AN INSURANCE CLAIM OR A CLAIM AGAINST A THIRD PARTY

Filing any type of damage claim may on the surface appear to be a simple process, but if not done properly it can result in not collecting on the claim. Perhaps there is nothing more upsetting than having a claim denied or not covered because basic steps were not followed.

First, the incident needs to be documented precisely, the more documentation the better.

All related materials (e.g. invoices, police reports, etc.) should be retained to be submitted to the insurance company or another third party.

If there are witnesses, obtain their names and telephone numbers.

Photographs and even video can help document damage. Photographs and videos are easily worth a thousand words when it comes to filing claims.

Notify the association's insurance provider as soon as possible that a claim file may need to be opened and the nature of the claim. Delaying notifying the insurance agent can cause irreparable issues that may negate the policy coverage. It may be advisable to notify the insurance agent even if the claim does not appear to have any merit or any liability to the association. Because of the liability that comes with all unnatural deaths, it is always advisable for the board to notify the insurance agent when an unnatural death occurs within the association.

Third-Party Claims - Third-party claims are claims such as a person running their automobile into the front entrance sign or a utility company damaging an association fence while installing a telephone pole. With an automobile accident, the police should always be called to write a police report. When the police are called, the person will have to show proof of insurance, and all the needed information from the driver can be obtained. With a third party such as a utility company, obtain the names of the crew who did the damage and their supervisor's name and number. Take a picture of the truck's license plate, since large utility companies may have many trucks out performing work.

Insurance Claims - If an incident reaches the standard and level of filing an insurance claim, the insurance company must be notified within a reasonable timeframe. Not notifying the insurance company within a reasonable amount of time can jeopardize the chances of the insurance company paying the claim. After notification, a claim number will be generated, and a claims adjuster will be assigned to resolve the matter.

■ ■ ■

THE RISKS IN CHANGING THE ASSOCIATION'S INSURANCE CARRIER

Comparing insurance carriers is a good practice to ensure that premiums are competitive. However, there are risks with changing carriers if the association has had a good claims history with their current carrier.

If an association has a good claims history over an extended period of time, this is worth something to the current carrier. For example, if an association has been with a carrier for 10 years without a significant claim, a large claim popping up may not negatively affect the relationship, negatively meaning a large spike in premiums or the coverage being cancelled. Being cancelled from a primary-market insurance carrier can result in an association having to obtain coverage from the secondary insurance market, such as Lloyd's of London.

Secondary insurance market premiums are usually as much or more than three times the primary market rates. The secondary market polices will, many times, have substantial deductibles of $50,000 to $100,000. Also, many times secondary market policies will exclude from coverage the particular claim issue(s) that caused the original cancellation. For instance, if fire sprinklers ruptured, Lloyd's would exclude coverage on any future fire sprinkler claims.

There are other risks, such as that the new carrier will lose their appetite for the particular line of business and not renew at the end of the term. For example, carriers might enter and exit the multifamily structure insurance market. However, most other risks pale in comparison with losing a good long-term claims history. An association that has been with an insurance carrier for a period of time with good service from a claims standpoint needs to think long and hard about changing carriers. The potential savings must be sufficient to offset this potential risk.

■ ■ ■

FIDELITY BOND

THE MANAGEMENT COMPANY FIDELITY BOND

A fidelity bond, while called a bond, is not actually a bond. It is an insurance policy that provides coverage for losses resulting from fraudulent acts. It is most commonly used for fraudulent acts of a management company's employee or agent. A fidelity bond protects the association's funds and other valuables from acts of fraud, dishonesty, forgery, theft, larceny, embezzlement, wrongful abstraction, willful misapplication, misappropriation and criminal acts from guilty parties. These guilty parties might be directors, board members, board officers, committee members, association employees, association volunteers or agents of the association.

Because insurance companies have varying underwriting guidelines for fidelity bonds, it is difficult to address specific coverage requirements and the various situations in which coverage would apply. The key point regarding fidelity bonds is that, without exception, the management company must have a fidelity bond. While some state statutes and association governing documents require the management company or managing agent to carry a fidelity bond, this may not always be the case. If a management company does not have a fidelity bond or tries to say that they have a crime provision in the company's insurance policy, this should be a concern to the board of directors. If a management company's corporate policy has a crime provision or crime rider, this, in most circumstances, only protects the management company's funds, not their association client's funds.

Adequate coverage is another consideration of the management company's fidelity bond. Even if a management company has a fidelity bond, there may be insufficient coverage because this bond provides coverage to all their clients. Because of the expense, many management companies carry coverage well under $250,000, while some larger management companies have a million-dollar fidelity bond.

A study by the Association of Certified Fraud Examiners (ACFE) found that the median embezzlement loss was $145,000. However, the same study found that 22% of embezzlement cases involved losses of at least $1 million. The fidelity bond coverage amount "comfort level" will vary from association to association, but a rule of thumb is two times the association's total annual assessment. Fortunately or unfortunately, depending upon how the matter is viewed, management company embezzlements usually involve multiple association clients and thus usually limit one individual association's overall loss because funds are stolen from multiple associations.

KEY FINDINGS OF THE ASSOCIATION OF CERTIFIED FRAUD EXAMINERS (ACFE) STUDY FINDINGS

- The median duration of time between when the fraud began and when it was detected was 18 months.
- Anti-fraud controls reduced losses and shortened the detection time. Losses were lower at companies that had implemented common anti-fraud controls, significantly lower than at companies who had no such controls.
- 28.8% of all companies with less than 100 employees had experienced fraud, with an average loss of $154,000.
- 23.6% of all companies with more than 100 employees had experienced fraud, with an average loss of $128,000.
- The study found that larger companies with anti-fraud controls detected fraud earlier, thus reducing the average fraud loss.

THE ASSOCIATION'S FIDELITY BOND

An association can have their own individual fidelity bond. It is important to make certain that the association's fidelity bond provides coverage for wrongdoing, not only by members of the board/association, but also by vendors or agents of the association. Agents and vendors coverage may need to be added. An association fidelity bond may not automatically provide coverage for the acts of non-association members. The premiums on an association fidelity bond are usually very reasonable, well under $1,000 annually.

■ ■ ■

Issues That Arise

■ ■ ■

COMMERCIAL ACTIVITY WITHIN THE ASSOCIATION

In this author's career, he has encountered an array of businesses operated within associations. Be it single-family home associations or multifamily associations, it seems like every association has had to deal with members operating businesses from their homes, at one time or another. The author has encountered everything from a multiple-chair hair salon to a telemarketing call center to a medical doctor seeing patients in their home. The most interesting was an association member who hosted Sunday morning church services from his home. This was discovered because of the ensuing parking issues.

The Internet has released a range of commercial activities within associations that were virtually unheard-of 10 years ago. Receiving a great deal of attention within associations are overnight rentals or weekly vacation rental services such as Airbnb, Vacation Rental by Owner (VRBO)and HomeAway. These commercial activities have been challenges to many associations. While some association governing documents do address short-term rentals, interestingly enough, the majority of association documents make no mention of the issue.

Difficulty may arise when attempting to prove that a commercial activity is actually occurring within a member's home or, more precisely, determining this business activity to a legal certainty, so that the association's governing documents can be enforced.

Affected association boards are routinely scrutinizing online sites such as Airbnb and VRBO for any short-term rental advertisements within their association. However, if a member is advertising on one of these sites, does that constitute legal proof that the member is "actually" renting out their home or part of their home? For example, the member advertising might admit, "Yes, I advertise, but I have never had anyone book." An attorney could possibly defend this action by stating that the governing documents do not prohibit advertising, only actually renting.

Another consideration is home offices. With many members working from home, does this constitute a business operated from their homes? What if a salesperson has a second phone line installed for a business phone or fax machine, but does not have an actual room within their home with an office setup?

The author had a situation where a telephone call center was being operating out of a single-family home. This call center operated for a number of months with about a dozen people coming in the morning and leaving in the late afternoon. Even with all of the automobiles and people coming and going, the only legal point or verifiable element that the association could make in court was that a commercial T3 communication telephone line had been installed at the residence. Fortunately, with the people arriving and leaving, the preponderance of the T3 line was deemed to be enough for the association to prevail.

Short-term rentals can be even more difficult to substantiate because of the low-profile nature of this online enterprise. The author had an association member who was "allegedly" renting her home out as a bed-and-breakfast. This was only discovered when a "guest" accidentally backed their car into a neighbor's car and discussions ensued. It could not be determined where or whether the association member was advertising her home for this purpose. The owner was called to a hearing before the board of directors to discuss the matter. During the hearing, the member denied that she was operating a bed-and-breakfast from her home and that she "just had a lot of different friends visiting." Nonetheless, after the board hearing, the member's many "friends" stopped visiting.

If questions arise about commercial activities, the first place to seek guidance is the association's governing documents, generally the CC&Rs. (Certain situations may arise that involve the articles of incorporation.) If there is language specifically addressing commercial activities, it may be similar to and as nonspecific as this:

"Section 7.8 - Commercial Activities. No commercial activities can be conducted on any lot or from any structure, common or private, within the association. No commercial vehicles can be maintained within the association."

The example language above is extremely broad and could be deemed vague.

One basic rule of contract law, as governing documents are essentially contracts between the association and the membership, is that contract conditions must be certain. This legal principle can more accurately be summarized as that contractual terms must be sufficiently certain and not too vague or ambiguous to be legally enforceable. It is usually advisable to avoid having a judge determine whether or not contract conditions are certain.

If there is no specific commercial activities language in the governing documents, a fall-back would be the nuisance clause for possible enforcement. An example of a nuisance clause:

"Section 7.2 - Nuisance. No obnoxious, offensive or unlawful activity shall be conducted within any home or lot, or on or about the Common Elements, nor shall anything be done thereon or therein which may be or which may become an annoyance or nuisance to the other Owners or endanger the health and safety of any Owner."

While the nuisance clause is better than nothing, it can be extremely broad, such as the commercial activities example noted previously. This nuisance clause language could be deemed legally unenforceable.

If the association's governing documents do not include language that specifically addresses commercial activities, many times the CC&Rs and articles of incorporation will have a statement of purpose or reason for establishing the association.

"Declarant is the owner of a parcel of real estate containing a total of approximately 417.67 acres located on Happy Glen Avenue near the intersection of Main Street in Springfield, Springfield County, as more particularly described on Exhibit A attached hereto (the "Land"). The Land has constructed 364 single family lots in which Declarant will constructed a total of 364 residential single-family homes..." "

This statement of purpose clearly establishes the association as a "residential" entity. In certain instances, this may be the only language in a set of governing documents giving the association authority or standing as solely a residential community.

If the governing documents do not provide specific authority regarding commercial activities or have enough teeth to enforce, pursuing a document amendment may be an option. While it is typically difficult to amend governing documents because of the high threshold of affirmative votes needed, many times this may be the association's only viable option. Working with the association's attorney on crafting the proper language that can survive being dissected by a judge is of paramount importance.

When it comes to restricting commercial enterprises, attorneys are tasked with writing amendments that are even more difficult to encapsulate. The gray area of this situation is what constitutes a commercial enterprise. Many times in governing documents there will be language similar to: "No commercial activities are permitted in which nonmembers will be entering and leaving members' homes such as what is found in a retail store operation." Thus, this wording in an amendment could forbid Tupperware parties.

Because of home offices and the occasional Tupperware party, attorneys will ideally craft wording that revolves around the problems created by commercial enterprises. If an enterprise is invisible from the street and neighbors, does not generate noise and does not cause traffic and parking issues, the attorney many times will craft the amendment language on the negative impact. This is generally done with emphasis on parking and traffic-related impacts or possible safety concerns.

If amending the association's governing documents is not a practical option, another possible less arduous path may be local ordinances or zoning. Most municipalities have ordnances restricting commercial activities within residential homes and residential communities. Certain activities might even fall under state regulatory agencies. While code enforcement or other governmental agencies may have broader enforcement abilities than the association, there is still a level of proof or evidence of an ordnance infraction that has to be met. Code enforcement officers often encounter the same issues that boards and association managers encounter: knowing that there is commercial activity being conducted, but being unable to prove this to a level of certainty in a court of law.

While commercial activities can be a very complex situation within any association, there are two main elements of resolution: first, governing document interpretation, plan of action and possibly seeking legal guidance from the association's attorney to clarify or address possible pitfalls; second, documentation of the business activity. The association manager, board members and neighbors need to document all activities witnessed or witnessed by others. Detailed and dated activity records on a number of occasions have been the critical element in boards being successful in hearings and court cases.

■ ■ ■

GOING GATED

There is occasional debate among boards and the association membership about the pros and cons regarding gated communities. The debate is over whether to become a gated community or to do away with the expense of being a gated community. When many think of a gated community, they think of aspects such as security, exclusivity and expensive homes. All the varied aspects of a gated community merit a more analytical review of the benefits and drawbacks.

In the United States, gated communities can be traced back two centuries to St. Louis. In Charles Savage's book, *Architecture of the Private Streets of St. Louis,* he details how "[f]or nearly sixty years, St. Louis' private streets remained the only defense against inadequate municipal protection available to the residents of the city." The first gated community in St. Louis was the development Lucas Place in 1851. However, it has only been since the 1980s that gated communities have become more prominent in the rest of the nation.

The additional security and privacy are the common characteristics that home buyers seek from gated communities. While these two characteristics can be argued, the gate can make it more difficult for nonmembers to access. Security experts also point to private roads with limited entrances and exits as a good crime deterrent. Even with a gate, there is still no certainty that the community would not succumb to criminal activity. The gate is nothing more than a deterrent, as are alarm systems. One proposed theory is that a gated community may not decrease crime, but, in fact, may increase crime since criminals may believe that a gated community has better things to steal.

Privacy may be enhanced by deterring door-to-door solicitations. Traffic can also be reduced by preventing non-community members from using the community's streets. Less traffic will equal less noise and safer driving conditions for the community. It is important to realize that gates are not a panacea for security, as piggybacking behind other cars entering through the gate is difficult to prevent and very common.

The premise in real estate about gated communities is that it increases property values, because of the exclusiveness and possible scarcity of homes because of the fewer homes within the community for sale at any given time.

While the benefits of a gated community are impressive, these benefits come at a price. The cost to just install an electronic gate can range from $15,000 to $50,000 depending upon use and other features. Features can range from cameras to bollards. Bollards are metal devises that spring up behind the car once the gate opens. Bollards are to prevent other cars from piggybacking behind a car entering.

The initial cost of the gate installation is probably not as big a budget hurdle for most associations as is the ongoing maintenance. Because of the nature of an automatic gate continuously moving and commonly being damaged by cars, the maintenance costs can be excessive. At a minimum, an annual budget for one gate's maintenance is typically $15,000 a year. Depending upon the size of the community and use, this gate maintenance can easily exceed $25,000 a year.

However, the largest budget concern is going to be street maintenance and repaving. If the streets are currently maintained by a municipality, the association will have to take ownership of or responsibility for the streets once a gate is installed. Public streets cannot be gated. Depending upon the condition of the roads and use, budgeting for repairs can be in the many thousands of dollars. A rule of thumb cost estimate for repaving a mile of road is $500,000. This dollar amount can vary based upon a number of factors, but this can be a starting point from which to calculate the future expense. If the streets are currently private, these costs should already be accounted for in the association's annual budget and reserve funding.

If an association is considering the installation of an entrance gate, one of the first steps should be seeking council from the association's attorney. The association's attorney will outline the steps that will need to be taken, which may require the CC&Rs to be amended.

While there are a number of benefits to living in a gated community, the increase in home values is probably the most impactful. The biggest proponents of living in a gated community will stress the lower traffic throughout the community and the feeling of additional security that the gate provides.

■ ■ ■

SHORT-TERM RENTALS

Short-term rentals, be they overnight stays or week-long rentals, seem to be becoming more prevalent in homeowner and condominium associations. Some blame the advent of online services that help facilitate these activities, or they could seem more prevalent because of the ease of finding out that a neighbor is advertising their home online under one of these services. Some of the most popular online short-term or vacation rentals services are Airbnb, Craigslist and VRBO.

Association members and, in some instances, tenants of members are renting out rooms or entire homes by posting home descriptions and photographs on these online services. Users book these homes online, many times, without ever meeting the owner. If they do meet the homeowner, it is upon arrival at the home. After the stay, the owner and short-term tenant can publically evaluate their experiences on the site.

The definition of short-term rentals can vary from just overnight lodging up to any length of stay less than 12 months. However, the most common definition of a short-term rental is any stay less than 30 days in length. Additionally, many municipalities have established definitions of and conditions for what is considered a short-term rental.

While some municipalities regulate or prohibit short-term rentals in residential homes, some association governing documents limit or prohibit short-term rentals as well. Municipalities are regulating short-term rentals more aggressively due to lost tax revenue (the Hospitality Tax that hotels collect) and lobbying from the hospitality industry concerning this online competition. Municipalities are using zoning and other accommodation regulations as the basis for fines and additional regulations.

Despite the hospitality industry's lobbying efforts, municipalities are becoming more open to short-term leases and vacation rentals. Until recently, Mount Pleasant, South Carolina, near Charleston did not allow residential short-term rentals. Now individuals in Mount Pleasant can purchase a one-time $50 retail license, pay the 12.5% hospitality tax and rent out individual rooms in their homes. The City of San Francisco up until last year strictly prohibited residential short-term leases and now has eliminated these restrictions and implemented regulations allowing the practice. For now, New York City appears to be one of the few large municipalities that continue to prohibit rentals of residences for less than 30 days.

In recent news stories, associations have been front-and-center in addressing some of the issues arising from short-term rentals. There is a well-known California court case involving an association member who was fined $106,000 for offering short-term rentals at his home. A San Diego Superior Court judge ruled that the member had knowingly violated the association's CC&Rs of no leases of less than 90 days in length and upheld the fine.

Another well-publicized Airbnb incident involved a Los Angeles interior designer who was liable for over $10,000 worth of damages after an Airbnb guest clogged her condominium unit's toilet. The Airbnb guest reportedly caused the toilet to overflow and failed to address the problem and thus allowed water to pour into the condominium hallways and other nearby units in the early hours of the morning. Unfortunately, this water leak was not the first incident that this homeowner had had with a short-term rental guest. An earlier guest had driven their car into a neighbor's garage, causing damage.

Who paid for the damages of these short-term rental guests? Airbnb has a program called Host Guarantee that offers up to $1 million in coverage. Unfortunately, Airbnb Host Guarantee only provides coverage for the actual short-term rental domicile. The coverage does not extend to outside the actual unit. In this case, the coverage only paid for the plumber who unclogged the toilet.

While there are a multitude of arguments pro and con for short-term rentals in an association, one of the most common arguments against is the transient atmosphere that is created. This type of atmosphere could be disruptive, but the common pro argument for short-term leases revolves around individual homeowner rights over their property.

Putting individual property rights aside, even if a municipality permits short-term rentals, associations may prevent association members from this activity if the governing documents have certain provisions. If the association's CC&Rs specifically deny short-term rentals and adequately define what a short-term rental is, enforcement can generally be straightforward. If the language on short-term rentals is vague, the association's attorney may need to be involved for clarification on how the matter can be enforced.

If the CC&Rs are void of any language specifically prohibiting short-term rentals, most governing documents have provisions limiting business activities or operating a business from a member's home. These are areas that many times require the association's attorney to expand upon and clarify for enforcement viability. If there are no CC&Rs in place or any other provisions that can be used to address the short-term rental issue, amending the association's governing documents may be the only avenue available.

Of course, if an association wishes to allow or has no ability to prevent short-term rentals, some considerations should be taken into account: first, if the association is going to sanction short-term rentals then the governing documents must not have a provision preventing them, as, obviously, the CC&Rs cannot be ignored; second, the association member who is going to be renting out their home must obtain the proper insurance to address any issues that may arise, and the association's insurance agent should be consulted on these additional insurance requirements as they relate to the association's insurance coverage: third, rules and guidelines must be established for both the association member who is renting and the guest who will be staying under the short-term lease.

Affected association boards are routinely checking these online sites for any short-term rental activity within their association. This virtual Internet world keeps everyone honest and also mitigates the pretext that "I just have a lot of friends coming over and staying with me."

■ ■ ■

WITHHOLDING DUES PAYMENTS

"I do not use the association swimming pool, so I am going to deduct $25 from my assessment" or "since the association is not keeping property values up, I am not going to pay my dues"—whatever the excuse or reasoning may be, associations are routinely challenged by members who feel that they can avoid paying the assessment. Whatever the reasoning, these members usually feel justified or sincere in their rebelliousness. Fortunately, association governing documents have provisions specifically spelling out the requirements of members and their assessments.

What follows is a sample of language taken out of an association's CC&Rs:

Section 8.2 Powers; Lien for Assessment. In the administration of the operation and management of the Property, the Association shall have and is hereby granted the authority and power to enforce the provisions of this Declaration, to levy and collect assessments in the manner provided in Article X below and in the Bylaws and adopt, promulgate and enforce such rules and regulations as the Association may deem to be in the best interest of the Owners in accordance with the Bylaws. Any sum assessed by the Association is due within thirty (30) days, without offset, and any sum remaining unpaid after a period of thirty (30) days or longer shall constitute a lien on the Unit, with respect to which such sum has been assessed upon filing in accordance with state statute and shall be enforceable by the Association in accordance with state statute and Section 8.7 of the Bylaws.

While no two sets of governing documents are written the same, deeded mandatory associations will have language similar to the above. These governing document provisions provide the association with the legal authority and ability to collect assessments. Without this type of language, the association would not have the legal authority to lien and collect assessments. Conversely, volunteer deeded associations or non-mandatory associations generally have no ability to lien for assessments, as members volunteer to pay assessments.

Assessment offsets or short-payments are no more allowed than refusing to pay the entire assessment amount. In the example above—"Any sum assessed...is due...without offset"—this wording specifically disallows offsets. Fortunately, even if there is no wording specifically prohibiting offsets, most judges will not condone any type of offset as it relates to properly applied assessments.

■ ■ ■

SQUATTERS RIGHTS/ ADVERSE POSSESSION

Squatters rights, or adverse possession, is an antiquated legal situation that occurs, with regard to homeowner associations, when someone moves into a vacant home and makes it their residence without the owner's permission. With adverse possession, a squatter can acquire another person's home without compensation by living in the home for a specific period of time. This time period can vary per individual state statute.

To make a claim for adverse possession, the squatter must overtly occupy the property wholly and maintain the property as their residence. To occupy the property wholly, the squatter must keep out all other parties, meaning that other squatters cannot be making the same claim and other parties cannot be coming and going.

Homeowner associations have been dealing with adverse possession since the beginning of the housing crisis in 2008. During the crisis, when some homeowners abandoned their homes, and in some instances even after financial institutions had foreclosed, squatters would move in and take up residence in these abandoned homes.

No community has been exempt. In 2013, a $2.5 million-dollar mansion in Boca Raton, Florida, was taken over by a squatter.

The mansion was a bank-owned foreclosure when a 23-year-old man took up residence, claiming adverse possession. Apparently no one saw the man break into the home, and thus it was a civil matter and not a criminal matter, so the police were unable to remove the man. In Florida at the time (Florida revised their adverse possession statutes in 2014), if a squatter could maintain adverse possession for seven years, the squatter could claim legal title to the home. The 23-year-old man in this case, being knowledgeable of the law, went as far as contacting the county appraiser's office to notify them of his possession and thus apparently his intent to stay for the required seven years.

Another current trend in the adverse possession situation is a squatter having a written lease to the home. If a neighbor inquires or if the police are called to address someone living in the "abandoned" home, a lease is produced. If the police are involved and a lease is produced, the matter usually becomes a civil legal issue, even if the writer of the lease is not the owner of record with the register of deeds.

There are at least two different "lease" situations that seem to arise: (1) the squatter has somehow come up with a lease to the property that they know is bogus; (2) the squatter has entered into what they believe is a valid lease with a third party, which represents that they have the legal authority to lease the property. The latter is a scam in which the squatter/tenant has been duped by a third party into renting an abandoned home or bank-owned home.

No matter which version of the two possible events occurs, it can be extremely difficult to evict the squatter, especially if the home is just abandoned and the original homeowner is not in the picture to pursue eviction. With a home that is completely bank-owned from a completed foreclosure, the bank can file for eviction. However, the lease, even a bogus lease, may have legal standing in a court of law under certain circumstances. With these legal hurdles, banks have been known to pay squatters or tenants to leave the property.

While most adverse possessions that arise in homeowner associations are rarely this extreme, there are still challenges that occur with abandoned homes and bank-foreclosed homes. Squatters taking up "residence" in these homes do not have the best interests of the individual properties or the overall association at heart.

While each state has their own specific statutes that govern adverse possession, there are, at a minimum, five basic conditions that generally have to be met in order to successfully gain legal ownership:

- Actual possession of the home: The person in adverse possession must physically use the property as a property owner would. This behavior, besides living in the home, could include maintaining the property, such as mowing the yard, repairing the structure or even changing locks.
- Non-permissive or hostile use of the home: The person in adverse possession must have entered the home without permission from the actual owner.
- Open and obvious use of the home: If the legal owner is aware of the adverse possession, this condition is met. However, this condition can also be met by the person in adverse possession simply posting a sign noting such in a window.

- Continuous use of the home: The person making a claim of adverse possession must hold the home continuously for the time period required by that state's governing statutes.
- Exclusive use of the home: The person claiming adverse possession must inhabit the home to the exclusion of the actual owner. If at any time the actual owner inhabits the home, either adverse possession cannot be claimed or the time requirement starts over from that point.

In most instances, posting "No Trespassing" signs in the front windows of bank-owned properties and making regular property inspections eliminate the ability of squatters to successfully claim adverse possession. Abandoned homes pose more of an issue. However, with foreclosure rates dropping, this is becoming less and less of an issue. Fortunately, in most jurisdictions in the United States squatters rarely can make successful legal claims for adverse possession, but getting squatters out of a home swiftly may still be a challenge.

■ ■ ■

TOO MANY BOARD MEMBERS

Occasionally, usually during or after an annual meeting election, adding an additional member to the board of directors is suggested. This most often comes up when there has been a close election and a high-quality candidate has barely lost their run for the board. While it is very fortunate for an association to have more than enough quality members willing to serve, just adding a board member is usually not a simple process.

First, do the association's governing documents allow for the board of directors to be expanded? The bylaws are normally the association governing document that would address adding board members, if this is addressed at all. If adding board members is addressed, the process set forth should be followed before any action is taken.

If adding board members is not addressed in the governing documents, the governing documents could possibly be amended. The section on how to amend the particular governing document is usually located towards the back of the particular governing document. The association's attorney should be consulted and involved in the amendment process in order to ensure that the process is completed properly.

It is important to recognize that, if the bylaws have wording similar to: "The board of directors will be comprised of five members," this means five or less, not six, seven, etc. The consequences of failing to follow the governing documents on the correct number of board members can be fraught with liability for the board of directors. This is imperative because just adding a board position without either the proper authority or amending the documents can delegitimize any actions that the entire board takes thereafter. For example, if the board votes to send a delinquent member to the attorney for collections, an improperly elected or appointed board member's vote could be challenged by the delinquent member's attorney.

More than likely, moving forward, all board decisions could be challenged. Even more concerning would be the directors and officers insurance coverage. If the board of directors is supposed to have a set number of members, the additional member may not have coverage.

Practical issues also arise with increasing the number of board members. Additional board members can make the voting process more difficult. For example, if the additional board member results in the board being an even number of members, this tie in board votes can hinder the association from moving issues forward. Board meetings can tend to run longer with additional members, as well.

Committees are one viable and productive alternative to increasing the number of board members. Placing high-quality association members on committees can be a huge benefit. Committees are a great way to prepare future board members while assisting the current board and community.

■ ■ ■

"The Man In The Arena"

"It is not the critic who counts; not the man who points out how the strong man stumbles, or where the doer of deeds could have done them better. The credit belongs to the man who is actually in the arena, whose face is marred by dust and sweat and blood; who strives valiantly; who errs, who comes short again and again, because there is no effort without error and shortcoming; but who does actually strive to do the deeds; who knows great enthusiasms, the great devotions; who spends himself in a worthy cause; who at the best knows in the end the triumph of high achievement, and who at the worst, if he fails, at least fails while daring greatly, so that his place shall never be with those cold and timid souls who neither know victory nor defeat."

Theodore Roosevelt - From his April 23, 1910, speech at the Sorbonne, Paris, France.

■ ■ ■

Appendix

Balance Sheet - Operating
Happy Glen Homeowners Association
End Date: 5/31/2017

Asset				
Assets				
	10-1001-0000	Cash - Operating	$3,691.71	
	10-1005-0000	Cash - Reserves	$70,933.97	
Total Assets:				$74,625.68
Total Assets:				**$74,625.68**
Liabilities & Equity				
Liabilities & Equity				
	25-2801-0000	Paving Reserves	$33,690.05	
	25-2802-0000	Plumbing Reserves	$16,217.97	
	25-2803-0000	Pool Reserves	$9,396.73	
	25-2902-0000	Wall Reserves	$11,587.21	
	25-2960-0000	Retained Earnings	$6,576.27	
Total Liabilities & Equity:				$77,468.23
		Net Income Gain /	($2,842.55)	
				($2,842.55)
Total Liabilities &				**$74,625.68**

(Unaudited) Income Statement - Operating

Happy Glen Homeowners Association
05/31/2017

Description	Current Period Actual	Current Period Budget	Current Period Variance	Year-to-date Actual	Year-to-date Budget	Year-to-date Variance	Annual Budget
OPERATING							
Income							
3001-0000 Regular Assessments	$ 9,150.00	$ 8,550.00	$ 600.00	$ 42,605.00	$ 42,750.00	($ 145.00)	$102,600.00
3004-0000 Late Fees	$ 160.00	-	$ 160.00	$ 440.00	-	$ 440.00	-
3010-0000 Interest - Reserves	$ 9.04	-	$ 9.04	$ 42.01	-	$ 42.01	-
Total Income	$ 9,319.04	$ 8,550.00	$ 769.04	$ 43,087.01	$ 42,750.00	$337.01	$102,600.00
Total OPERATING	**$ 9,319.04**	**$ 8,550.00**	**$ 769.04**	**$ 43,087.01**	**$ 42,750.00**	**$ 337.01**	**$102,600.00**
OPERATING							
Expense							
4008-0000 General Exterior	-	$ 20.83	$ 20.83	-	$ 104.15	$ 104.15	$ 250.00
4033-0000 Plumbing Repairs	-	$ 312.50	$ 312.50	-	$ 1,562.50	$ 1,562.50	$ 3,750.00
4037-0000 Electrical Repairs	-	$ 16.67	$ 16.67	-	$ 83.35	$ 83.35	$ 200.00
4038-0000 Outside Lighting Repairs	-	$ 16.67	$ 16.67	-	$ 83.35	$ 83.35	$ 200.00
4048-0000 Streets & Paving	-	$ 41.67	$ 41.67	-	$ 208.35	$ 208.35	$ 500.00
5000-0000 Landscape Contract	$ 2,883.25	$ 1,541.67	($ 1,341.58)	$ 7,498.00	$ 7,708.35	$ 210.35	$ 18,500.00
5003-0000 Tree Trimming &	-	$ 250.00	$ 250.00	$ 1,065.00	$ 1,250.00	$ 185.00	$ 3,000.00
5004-0000 Landscape	-	$ 273.58	$ 273.58	-	$ 1,367.90	$ 1,367.90	$ 3,283.00
5005-0000 Landscape - Other	$ 13,254.00	$ 291.67	($12,962.33)	$ 15,500.00	$ 1,458.35	($14,041.65)	$ 3,500.00
5007-0000 Pine Needles - Straw	-	$ 350.00	$ 350.00	$ 189.00	$ 1,750.00	$ 1,561.00	$ 4,200.00
5016-0000 Irrigation System &	-	$ 20.83	$ 20.83	-	$ 104.15	$ 104.15	$ 250.00
5400-0000 Pool Service Contract	-	$ 191.67	$ 191.67	-	$ 958.35	$ 958.35	$ 2,300.00
5404-0000 Pool Repairs	$ 3,056.63	$ 20.83	($ 3,035.80)	$ 3,056.63	$ 104.15	($ 2,952.48)	$ 250.00
5406-0000 Pool Supplies &	-	$ 166.67	$ 166.67	-	$ 833.35	$ 833.35	$ 2,000.00
6002-0000 Utilities - Electric	$ 165.00	$ 225.00	$ 60.00	$ 541.69	$ 1,125.00	$ 583.31	$ 2,700.00
6004-0000 Utilities - Water &	$ 1,312.33	$ 2,000.00	$ 687.67	$ 5,042.16	$ 10,000.00	$ 4,957.84	$ 24,000.00
6005-0000 Utilities - Storm Water	$ 218.56	$ 166.67	($ 51.89)	$ 1,092.82	$ 833.35	($ 259.47)	$ 2,000.00
6012-0000 Utilities - Telephone	-	$ 47.92	$ 47.92	$ 263.72	$ 239.60	($ 24.12)	$ 575.00
7042-0000 Snow Removal	-	-	-	$ 1,025.00	-	($ 1,025.00)	-
Total Expenses - Buildings & Grounds	$ 20,889.77	$ 5,954.85	($14,934.92)	$ 35,274.02	$ 29,774.25	($5,499.77)	$ 71,458.00
Expense							
8002-0000 Office	$ 26.57	$ 27.08	$ 0.51	$ 74.90	$ 135.40	$ 60.50	$ 325.00
8005-0000 Professional Services	-	$ 16.67	$ 16.67	-	$ 83.35	$ 83.35	$ 200.00
8006-0000 Accounting Expense	-	$ 79.17	$ 79.17	-	$ 395.85	$ 395.85	$ 950.00
8008-0000 Legal Expense	-	$ 41.67	$ 41.67	-	$ 208.35	$ 208.35	$ 500.00
8010-0000 Insurance Premiums	$ 169.22	$ 125.00	($ 44.22)	$ 846.10	$ 625.00	($ 221.10)	$ 1,500.00
8014-0000 Management Fees	$ 420.00	$ 420.00	-	$ 2,100.00	$ 2,100.00	-	$ 5,040.00
8016-0000 Printing, Newsletter,	$ 6.66	$ 8.33	$ 1.67	$ 87.18	$ 41.65	($ 45.53)	$ 100.00
8018-0000 Pool License/Permits	-	$ 10.42	$ 10.42	-	$ 52.10	$ 52.10	$ 125.00
8024-0000 Late Fees Paid to Management	$ 70.00	-	($ 70.00)	$ 180.00	-	($ 180.00)	-
8073-0000 Meetings &	-	$ 16.67	$ 16.67	-	$ 83.35	$ 83.35	$ 200.00
8083-0000 Social Committee	-	$ 8.33	$ 8.33	-	$ 41.65	$ 41.65	$ 100.00
Total Expenses - Administrative	$ 692.45	$ 753.34	$ 60.89	$ 3,288.18	$ 3,766.70	$478.52	$ 9,040.00
Expense							
9801-0000 Paving Reserves	-	$ 909.67	$ 909.67	$ 3,638.68	$ 4,548.35	$ 909.67	$ 10,916.00
9802-0000 Plumbing Reserves	-	$ 541.67	$ 541.67	$ 2,166.68	$ 2,708.35	$ 541.67	$ 6,500.00
9803-0000 Pool Reserves	-	$ 195.25	$ 195.25	$ 781.00	$ 976.25	$ 195.25	$ 2,343.00
9902-0000 Wall Reserves	-	$ 195.25	$ 195.25	$ 781.00	$ 976.25	$ 195.25	$ 2,343.00
Total Expenses - Reserves Funded	-	$ 1,841.84	$ 1,841.84	$ 7,367.36	$ 9,209.20	$1,841.84	$ 22,102.00
Total OPERATING	**$ 21,582.22**	**$ 8,550.03**	**($13,032.19)**	**$ 45,929.56**	**$ 42,750.15**	**($ 3,179.41)**	**$102,600.00**
Net Income:	**($12,263.18)**	**($ 0.03)**	**($12,263.15)**	**($ 2,842.55)**	**($ 0.15)**	**($ 2,842.40)**	**$ 0.00**

Cash Disbursement
Happy Glen Homeowners Association
5/1/2017 - 5/31/2017

Date	Check #	Payee		Amount
10-1001-00 Cash - Operating				
10/01/2017	1055	WD Management Company		$1,222.00
		80-8014-00 Management Fee - Current Month	$1,222.00	
10/03/2017	1056	WD Management Company		$95.88
		80-8024-00 September Expense Reimburse; Pool Software	$55.00	
		80-8002-00 September Expense Reimburset; Copies	$4.00	
		80-8002-00 September Expense Reimburse; A/P Post	$6.16	
		80-8002-00 September Expense Reimburse; Postage	$30.72	
10/01/2017	1057	C&C Municipal Utility		$554.54
		40-6004-00 Utilities - Water & Sewer; 62268675-333322303	$23.44	
		40-6004-00 Utilities - Water & Sewer; 62268675-320733338	$210.03	
		40-6004-00 Utilities - Water & Sewer; 62268675-320739331	$298.57	
		40-6004-00 Utilities - Water & Sewer; 62268675-347334330	$22.50	
10/01/2017	1058	Allied Waste Services		$313.02
		40-7008-00 acct# 30742011015786; acct# 30742345015786	$313.02	
10/01/2017	1059	Providence Community Building		$75.00
		80-8073-00 Donation for room rental annual meeting	$75.00	
10/01/2017	1060	Association - Reserve		$819.59
		90-9607-00 Roof Reserves	$375.00	
		90-9705-00 Lighting Reserves	$444.59	
10/01/2017	1061	Bill Smith		$70.00
		80-8073-00 Reimb: Supplies for annual meeting; Reimb:	$70.00	
10/01/2017	1062	Duke Energy		$46.19
		40-6002-00 Utilities - Electric; 205413351177	$23.45	
		40-6002-00 Utilities - Electric; 196878454571	$22.74	
10/01/2017	1063	American Turf Management Company, Inc.		$1,815.00
		40-5000-00 Multiple Invoices; Monthly grounds maintenance	$840.00	
		40-5005-00 Multiple Invoices; Straw & seed for bare areas	$160.00	
		40-5005-00 Multiple Invoices; Soil amendments & flower i	$815.00	
10/01/2017	1064	Pet Services Inc.		$35.00
		40-4019-00 Emptying of the doggie station; Emptying	$35.00	
			Association Total:	**$5,046.22**

■ ■ ■

AFFIDAVIT OF MAILING

I, ______________________________, of lawful age, upon my oath depose and say: that I mailed to all ______________________________ property owners of record, as of ______________________, a letter containing information regarding the Annual Meeting of said Association to be held on this application on ______________________________. A copy of the typical letter and names and addresses of all ______________________________ property owners of record are attached and made a part of this Affidavit. This said mailing was made on ______________________.

____
Signature

STATE OF NORTH CAROLINA)
)
COUNTY OF __________________)

The above and foregoing Affidavit is subscribed before me on this______day of______, ______, A.D. personally by______________.

____
Notary Public

BID SHEET – ASPHALT REPAIR & SEAL COAT

Main Street Condominium, Inc. is soliciting proposals for asphalt repair and seal coat work to be done between June 15th and August 15, 2008 with at least two weeks advance notice. The Board of Directors of the Association will select a contractor for the project.

The yardages given are estimates. The job will have to be field measured before submitting your proposal.

Contractor must provide certificate of insurance evidencing workers' compensation and employee's liability insurance as required by law and general liability insurance covering both public liability and motor vehicle liability with single liability limit of not less than $500,000.00.

The work to be performed is as follows:

1) Thorough cleaning of all asphalt surfaces by brooming, washing, and air blowing.
2) Remove oil and grease deposits by scraping and scrubbing with chemicals compatible with sealing material.
3) Dig out sections of asphalt which have an alligatored appearance in rectangular shape to neat even lines; install new aggregate base; install and compact new asphalt.
4) Protect all utility covers from seal by oiling or other means prior to sealing. All covers to be cleaned by contractor after sealing is complete.
5) Apply two coats of sealing material in accordance with manufacturer's instructions.
6) Prevent excessive buildup or unsightly appearance.

BID SHEET – PAINTING

Community Name: Main Street HOA

Location: 1001 Paintbrush Court, Charlotte, NC 28209

Description: Community association with office/recreation center

Contact: John Smith, Property Manager

General Information: By September 15, the Main Street HOA Board of Directors will choose a contractor to paint the exterior of its office/recreation center. Work will include all materials, equipment, supplies, labor, and supervision to perform the work required. Work will begin by October 1 and end by October 20.

PAINTING SPECIFICATIONS

Contractor shall:

1. Apply Olympic Supreme primer and paint to all wood trim and wood siding.
2. Not prime or paint gutters or down spouts.
3. Clean primer and paint from all adjacent surfaces.
4. Replace and prime/paint rotten wood

WORK SPECIFICATIONS

1. Work shall be performed Monday through Friday between the hours of 8 AM and 5 PM.
2. Contractor shall furnish qualified supervision to oversee all work.

BID SHEET – POOL MAINTENANCE

Company Name __________________ Phone No. __________________

Address _________________________ Tax ID No. __________________

____

____

Please provide three community association references.

____

OPENING POOL .... $________

FIRST CLEANING .... $________

WEEKLY MAINTENANCE (7x per wk. for 16 weeks)..... $________

CLOSING .... $________

TOTAL AMOUNT OF CONTRACT .... $________

ADDITIONAL EMERGENCY SERVICE RATES .... $______/hr

AGREED: __________________________________ DATE: ____________
Contractor

AGREED: __________________________________ DATE: ____________
Manager

BID SHEET – LANDSCAPE MAINTENANCE

Mail To:

Property Name ________________________________

Property Address & Directions ________________________

____

Landscape Contractor ___________________________
Liability And Workers Compensation (Enclose Certificate Of Insurance)
Contractors-Phone/Office#____________Mobile#___________
Beeper#____________Nextel#___________________

Section I Fixed Monthly Expense

	Monthly		Annual
1) Monthly Labor Expense.	$_____	X 12	$____
2) Any Other Fixed Expense Specify			
Total Fixed Expenses	$_____	X 12	$____

Section II Variable Expense (Cost Estimates)

1) Pine straw: Estimate Number Of Bales.	$______	
Cost Per Bail	$______	
Total Cost	$______	
Number Of Applications	______	
Annual Total Cost (**Pinestraw**)		$________

2) <u>Fertilizer</u>: Cost Per Application. $______
Number Of Applications ______
Annual Total Cost (**Fertilizer**) $_______

3) <u>Grass Seed</u>: Cost Per Pound $______
Estimate Number Of Pounds _______
Cost Per Application $______
Number Of Application ______
Annual Total Cost (**Grass Seed**) $_______

4) <u>Other Materials</u>
Such As "Round-Up", Etc. $______ $_______
Pre-emergent Herbicide. $______ $_______

5) Inspect Cycle, And Make Minor Repairs
For Any <u>Irrigation System</u> $______ $_______

<u>Bottom Line Cost</u> $______ $_______

This Contract May Be Cancelled With 30 Days Written Notice From Either Party.
Accepted As Of ________Contract To Start ________End ________
Property Representative ______ Landscape Representative ______

LAWN CARE

1) Mowing:
   A. Frequency: 1 time per week or as required (___times per year minimum under normal conditions) to maintain a neat and attractive appearance year round.
   B. Specifications: Cutting height 3" unless conditions dictate another height. Mowing blade must be sharp, no more than 1/3 of the blade should be cut off at any one time.
   C. Schedule: To be determined by the judgment of the landscape contractor. One time per week in the growing season, according to need at other times. If the regularly scheduled day is missed because of weather, the sub-contractor will perform the work on the next day that the weather permits. All areas that cannot be cut with a mower will be trimmed to the same height.
2) Edging:
   A. Specifications: All curbs, walks and A.C. pads will be mechanically edged to form a distinct separation between grass and concrete, with each cutting.
3) Trimming:
   A. Specifications: All trees, building, beds, and other obstacles will be trimmed around, with each cutting.
4) Blowing Cut Grass:
   A. Frequency: With each cutting. **DO NOT BLOW DEBRIS TOWARDS BEDS.**
   B. Specifications: All grass and other debris caused by contractor will be blown from sidewalks, curbs, and parking areas.

5) Litter Removal:
   A. Frequency: Before each cutting and one time per week during the non-cutting season.
   B. Specifications: Litter will be removed from all parking lots, walks, and breezeways.
   C. Blow stairway, landing, and stairwell **Yes**_______**NO**________ Show cost under Section I "Other Fixed Expense".
6) Leaf Removal:
   A. Frequency: As needed. At least one time per month in October, November, December, and January. Be sure lawn is clean just before Thanksgiving and Christmas.
   B. Specifications: Leaves will not be allowed to accumulate in a manner which might result in turf damage. Leaves will be disposed of on-site as mulch in natural areas or off-site. Leaves **MAY NOT** be disposed of in trash can areas, dumpster, ect.
7) Turf Fertilization:
   A. Frequency: Two times per year.
   B. Specifications:
      1. Month of first application: April
      2. Type fertilizer: Slow release high nitrogen fertilizer (13-2-5) or suitable substitute. If substituting, please specify______
      3. Rate to be applied: 250 lbs. per acre.
      4. Month of 2nd application: October
      5. Type fertilizer: High phosphorous fertilizer (18-24-12) or suitable substitute. If substituting, please specify_________
      6. Rate to be applied: 200 lbs. per acre.
   C. Restrictions: Fertilizer to be applied evenly and only when grass is dry, preferably when rainfall is predicted.

8) Weed Control: If using suitable substitute, please specify____________.
   A. Preemergent:
      1. Month: March 1st and April 15th.
      2. Type: Dacthal Granular
      3. Rate: 12 lbs./acre active ingredient each application.
   B. Postemergent:
      1. Month: June 15th and August 15th.
      2. Type: 2-4 Damine
      3. Rate: 1 lb/acre active ingredient for each application.
9) Reseeding, Aeration, Liming:
   A. Frequency:
      1. Reseeding: One time per year.
      2. Aeration: One time per year.
      3. Liming: As needed to maintain a 6.0 ph.
   B. Specifications: All grass areas will be aerated and over seeded in the fall with a Rebel II quality Fescue blended grass seed at the rate of 130 lbs per acre. There will be additional expenses involved for bare areas which will involve doubling the amounts of seed and fertilizer, with an application of straw. These areas will be brought to the attention of William Douglas Management Company for approval before the work is begun along with a cost estimate.
10) Insect Treatment and Disease Treatment:
   A. All turf areas shall be inspected monthly for signs of development of any pathogen which might adversely affect the growth and normal development of the turf areas. Immediately upon finding any such problems, the Landscape Contractor shall notify William Douglas Management Company and take steps to control the problem(s) as they exist, along with a cost estimate.

Plant And Shrub Care

11) Remulching Of Beds With Pine Straw:
    A. Frequency: 1 time per year.
    B. Month: January
    C. Quantity: __________bales of high quality fresh pine needles. The count is to be verified by a representative of the Association.
    D. No pine needles will be left on shrubbery. Wire or yarn from the bales shall be removed from the sight by the contractor.
    E. Beds will be kept clean of trash and leaves all the time.
12) Weed Control:
    A. Specifications: All beds and curbs will be kept free of all unwanted vegetation by hand weeding and the use of herbicides. All herbicides to be applied by a trained applicator. No application of Round-Up or any other herbicide may be applied in windy conditions which will cause spray to be blown onto surrounding plants.
    B. Preemergent will be applied if requested by the Association.
13) Pruning: (Trimming)
    A. Frequency: Two times per year.
    B. Specifications: The existing shape of the shrubbery will be maintained by pruning. Major cut back of shrubbery will be quoted on an as-needed basis.
14) Insect and Disease Control:
    A. Frequency: As needed.
    B. Contractor is responsible to monitor plants, notify management company, and take appropriate action in the case of disease or infestation.

15) Dead Shrubbery:
    A. Dead shrubbery will be removed and management notified per occurance.
    Labor for plant installation will be furnished as requested by the management company at an additional charge.
16) Fertilization:
    A. All shrubbery will be fertilized in the spring with a slow release fertilizer.

Trees

17) Insect and Disease Control:
    A. Frequency: As needed.
    B. Specifications: Contractor is responsible to monitor trees, notify management company, and take appropriate action in the case of disease or infestation.
18) Pruning:
    A. Small trees will be pruned as needed to remove sucker growth.
    B. Large trees, Can you provide trimming service.
    Yes__________No__________

Irrigation System

19) A. Irrigation System Start-Up and Shut-Down Annually.
    B. Monitor the system by the manager on each visit.
    C. Cycle the system monthly by manager to insure proper cycle time and direction of watering head.
20) State herbicide applicator license number: #________________
21) Number of years in business: ____________________________
    Number of years present management has run business: ____

Will an owner of the business be on site when work is being done?
Yes__________No________.

What target day of the week will service be performed? _____

22) On each billing, the contractor will furnish dates of mowing, edging, herbicide application, fertilization, and any other pertinent facts.

23) Include a minimum of three references including addresses and telephone numbers.
   1. ____
   2. ____
   3. ____

Snow & Ice

24) Ice Melt **Yes______No______**
   A. Ice melt stored on site **Yes______No______**
   B. Initiating contact? **Name**________________________________
   C. Ice Melt to be applied by outside contractor **Yes______No______**

25) Snow Shoveled off steps and walks **Yes______No______**

   A. Clean off the complete steps and walks **Yes______No______**

   B. Just clean off a path on steps and walks **Yes______No______**

   (this option is less expensive)

26) Plowing Parking Lots and Entrance Ways: **Yes**_____ **No**_____

A. Parking lots plowed (Very Expensive) **Yes**_____ **No**_____

B. Entrance to main road to be plowed **Yes**_____ **No**_____

27) Estimate Rate Per Hour Per Man $_________ For Snow Removal
Equipment rate per hour:
A. (Plow)________________________ $___________________
B. (Other)_______________________ $___________________

28) Time commitment to start Snow or Ice Removal work, work will commence within____________ hours after the storm has stopped, and the contractor has been given permission to start by # 24-B above.

About the Author

Since 2003 Chris has been the president of William Douglas Management, Inc., an association management company with offices in North Carolina, South Carolina, and Georgia. He received a BA in Business Management from North Carolina State University. Chris resides with his family in North Carolina.

www.ingramcontent.com/pod-product-compliance
Lightning Source LLC
Chambersburg PA
CBHW050450270326
41927CB00009B/1677

* 9 7 8 0 6 9 2 9 1 8 9 4 4 *